teach®
yourself

Islam
ruqaiyyah waris maqsood

teach yourself
70
1938
2008
celebrate
with us

Launched in 1938, the **teach yourself** series grew rapidly in response to the world's wartime needs. Loved and trusted by over 50 million readers, the series has continued to respond to society's changing interests and passions and now, 70 years on, includes over 500 titles, from Arabic and Beekeeping to Yoga and Zulu. What would you like to learn?

be where you want to be with **teach yourself**

For UK order enquiries: please contact Bookpoint Ltd, 130 Milton Park, Abingdon, Oxon, OX14 4SB. Telephone: +44 (0) 1235 827720. Fax: +44 (0) 1235 400454. Lines are open 09.00–17.00, Monday to Saturday, with a 24-hour message answering service. Details about our titles and how to order are available at www.teachyourself.co.uk

For USA order enquiries: please contact McGraw-Hill Customer Services, PO Box 545, Blacklick, OH 43004-0545, USA. Telephone: 1-800-722-4726. Fax: 1-614-755-5645.

For Canada order enquiries: please contact McGraw-Hill Ryerson Ltd, 300 Water St, Whitby, Ontario, L1N 9B6, Canada. Telephone: 905 430 5000. Fax: 905 430 5020.

Long renowned as the authoritative source for self-guided learning – with more than 50 million copies sold worldwide – the **teach yourself** series includes over 500 titles in the fields of languages, crafts, hobbies, business, computing and education.

British Library Cataloguing in Publication Data: a catalogue record for this title is available from the British Library.

Library of Congress Catalog Card Number: on file.

First published in UK 1994 by Hodder Education, part of Hachette Live UK, 338 Euston Road, London, NW1 3BH.

First published in US 1994 by The McGraw-Hill Companies, Inc.

This edition published 2006.

The **teach yourself** name is a registered trade mark of Hodder Headline.

Copyright © 1994, 2003, 2006 Ruqaiyyah Waris Maqsood

Typeset by Transet Limited, Coventry, England.
Printed in Great Britain for Hodder Education, an Hachette Livre UK Company, 338 Euston Road, London NW1 3BH, by Cox & Wyman Ltd, Reading, Berkshire.

The publisher has used its best endeavours to ensure that the URLs for external websites referred to in this book are correct and active at the time of going to press. However, the publisher and the author have no responsibility for the websites and can make no guarantee that a site will remain live or that the content will remain relevant, decent or appropriate.

Hachette Livre UK's policy is to use papers that are natural, renewable and recyclable products and made from wood grown in sustainable forests. The logging and manufacturing processes are expected to conform to the environmental regulations of the country of origin.

Impression number   10 9 8 7
Year   2010

contents

Notes

As a mark of respect, Muslims may add 'Peace be upon him' when they refer to the Prophet Muhammad and other prophets. In this book it is abbreviated as ﷺ.

Dates from the Muslim calendar are shown as AH (*Anno Hegira*), others are shown as CE (Common Era) which is equivalent to AD in the Christian calendar.

Quotations from the Qur'an have been printed in italics, whereas teachings of the Prophet ﷺ himself are in normal script.

What is Islam?

Islam is one of the three great faiths that sprang from the harsh land and deep silences of the Middle Eastern deserts. The other two are Judaism and Christianity and all three are interlinked because they are, in reality, worshipping the same One God. In historical terms, Islam is the youngest of the three, although Muslims argue that it is the earliest and forms the basis of all three.

Being a Muslim (a follower of Islam) has nothing to do with being an Arab. The word 'Muslim' means simply 'one who submits'. The creed of Islam is a simple statement in two parts, *'La ilaha ilallah wa Muhammadur rasul al-Lah'* ('There is no God but the Almighty, and Muhammad ﷺ is the messenger of God'). Muslims accept these two basic things in the heart; that there really is One God, Supreme and Unique; and that the revelation given through the Arab prophet Muhammad ﷺ is the genuine, final and complete revelation from this God, and supersedes all revelations that came before it.

Being a Muslim is essentially a very personal experience. It cannot be done 'second-hand'. It involves a moment (known as *ihsan* or realization) of being 'born anew'. Every Muslim has to experience this if their Islam is to be a truly living thing.

Most people, once they become aware that God exists, rapidly develop *taqwa* or 'God-consciousness'. They become aware that everything they do, think or say, is done under the 'eyes of God'. It alters everything, from the simplest of deeds to the most momentous, because with *taqwa* there is a goal to be aimed at: to please God, who can see them at every instant and knows every detail about them, even the secret unspoken thoughts of their hearts.

This God, by definition, is the Supreme, the Almighty One. It is not possible for there to be *two* Almighties, so there is only One God. This is the basic concept of Islam known as *tawhid* or 'one-ness', which is expressed in theological terms as monotheism (the belief that there can only be One God).

God, the Creator and Organizer of the universe, is so far above and beyond the limitation of the human mind that it would be impossible for anyone to grasp anything about Him at all, were it not for His desire that human beings should know and love Him, and try to live in a way that will bring them success and happiness. This is the second basic concept of Islam, known as *risalah* or 'prophecy'. God sends revealers, or messengers.

Muslims believe that there has never been a time since the creation of human beings capable of conscious thought when there were not revealers and people of insight. Many of these were the prophets named in the Bible. Most Muslims regard Adam ﷺ as God's first prophet, and the builder of the first shrine dedicated to God's worship on earth.

The third basic concept of Islam is *akhirah* or 'life after death'. Muslims believe that life on this earth is very far from being all that there is. Human life does not begin at birth, but at whatever stage God chose to create the living soul; it does not end at 'death', but at whatever stage God chooses to disintegrate that soul, if it is His will. The short period of time spent as a human being on this earth is for a reason: it provides a series of lessons and tests, the outcome of which is most important for each individual.

To develop from the training, which will sometimes involve much suffering, or perhaps being faced with the temptations of easy or corrupt living, a person needs a standard by which he or she can be guided. Each messenger or revealer of God did his or her best to teach this standard, but somewhere along the way followers with particular beliefs of their own, or with certain vested interests, coloured these teachings and diluted them. Muslims believe this is what happened to the pure teaching of the messenger Jesus ﷺ. The message revealed to the Prophet Muhammad ﷺ came in the form of words that had to be learned by heart and recorded with the utmost care and precision, and never altered in any way, so that there should be no doubt about them.

This revelation was given to the Prophet ﷺ over a period of some 23 years commencing in 610 CE, and is now collected into book form, the book known as the *Holy Qur'an*. Muslims believe that the sacred words in the Arabic text of the Qur'an (obviously, it is a different matter for translations) are exactly as they were revealed to the Prophet ﷺ, and have never been altered, edited, added to or taken away from, since he was given the messages in the sixth century CE. They are there for all time, a standard and a guide for the whole of life.

Although Islam began in the Middle East, and the revelation to the Prophet ﷺ applied in the first instance to Arab people, it is a universal faith and has nothing to do with a person's nationality. Nowadays there are many millions of Muslims all over the earth, of diverse races from Eskimo to Aborigine, and Arab Muslims form only a small percentage of this vast *ummah* or 'family'.

There is only one form of superiority in Islam, and that is of genuine piety and humility, and desire to serve God. True service of God does not consist of rituals and recitations, which are only symbols or manifestations of religious awareness, but is a matter of the heart, the mind and the soul. The most brilliant scientific discoverer with his flash of insight, and the most long-suffering ascetic saint with all his hours of pain and prayer, are not superior to the most simple goat-herd who is aware of God watching him while he watches his flock. They are of equal value to Him who created all of them, set them in their individual paths, and who loves them – despite their faults – with an intensity no human being can ever fully comprehend.

So that is the message and the 'ground-plan' of Islam. There *is* a God for real, and no God but the One, and the words and insights given to the Messenger Muhammad ﷺ consist of true and genuine revelations from this Being, as relevant today as they were when they were first uttered some 1,400 years ago.

> 'Righteousness is not a matter of turning your faces to the East or West; but this is (true) righteousness – to believe in God and the Last Day, and the angels, and the Book, and the messengers; to use your resources – out of love for Him – for your family, for those without family, for those in need, for the refugee, for those who ask (for your help), and for setting slaves free; to practise prayer and giving in charity on a regular basis; to keep all the promises you have made; to be steadfast and patient in pain and adversity, and throughout all periods of panic. Such are the people of truth, the God-fearing.'
>
> (Surah 2.177)

The Ka'bah Mosque at Makkah, full to overflowing with Hajj pilgrims.

01

the life of the blessed Prophet Muhammad ﷺ

In this chapter you will learn about:
- the main events of the Prophet's ﷺ life
- his character
- the significance of various historical events.

His birth and early life

The Prophet Muhammad ﷺ was born in Makkah, Saudi Arabia, in around 570 CE, a member of the Hashim clan of the Quraysh tribe. His father, Abdullah, a merchant, died before he was born, and his mother, Amina, died when he was only six years old, leaving him an orphan. He was reared first by his grandfather, Abd al-Muttalib, a man famous for his saintly life, and then by his merchant uncle, Abu Talib. The only person with him from his first breath to his last was his Abyssinian nurse Barakah (Umm Ayman), who he always called 'Mother'.

At this time, the people of Arabia were mainly superstitious pagans with a few notable monotheist exceptions, such as Abd al-Muttalib. There were also considerable numbers of Jews and Christians in Arabia, especially on the border with Syria, the north-east, and the Yemen. Many Arabs lived nomadic lives on traditionally claimed territories, and there were only a few key cities such as Makkah, Yathrib and Taif. Makkah was a wealthy trading post that also happened to be the most important shrine for the Arab idols.

The cube-shaped Ka'bah temple claimed a very ancient history; it was said to have been built in the first place by Adam ﷺ, the first prophet, and then rebuilt by Ibrahim ﷺ and his son Isma'il ﷺ (Heb. Abraham, Ishmael). Originally, it had been a temple dedicated to the One True God, but over the centuries the Baal cults had predominated and at the time of the Prophet ﷺ it was said to have contained no less than 360 statuettes and cult objects to minor deities, including icons of the Virgin Mary and Jesus ﷺ, and the Prophet Ibrahim ﷺ.

The Prophet Muhammad ﷺ grew up a particularly devout and honourable man, a believer in One God, like his grandfather. He worked first as a shepherd, and then as a merchant, working for his uncle, Abu Talib. He became well known and well liked, and earned the nickname 'al-Amin' ('the Trustworthy One') for his piety, honesty, fair dealing, and practical common-sense. He became a leading member of an Order of Chivalry (the Hilf al-Fudul) dedicated to bringing justice and protecting the rights of the poor and weak.

Later, he was employed by a wealthy tradeswoman, Khadijah, who, after a short while, offered herself in marriage to him, although she was in her forties and he was about 25 years old. She had been married twice before and had at least five existing children. Despite the age difference, they were very happily married and had at least six children of their own. Their two sons (Qasim and Abdullah) died as infants, leaving the Prophet ﷺ with four daughters – Zaynab, Ruqaiyyah, Umm Kulthum and Fatimah. Only Fatimah survived him, and only by a few months.

He fostered two boys, his cousin Ali from the age of four, and a slave Zayd ibn Harithah from the age of 14. In due course Ali married Fatimah. Even though polygamy was normal among Arabs at this time, the Prophet ﷺ never considered any other marriage while Khadijah lived.

His call to be a prophet

His new position gave him security and much more time to devote to prayer and meditation. It was his habit to go off alone to the mountains around Makkah, and to meditate for long periods of time. Sometimes he would stay away for several days. He particularly used to favour the Cave of Hira on Jabal Nur (the 'Mount of Light') overlooking Makkah. On one of these occasions, in the year 610 CE, when he was around 40 years old, something happened that changed his life entirely.

A presence he identified as the angel Jibril (Gabriel) was suddenly there with him, and he was shown words and ordered to recite them. He protested that he was not a learned man and could not read them, but the angel insisted, and suddenly the Prophet ﷺ was given to understand what the words said. He was ordered to learn them, and repeat them to others. Thus came the first revelation of verses of the Book now known as the Qur'an (the Recitation).

The night this happened was towards the end of the month of Ramadan, which later became the Islamic month of fasting. The night is known as *Laylat ul-Qadr*. It is usually celebrated on the 27th night of Ramadan, although the exact date is not known.

From this moment of calling, Muhammad's ﷺ life was no longer his own, but in the hands of Him who had called him to be a prophet, and to spend the rest of his days in His service, repeating His messages.

After the first few visions, the Prophet ﷺ had no further revelations for some time, and went through a period of trial and testing when he was not sure of the implications of what had happened to him. Then, after around two years, the messages began again, and continued for the rest of his life, a period of some 23 years from the first revelation to the last.

The first convert was a woman, his wife Khadijah; the first male convert was his cousin Ali (then aged ten), and the first adult male was his best friend, the merchant Abu Bakr.

The way of life he taught became known as 'Islam', which means 'submission to the will of God', and his followers were known as Muslims, 'those who submit'. Allah, the Muslim name for God, simply means 'the Almighty'.

The Revelations

The Prophet ﷺ did not always see the angel Jibril when he had his revelations, and when he did, the angel did not always keep exactly the same form. Sometimes the angel was huge, filling the horizon, and sometimes the Prophet ﷺ was only aware of eyes watching him. Occasionally, he just heard a voice speaking to him. Sometimes he revealed that the message did not come through clearly, but there was a sound like muffled bells, and this gave him a headache. At other times, the message was as clear and direct as if another person was just standing by him.

Sometimes he received the revelations when he was in deep prayer, but at other times they occurred 'spontaneously' while he was engaged in everyday life, out riding, or involved in conversation concerning the subject.

Every time he received a revelation, there was no doubt either in his mind or the minds of those observing him – he would suffer physical symptoms, like heavy sweating or a trance-like state, and he reported that he frequently felt as if he was going to 'have his soul snatched away'. Those who were with him could tell quite clearly when his revelations started and when they finished.

Many of those who rejected belief in what was happening to the Prophet ﷺ accused him of being mad, demon possessed or suffering from a disease, such as epilepsy; but there is no evidence whatsoever of that. A study of his life as revealed in the *hadith* (his own sayings, and reports of his teachings and way of life) show him to have been an immensely sane, kind, warm-hearted, down-to-earth person, and later an eminent and astute leader of his nation.

His early mission

At first, the Prophet ﷺ did not preach in public, but spoke privately to those who were interested, or who had noticed the change in him. The particular way of Muslim prayer was revealed to him, and he began to practise this daily, which again drew comment from those who saw him. When he was given the instruction to begin preaching in public, he was ridiculed and abused as people scoffed at what he was saying and doing.

Also, many of the Quraysh tribesmen – who had a vested interest in the Ka'bah shrine, since they provided the many pilgrims with food, water, lodging and protection en route – were seriously alarmed as they realized his insistence on the One True God would undermine the prestige and credibility of the shrine, if people were converted to the Prophet's ﷺ ways and began to abandon the worship of idols.

Some of the Prophet's ﷺ own uncles (such as Abu Lahab) became his chief opponents, vilifying and ridiculing him, and stirring up trouble for those who had been converted. There were many instances of torture and abuse, particularly against slaves and women who joined the 'new' religion. The first martyr of Islam was a slave-woman, Sumayyah, and the first *mu'adhin* (caller to prayer) was a negro slave, Bilal, who was rescued from being left to die in the blazing sun with a huge rock on his chest.

Two large groups of early Muslims migrated to Abyssinia, where they took refuge with the Christian ruler, the Negus, who was so impressed with their teachings and way of life that he agreed to protect them, and later became Muslim himself.

The Quraysh tribes decided to boycott the clan Hashim, and for three years they were excluded from all trade, help, business and marriage arrangements, and were refused access to Makkah. It was a very difficult time, and many Muslims were reduced to absolute penury.

The Year of Sorrow

In the year 619, the Prophet's ﷺ beloved wife, Khadijah, died. She had been his most ardent supporter and helper. In the same year his uncle Abu Talib, an eminent sheikh able to protect him from the worst persecution of the tribes, also died. The grief-stricken Prophet ﷺ left Makkah and tried to make a fresh start in the town of Taif, but was rejected there also.

He had no wish to re-marry but struggled as the 'single parent' of his teenage daughters and foster sons. A female friend arranged for him to marry a devout widow, Sawdah, who was a suitable person to look after them and had been one of the first Muslim converts. She also suggested Aishah, the little daughter of his friend Abu Bakr, who had known and loved the Prophet ﷺ all her life. She was far too young for physical marriage at this time, but was engaged in a non-physical relationship that was quite traditional.

The 'Night of Ascent'

It was during this same year that the Prophet ﷺ experienced the second most important night of his life, the *Laylat ul-Miraj* or 'Night of Ascent'.

This experience bore no resemblance to the Christian belief in the Ascension to Heaven of the body of Jesus ﷺ after his death and resurrection. The Prophet's ﷺ experience occurred during his lifetime. It is not clear whether it was a vision, dream or psychic happening, but in it he was woken from where he lay sleeping, and taken by a *buraq*, a miraculous beast, to Jerusalem. (Marks or impressions of footprints 'marking the spot' are symbolic of where he stood, not miraculous imprints.) The ruins of the old Jewish Temple on Mount Zion, a way was opened for him through the heavens until he approached the Throne of God, in a region which even he and the angel Jibril, who was accompanying him, were not allowed to enter.

figure 1.1 the dome of the Rock Mosque, Jerusalem (also known as al'Quds)

It was during this night that the rules for the compulsory prayer five times per day (the *salat*) were revealed to him. They became the central part of the faith and have formed the keystone for Muslim life ever since.

He was also said to have seen and spoken to the still-existing souls of other prophets from the past, including Jesus, Moses and Abraham (Ar. Isa, Musa, Ibrahim – peace be upon all of them), and left interesting descriptions. The experience brought great comfort and strength to the Prophet ﷺ and confirmed that Allah had not deserted him, or left him to suffer alone. After this night, he lived for another 12 years, with no similar experience.

The hijrah – migration to Madinah

The Prophet's ﷺ fortunes now changed drastically. Although he was still persecuted and ridiculed in Makkah, his message had been heard by people outside the region. Some of the elders of the town of Yathrib invited him to leave Makkah and move to their town, where he would be honoured as their leader and judge. This town was the home of both Arab and Jewish people and there had been constant conflict between them. They hoped Muhammad ﷺ would bring them peace.

The Prophet ﷺ immediately advised many of his Muslim followers to move to Yathrib, while he remained in Makkah as long as possible to allay suspicions. Without the restraining hand of Abu Talib, the Quraysh were free to attack him, even to kill him, and this is what he realized they intended to do. They had no intention of letting him leave the city, or be received with honour anywhere else.

The Prophet's ﷺ move was not without some drama. Ali, his nephew, bravely volunteered to stay in his bed as a decoy, and the Prophet ﷺ evaded capture by using his knowledge of desert conditions. On a couple of occasions the Quraysh were nearly successful in capturing him, but eventually the Prophet ﷺ arrived at the outskirts of Yathrib. This emigration was known as the *hijrah*.

So many people rushed out to offer him refuge in their homes that he was embarrassed by their kindness, and left the choice of place to his camel. The camel stopped by a place where dates were spread out to dry, and this was instantly donated to the Prophet ﷺ to build his new home. The town took a new name – Madinat al-Nabi, the 'town of the Prophet' – which is now shortened to Madinah.

The people who had left Makkah and made their own hijrah were known as Muhajirun, the 'emigrants'. They were in the position of refugees, having left all their belongings in Makkah. The Prophet ﷺ appealed to the people of Madinah to take them in and offer them homes. All those who volunteered to help the Makkan Muslims became known as Ansars, the 'helpers'.

The Prophet ﷺ as ruler

The Prophet ﷺ then set about creating a charter which would enable all the disputing tribes and factions in Madinah to accept him as head of state and abide by his decisions. He ruled that all the citizens should be free to practise their own religion in peaceful co-existence, without fear of persecution or ill-favour. He asked only that if there was any aggression or tyranny, they should join together and cooperate in the face of the enemy. The whole text of the Charter was recorded, word for word, by Ibn Ishaq and Abu Ubaid in their respective books from the original preserved by Ibn Abi Khithamah.

The previous tribal laws of both Arabs and Jews were replaced by the basic principle of general justice for all, irrespective of class, colour or creed. At first, the Jewish tribespeople of Madinah accepted the Prophet's ﷺ rule; no Jew was ever forced to become a Muslim, and they were treated as equal citizens of Madinah and their own faith was protected. Later, trouble broke out when certain of the Jewish tribes did not keep the principle of supporting Madinah against attacks from outside, and these individuals were condemned as traitors.

The Prophet's ﷺ way of life

Every act and detail of the Prophet's ﷺ life was of the greatest interest to those around him; his recorded deeds and sayings, the hadiths, ran into many thousands.

Although he was now ruler of a city-state, and in receipt of increasing wealth and influence, the Prophet ﷺ never lived like a king. His home consisted of simple mud-brick houses that were built for his wives; he never actually had even a room of his own. Adjacent to these little houses was a courtyard with a well that became the mosque, the meeting place for the Muslim faithful.

It was taken for granted that the Prophet's ﷺ life was 'public property'; the origin of the *hijab* or 'veil' grew out of the habit of the public claiming constant access to him and his hospitality, and the need to allow his family a little privacy. The original veil was a curtain separating their private quarters from the area where people came and went. The Prophet ﷺ later taught that no one had the right to enter, or even to look into, other people's houses without permission.

He believed strongly in good manners, always greeting people kindly, showing respect to elders, and balancing his serious teachings and reprimands with gentle good humour. He once said: 'The dearest of you to me are those who have good manners; the most offensive to me are the most boring and the long-winded!'

He was never arrogant or superior, despite his position as leader; he never made people feel small, unwanted or embarrassed. He urged his followers to live kindly and humbly, releasing slaves as far as they were able, and generally showing practical charity, without thinking of reward. He said: 'Feed, for the love of Allah, the destitute, the orphan and the prisoner, saying: We feed you for the sake of Allah alone, desiring no reward from you, or thanks.' Much of his time was spent visiting the sick, comforting the bereaved, and counselling people with personal, family and marital problems.

His personal habits were extremely abstemious; he ate little, only simple food, and made it his practice never to fill his stomach. In hard times he ate nothing but raw food for days. He slept on a very simple mattress on the floor, and allowed virtually nothing in the way of home comforts or decorations. He did not regard it as right to sit down idly while others were working, and used to join in the housework with his wives, and helped in the various labour projects of his friends.

He was sent many rich garments but did not keep them; he used to sew and patch his old clothes and shoes whenever the need arose. He regarded all material things as being no more than loans from Allah, to be used in His service, so whenever he was given anything, he usually gave it away to the needy. He and his family supervised the distribution of food and charity on a daily basis.

All his recorded words and actions reveal him as a man of great gentleness, kindness, good humour and excellent common sense, who had a great love for animals and for all people, especially children. He had an implacable sense of justice, but ruled with humility and compassion. He was not only treated by his followers with enormous respect – he was deeply loved.

The Prophet's ﷺ life of prayer

The Prophet's ﷺ life was spent virtually in a constant state of prayer, and in teaching his followers. Apart from the five compulsory prayers, which he led in the mosque, the Prophet ﷺ also spent many hours in private prayer and contemplation, sometimes during the greater part of the night.

His wives prayed some of the extra night prayers with him, but after they had retired to sleep he could be found standing or sitting in contemplation for many hours, snatching a little sleep towards the end of the night, before being woken for the pre-sunrise prayer (the *fajr*).

figure 1.2 a pilgrim making personal prayer

Like many in the hot climate of the Middle East, the Prophet ﷺ made up for loss of sleep by taking a siesta during the heat of the day, after the midday prayer (the *zuhr*). Late afternoon was the time when the heat dropped again, and a major time of prayer – with the *asr* as the light began to change, and the *maghrib* after sunset. The last formal prayer was during the hours of darkness, the *isha*.

One of his most famous prayers is known as the 'Prayer of Light':

> 'O Allah, place light in my heart, light in my sight, light in my hearing, light on my right hand and on my left, light above me, light below me, light behind me and light before me. O Allah, Who knows the innermost secrets of our hearts, lead me out of the darkness into the Light.'

The Prophet's ﷺ family

In the last ten years of his life the Prophet ﷺ took at least 12 other women and their children into his household, all but one of whom had suffered the loss of their original spouses through death or divorce. (The Prophet ﷺ took on four small children when he married Umm Salamah, for example, and Sawdah may have had six.) In three cases, the wives were daughters of eminent defeated enemies. Two of his wives were Jewish, one was a Christian. It is worth making the comment that people who have not studied the Prophet ﷺ sometimes assume he must have been a sexual athlete, wanting intimacy with a selection of pretty girls. (If so, he was lucky to have started being such an athlete when he turned 50, having turned down any previous opportunity for a second wife besides Khadijah, or sexual intimacy with slaves and captives.)

The Prophet's ﷺ wives had no luxuries but were expected to share his devout and simple way of life, and to make enormous personal sacrifice. They became known as the 'Mothers of the Faithful', and lived together in small apartments alongside the Prophet's ﷺ mosque, at the centre of the Muslim religious community.

It is on record that all of his wives were once offered the free choice of whether they wished to live like this, or to leave him. All but one chose to stay, even those with whom he had no sexual relationship at all. The Prophet ﷺ granted one divorce, to Aliyyah bint Zabyan (Ibn Kathir, *Sirah* 4.586–87), her own choice, and she was returned to her people.

By these later wives, the Prophet ﷺ only had one further child of his own, a son Ibrahim, who, like his two sons by Khadijah, died in infancy.

His four daughters all married and three of them bore children. Of them, the most famous was his youngest daughter, Fatimah, who married Ali and gave him two grandsons, Hasan and Hussain, and two granddaughters Zaynab and Umm Kulthum.

The Prophet's ﷺ wives

1 Khadijah bt. Khuwaylid
2 Sawdah bt. Zama'a
3 Aishah bt. Abu Bakr
4 Hafsah bt. Umar
5 Zaynab bt. Khuzaymah
6 Hind (Umm Salamah) bt. Abu Umayyah
7 Zaynab bt. Jahsh
8 Juwayriyyah bt. Harith
9 Ramlah (Umm Habibah) bt. Abu Sufyan
10 Zaynab (Safiyyah) bt. Huyayy
11 Rayhanah bt. Zayd
12 Maymunah bt. Harith
13 Maryam Qibtiyyah

Khadijah and Zaynab bint Khuzaymah both died before the Prophet ﷺ. Some scholars debate the status of Rayhanah and Maryam Qibtiyyah as full wives. Before Islam, men did take advantage of sexual intimacy with their servants, but this was forbidden to Muslims. If they married a servant ('one whom their right hand possessed') she might receive her freedom in lieu of the dowry given to free women upon marriage.

Jihad

The Prophet ﷺ was a man of peace and reconciliation, and would have preferred it if he had been left in peace in Madinah, but sadly, the opposition from the Quraysh tribes continued and he was obliged to take part in sporadic warfare. Even so, the total amount of time he spent fighting only came to a few months.

His two most important early battles – Badr and Uhud – only took a single day. The Muslims won the first, but the second was a stalemate. As a result of this warfare, the many rules of conduct of war and treatment of prisoners were laid down for Muslims, the rules of *jihad*.

Jihad was never to be military activity for the sake of nationalism, tyranny or aggrandizement, but primarily for defensive reasons, and only until the enemy could be brought to peace. During the Prophet's ﷺ battles, many of the enemy were converted to his side, impressed by the Muslim chivalry, courage and faith in God.

In March 627, his enemy, Abu Sufyan, raised a massive force of 10,000 men and advanced on Madinah, buoyed up by support from a Jewish tribe that had agreed to the Madinah charter, but then turned traitor and decided to oust the Prophet ﷺ. This was called the Battle of the Trench, since the Prophet ﷺ had a huge ditch speedily constructed to protect the city. After a two-week siege, the opposition withdrew, giving the Prophet ﷺ a moral victory, for the eyes of Arabia had been upon him, and he had shown that even this vast army could not defeat him.

In the aftermath, the renegade Jewish tribe was dealt with severely. The Prophet ﷺ always counselled mercy for defeated enemies, and never forced anyone to accept the faith of Islam against their will. On this occasion, however, it was a serious matter because the Jewish tribespeople were citizens of Madinah and, therefore, under his charter. They had signed the pledge of loyalty. The Prophet ﷺ agreed to spare their lives so long as they repented their treachery and agreed to abide by the laws of Islam, but this they refused to do.

They were then allowed to appoint their own judge; but this judge had been so shocked by their treachery that he said he would apply their own ancient law to them, and quoted Deuteronomy 7:2:

> 'When the Lord your God gives them over to you, and you defeat them, then you must utterly destroy them, and make no covenant with them and show no mercy to them.'

All the men of the tribe were then put to the sword. It was intended to underline the point the Prophet ﷺ was trying to make: that the laws of Islam had superseded those from the ancient past.

The incident had nothing to do with anti-Semitism, and shortly afterwards, as if to prove the point, the Prophet ﷺ married one of the Jewish widows, Rayhanah bint Zayd. No Jews who accepted the charter were persecuted, or pressured to leave Madinah or to accept Islam.

Pilgrimage to Makkah

In March 628 the Prophet ﷺ dreamed of returning to Makkah, and decided to make this dream reality. He set out with some 1,400 followers, all unarmed, in pilgrim dress of two simple white cloths. Although an increasing number of the citizens of Makkah had by now accepted Islam, the Prophet's ﷺ followers were refused entry. Instead of making trouble, they offered their sacrifices outside Makkah, at a place called Hudaybiyah. The Quraysh chief, Suhayl, who had replaced Abu Sufyan, came out and negotiated a treaty to keep the peace for ten years.

The Muslims repeated the pilgrimage in 629, and were allowed to visit the ancient tribal holy places undisturbed.

The surrender of Makkah and the Final Pilgrimage

The Prophet ﷺ then began to plan for the spread of Islam. He sent letters to the celebrities of the surrounding kingdoms, inviting them to consider Islam – the Roman Byzantine Emperor, the Persian Emperor, the rulers of Egypt, Abyssinia and many leading chiefs – but only the Abyssinian accepted and was converted. However, many Christian Arabs soon did. It is claimed that some of these letters still exist, notably the letter to the Muqawqis of Egypt which may be seen in the Topkapi Museum, Istanbul.

The truce of Hudaybiyah did not hold; in November 629 the Makkans attacked one of the tribes that allied with the Muslims. The Prophet ﷺ, who now had grounds for marching on Makkah, gathered a force of 10,000 men, the largest army that had ever left Madinah. They marched to Makkah, camped outside the city, and Abu Sufyan (whose widowed daughter Umm Habibah had left him and became one of the Prophet's ﷺ wives!) came over to his side. The Prophet ﷺ promised a general amnesty if the Makkans would formally submit, declaring that all who took refuge with Abu Sufyan or who shut their doors on the battle would be safe. In the event, there was only one skirmish in which 11 people lost their lives before the surrender.

The Prophet ﷺ entered the city in triumph, went straight to the Ka'bah, and performed the ritual circumambulation seven times. He then entered the shrine and destroyed all the idols.

All the hereditary territories were left in the hands of their accustomed guardians, and the Prophet ﷺ asked his followers who had originally abandoned property in Makkah when they moved to Madinah not to claim it back. Uthman ibn Talhah, who had once refused Muhammad ﷺ entry to the Ka'bah and persecuted him, was given back the key to the shrine, and it remains with his family to this day. One by one the Quraysh swore their fealty to the Prophet ﷺ, and were pardoned. Only ten people who were guilty of murder or incitement to murder were condemned to death, but even of these only four were actually executed.

The Last Sermon

The Prophet ﷺ did not live long to enjoy a peaceful rule. He returned to his home in Madinah, but his army was obliged to conduct further warfare against tribes that attacked them – tribes that had been shocked by the desecration of their idols at Makkah.

Events outside Arabia worked to the advantage of Islam. The western part of the Roman Empire was overrun by barbarians, and in the east the Byzantines at Constantinople had fallen into confusion through internal conflicts and inefficient rule. The Persian Sassanid Empire (which reached from Iraq to Afghanistan) had engaged the Byzantines in conflict for some 30 years, and had successfully attacked Jerusalem. By 630 the Byzantines had retaken Jerusalem, and the Persian influence was low, leaving a political vacuum for the warriors of Islam to occupy.

In March 632 the Prophet ﷺ made his one complete Muslim *Hajj* to the Ka'bah shrine, known as the Hajjat ul-Wida, the Final Pilgrimage. During this pilgrimage the revelations about the rules of the Hajj were given to him, which are followed by all Muslims to this day. Up to this time pagans had been allowed to visit the Ka'bah as well as Muslims, but now all pagan influence was removed, and only Muslims were allowed into the city.

When the Prophet ﷺ arrived at Mount Arafat for the 'Stand before Allah' (see page 94), he delivered what is known as his 'Final Sermon'. The summarized text of this famous teaching can be found in mosques all over the world:

'O people, listen carefully to what I say, for I do not know whether, after this year, I shall ever be amongst you again. Listen carefully, and report my words to those who cannot be here today.

figure 1.3 pilgrims gather at the Ka'bah

Regard the life and property of every Muslim as a sacred trust . . . Hurt no one, so that no one may hurt you. Remember that you will indeed meet your Lord, and that He will reckon your deeds . . . You will neither inflict nor suffer injustice . . . O men, remember that you have rights with regard to your women, but they also have rights over you. Remember that you have taken them as your wives only under Allah's trust and with His permission . . . Treat them well and be kind to them, for they are your partners and committed helpers . . .

O believers, worship Allah, say your five daily prayers; fast during the month of Ramadan, and give your wealth in zakah. Perform Hajj, if you can afford to . . . An Arab has no superiority over a non-Arab; a white has no superiority over a black, nor a black over a white, except by piety and good deeds. Every Muslim is a brother (or sister) to every other Muslim . . .

No prophet or apostle will come after me, and no new faith will be born . . . I leave behind me two things, the Qur'an and the Sunnah; if you follow these, you will never go astray.'[1]

[1]Shi'ite sources specify the two things as the Qur'an and his descendants.

At the end, he received his final revelation:

'Today I have perfected your religion for you, and I have completed My blessing upon you; and I have approved Islam as your religion.'

(Surah 5:5)

There was a silence, and then the voice of Bilal rose over the hushed enormous crowd, calling them to prayer.

The death of the Prophet ﷺ

When he returned home to Madinah, he began making preparations for an expedition to the Syrian border, but he became ill and developed a heavy fever. He continued to attend and lead the prayers in the mosque as far as he was able, supported by Ali, and when too ill he requested Abu Bakr to take his place. The army was entrusted to Usamah, the 17-year-old son of Zayd by the Prophet's ﷺ nurse Umm Ayman.

He did not recover, and eventually collapsed. His wives realized that he wished to be with Aishah, and moved him to her room, where he died in her arms* on 8 June 632 (in the Muslim calendar this is 12 Rabi'ul Awwal, 11 AH).

He was not an old man, only 63 years old. His last words were said to have been: 'I have chosen the most exalted companions, in Paradise.'

Umar and other companions found it hard to believe their Prophet ﷺ could have died like a mortal man, but Abu Bakr reminded them of the revelation after Uhud:

'Muhammad is but a messenger, and messengers have passed away before him. If he die, or is slain, will you then turn back?'

(Surah 3:144)

He was buried in Aishah's room, which is now a shrine and part of the modern mosque complex at Madinah. May peace be upon him.

*Shi'ite sources state he died in Ali's arms. Both were present at this sad time.

figure 1.4 the Prophet's ﷺ mosque. The dome covers the site of his tomb, Madinah

02

the succession

In this chapter you will
learn about:
- the four 'Rightly-Guided'
  Caliphs
- the conflict between the
  Prophet's ﷺ descendants
  and the Umayyads
- the Battle of Karbala and
  Shi'ite Islam.

The 'Rightly-Guided' Caliphs

After the death of the Prophet ﷺ the new *Caliph* (successor) was to be someone who had been with him in both Makkah and Madinah, qualified to pass on correct hadith, and whose life was so similar to the Prophet's ﷺ that it exemplified the sunnah. Such a person would be able to make decisions as binding as those of Muhammad ﷺ himself; the majority of Muslims believe that the first four Caliphs fulfilled these criteria, and are therefore known as the 'Rightly-Guided' Caliphs or *Rashidin*.

Although the Caliphs increasingly had access to enormous wealth, they continued to live simple lives, as the Prophet ﷺ had done, and were famous for their saintliness and humility.

Abu Bakr (632–4)

During his lifetime the Prophet ﷺ had given several indications that his cousin and son-in-law Ali should have been the next leader, but he requested Abu Bakr to lead the prayer when he was too ill, and there was strong feeling that the leadership should go to one of the 'elders' in the traditional Arabic manner. Leadership rarely passed to eldest son, but to the most capable and reliable candidate. Abu Bakr, then in his sixties, had been the Prophet's ﷺ first adult male convert and was the father of his dearly loved wife Aishah. He was respected for his gentleness, wisdom, piety and humility. As Caliph, he was known as As-Siddiq (the Witness to the Truth) and Amirul Muminim (Ruler of the Believers).

His short reign consisted largely of warfare (known as the Ridda Wars), mainly against those Arab tribes that decided to turn against Islam and refused to pay the *zakah* once the Prophet ﷺ had died.

On his deathbed, Abu Bakr did not give the community the chance to elect the next Caliph, but nominated Umar. Ali was disappointed, but accepted the decision.

Umar (634–44)

Umar's Caliphate saw the rapid spread of Islam, and war with surrounding territories. However, most of the populaces felt liberated and were happy to accept Muslim rulers instead of the previous cruel and corrupt rulers. Jerusalem fell in 638, the Christian ruler Sophronius declaring that he would surrender to none other than Umar himself. Umar behaved with great consideration to the Christians by refraining from offering prayer in the Shrine of the Holy Sepulchre, so that it was not turned into a mosque.

Although the Muslim army conquered territory successfully, no individual was forced to be converted to Islam at the point of the sword, as is often suggested. The Qur'an specified quite clearly: '*Let there be no compulsion in religion. Truth stands out clear from error.*' (Surah 2:256). The formula was 'Islam, tribute, or the sword', the sword being reserved for those who refused to pay the appropriate taxes. Those who did convert to Islam lived tax-free.

In 644 Umar was assassinated by a Firoz, a Persian Christian slave, who had been brought to Madinah to embellish the simple mud dwellings that had been the home of the Prophet ﷺ. Umar was stabbed six times at the dawn prayer, and died three days later.

Uthman (644–56)

As Umar lay dying, he elected a group of six people to choose the next leader, one of whom was Ali, but Uthman (who had been the husband of two of the Prophet's ﷺ daughters) was chosen. In his reign the Muslim empire spread west across North Africa and east to the boundary of China and the Indus Valley.

Although Uthman was a saintly man, he was also a wealthy member of the Umayyad clan of the Quraysh, and in his rush to provide governors for the newly acquired territories, he promoted too many of his own relatives, and was accused of nepotism. For example, his cousin Mu'awiyah, the son of Abu Sufyan, was created Governor of Syria, and another cousin, Amir, was Governor of Egypt.

The Muslims of Kufa and Fustat protested, and tried to persuade the 80-year-old Uthman to abdicate. Uthman preached a fiery sermon against them, in the face of all good advice. Soon afterwards, while he was reading his Qur'an, a group of Egyptians killed him. His wife Nailah tried to protect him, but her fingers were cut off. She sent them, with her plea for help, to Mu'awiyah in Syria.

Ali (656–61)

Twenty-four years after the Prophet's ﷺ death, Ali (also known as Asadullah – the Lion of God) claimed to be the rightful successor, but Aishah still opposed him, supported by the Prophet's ﷺ cousins Talhah and Zubayr. She accused him of being lax in applying justice, because he did not seek out the killer of Uthman. Aishah personally led an army against him, but was defeated in the Battle of the Camel in 656. She was captured, but treated with respect and returned safely to her friends in Madinah, where she lived until she died.

Next, Ali was opposed by Mu'awiyah, who had by now been Governor of Damascus for 20 years, who also refused to recognize him until the assassins of Uthman had been brought to justice. The implication was that Ali had supported them, since he had not tried to track them down and punish them. Their armies met at the Battle of Siffin, but Mu'awiyah made his troops put leaves of the Qur'an on the end of their spears, so Ali's pious soldiers refused to strike them down. Ali agreed to accept arbitration, in which both sides should stand down and face new elections, but this was tantamount to accepting that he was not the rightful Caliph. His most pious warriors were shocked that Ali should have agreed to this and seceded from his ranks, becoming known as the *Kharijites* (Seceders – the fore-runners of later extremists who were prepared to kill or die rather than compromise their sectarian attitudes and beliefs).

Ali was given many premonitions of his fate, including even the name of the man destined to kill him. Despite this he refused to hide or run away. He was struck down by a Kharijite while praying in the mosque at Kufa, and during the three days it took him to die, he protected and fed his assassin, ordering that he should be spared if he lived, and killed with one stroke if he died. He was buried at Najaf.

Mu'awiyah and the Umayyads

Mu'awiyah seized the chance to have himself elected Caliph. Ali's son Hasan agreed to waive his rights and accept a pension; Ali's second son, Hussain, agreed to leave his claim until the death of Mu'awiyah. Instead of Caliph, both Hasan and Hussain took the title *Imam*.

Mu'awiyah decided not to move to Madinah, and Damascus became the capital of the Muslim world. On his deathbed he nominated his son Yazid as successor instead of Hussain. From Mu'awiyah onwards, the Caliphate became hereditary. The first dynasty is known as the *Umayyad*.

Hussain's supporters never accepted Yazid, however, and formed the Shi'at Ali (Party of Ali and his descendants). The Shi'ite revolt peaked with the Battle of Karbala, in which Hussain and a few hundred followers faced a huge army, and were massacred.

The martyrdom of Hussain

In 680 CE/61 AH, Hussain and his supporters were surrounded by Yazid's army of 4,000 warriors at Karbala. They were in sight of the River Euphrates, but Yazid's army tormented them by denying them any access to the water and watched them die of thirst.

For eight days they tried to negotiate Hussain's unconditional surrender, but his belief in his right to be Caliph was strong. He refused to give way, even when it meant his defeat and death. Hussain had already foreseen his martyrdom in a vision.

On 10th Muharram, Hussain put on the mantle of his grandfather the Prophet ﷺ, and went out to die. Hopelessly outnumbered, his followers fell, one by one. When Hussain held out his baby son Ali Asghar for mercy, an arrow fired through the baby's neck and pinned him to Hussain's arm.

At the end, the Prophet's ﷺ family was almost wiped out, with over 70 of his relatives slain. The body of Hussain, riddled with arrows, was trampled in the mud. His head was hacked off and taken to Damascus, but Yazid did eventually return it for burial.

Yazid allowed safe passage to Madinah for the surviving women, plus Hussain's son Ali Zayn al Abidin, whom the troops had left for dead on the battlefield. He was nursed back to health by Hussain's sister Zaynab, who led the Shi'ites until he recovered. Also saved was Ali Zayn's four-year-old son Muhammad al Baqir. They became the next Imams of the Shi'a.

The shrine where Hussain was buried, at Karbala, became a holy place that rivalled Makkah. Shi'ites hold a ten-day festival there every year, in remembrance of his martyrdom. During the festival the people weep for the seeming triumph of tyranny and evil (symbolized by the corrupt, cynical Yazid) over the good (symbolized by the piety and refusal to compromise of Hussain). They pledge themselves to keep up the fight to defend their faith and principles.

The main feature of the festival, which takes place in the month of Muharram, is a series of processions and passion plays commemorating the terrible deaths of Hussain and the Prophet's ﷺ family. There are daily gatherings, or *rawdahs*, in which emotions are stirred up until everyone weeps and dedicates their lives anew – see Ashura, page 111.

Sometimes the men in the processions gash themselves with knives and beat their backs with chains, in memory of the martyr's wounds.

Shi'ite Islam

Some 20 per cent of the world's Muslims are Shi'ites. Shi'ites claim that Sunni Islam is the creation of the lax and worldly Umayyad Caliphs backed up by the eminent but rather pedantic Muslim jurists of the ninth and tenth centuries CE, and that Shi'ite Islam is actually older and more closely based on the political practices of the Prophet ﷺ and the original four Caliphs. Sunnis reject this point of view, and claim that they represent authentic Islam – which is practical, tolerant and compassionate – and that the Shi'ites, in their quest for personal purity and interest in the theology of that which lies beyond human understanding, represent a speculative and extremist form of Islam.

Both Sunni and Shi'ite extremists are frequently regarded as troublemakers in the West because they will not compromise or accept a status quo that goes against their principles; their zealots preach revolution against tyranny and corruption, and have stirred up numerous uprisings and civil wars, interpreting the verses about jihad in the Qur'an to mean that they should put all their energy into conversion of the world by driving away the devil and all his works. (The West has typically been regarded as corrupt – through sexual freedoms, drugs, and American politics – and known as 'the Great Satan'.)

Shi'ite Muslims claim that the Prophet ﷺ had always intended Ali to be his successor after his death, and had declared it at a huge gathering at Ghadir Khum after his final pilgrimage, but while Ali was involved in burying him, the Prophet's ﷺ close friend Abu Bakr (father of the Prophet's ﷺ wife Aishah) took control. They therefore reject the Caliphate of Abu Bakr and his successors. (Sunnis interpret the speech at Ghadir Khum as being no more than an acknowledgement of Ali's merit, and not a nomination for succession.)

Ever since the Caliphate passed to Mu'awiyah and other Umayyads after him, who were not direct descendants of the

Prophet ﷺ, the Shi'ites have agitated to replace them with a true descendant on the throne of a united Islamic Empire.

They reject the Sunni principle of 'the consensus of the community' (ijma) and substitute the doctrine of the Imam or spiritual head directly descended from Ali. Shi'ites believe the choice of these Imams was divinely determined by birth, not left to human error. They were blessed with divinely inspired knowledge, which was infallible.

The Shi'ites later divided into two major branches known as Seveners or Twelvers according to whether they believed in 12 or seven Imams. In each group, they claim that the last of their Imams mysteriously disappeared without dying, and now follows the course of history in a mystical way. They believe that their 'Hidden Imam' (or Mahdi) is forever present in the world, although unseen, appearing to the faithful in their times of need and sending out his light to convert all mankind. He appears to people in prayer and strengthens the faithful in times of persecution. He will eventually return to establish righteous rule and bring about the end of the world. The Seveners and Twelvers then split into further sub-sects, notably the Isma'ilis.

Other key Shi'ite differences from Sunni Islam are their belief that God has foreknowledge of all human action, but does not predestine it; a different form of call to prayer and ritual ablution before prayer; the permission of temporary marriage (mutah) which was repealed by the Prophet ﷺ after initially allowing it; the veneration of shrines and tombs of Imams, and the permission to conceal their beliefs (taqiyya) in order to avoid persecution and suffering, or argument with the mainstream Sunni, who regard all these things as incorrect.

Iranian Shi'ism (perhaps from a Persian Zoroastrian background) draws sharp boundaries between the worlds of light and darkness, black and white, haq (truth) and batel (falsehood), and is undergirded by a conviction that the world is unsafe for Shi'ites. Neither the Prophet ﷺ, his family, nor any of the 12 Shi'a Imams died a natural death (they believe the Prophet ﷺ died as the result of poisoning), which contributes to the tendency to feel relentlessly persecuted.

The chief Shi'ite holy cities are Najaf in Iraq, (the burial place of Ali – the tomb is located four miles from Kufa where Ali was felled by Kharijite assassins in 661), and Karbala, the site of the martydom of the Prophet's ﷺ grandson Hussein.

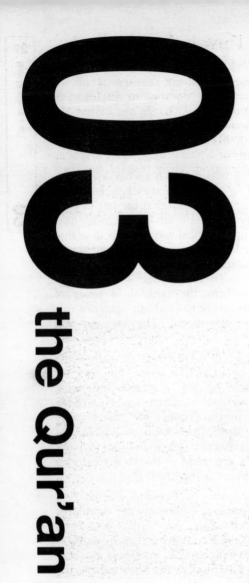

03

the Qur'an

In this chapter you will
learn about:
- facts about the Qu'ran
- the compilation of the Qu'ran
- how Muslims respect the
  Qu'ran.

Writing down the Revelations

The Qur'an was revealed to the Prophet ﷺ bit by bit over a period of some 23 years. Muslims believe that it is the Word of Allah, exactly as the Prophet ﷺ received it, and in this sense it is different from any other of the world's holy books, since they were all created by human authors many years after the deaths of the prophets involved, and were then edited and revised and added to by disciples. The Qur'an contains nothing but the direct revelations from Allah, through the angel Jibril, not one word of it being the creation of the Prophet ﷺ. He was nothing more than the transmitter. (The Prophet's ﷺ own teachings and sayings run into many thousands and are known as *hadiths*.)

As each revelation was given, the verses were learnt by heart and jotted down on whatever materials came to hand – dried-out palm leaves, pieces of broken pottery, ribs and shoulder bones of sheep, bits of animal skin and flat stones.

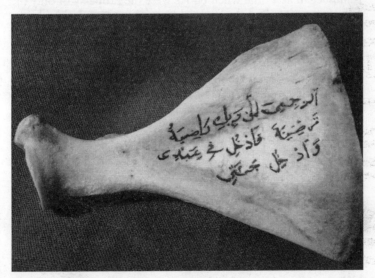

figure 3.1 a verse of the Qur'an on a sheep's shoulder bone

A single verse is known as an *ayah* (meaning a 'sign'), and a chapter is a *surah* (a step up). There are 114 surahs of varying lengths (all except the ninth beginning with the words '*In the Name of Allah, the Most Compassionate, the Most Merciful*'), and 6,616 ayahs – a total of 78,000 words in Arabic.

The surahs are not in chronological order, however. It is generally accepted that the first words are in surah 96:1–5 and the final words are in surah 5. The order was also something revealed to the Prophet ﷺ, who had to recite the whole collection revealed so far to the angel every Ramadan, and the entire text was checked with the angel twice, shortly before the Prophet ﷺ died.

The first surah is called *al-Fatihah* (the Opening). Each surah is named after some striking incident or word in it, so some have strange names like *al-Baqarah* (the Cow) and *al-Ankabut* (the Spider). Others have names of Allah, for example, *al-Nur* (the Light), *al-Rahman* (the Merciful). The Cow is actually about religious duties, divorce laws and rules governing fair conduct of war.

Compiled as a book

Islam began at a time when books were the property of only the rich, and people had the habit of learning a great deal by heart. Anyone who knew the full text of the Qur'an was known as a *hafiz* (plural *huffaz*).

After the Prophet's ﷺ death, Abu Bakr, requested the Prophet's ﷺ Companion Zayd ibn Thabit to put together the first complete written version in one Book. Zayd had been the Prophet's ﷺ secretary from the age of 12. He was reluctant to do something the Prophet ﷺ had not authorized, but was eventually persuaded, and gathered the text 'from the leaves of the date, and white stones, and the breasts of people that remembered it', of whom he was one.

He did not alter the messages in any way; no explanations or editorial comments were added. The pages of this text were kept by Abu Bakr, passed to Umar, and then to his daughter, Hafsah the Prophet's ﷺ widow, and were known as the *mushaf* of Hafsah.

Uthman's 'recension'

When many of the original huffaz had passed away, and Muslims were beginning to write down verses in their dialects, this brought with it a danger of personal interpretation, misinterpretation, and alternative versions (*qira'ah*). Uthman realized the danger of the Revelation being corrupted, since all translations and editions were dependent upon the skills of the translator or editor; so in 651 he ordered that all texts which individuals owned were either checked for full agreement against Hafsah's text, or destroyed.

Uthman had six copies of this 'standard' text inscribed on the specially prepared skins of sacrificed goats. He kept one for himself in Madinah, and sent the others to the chief Muslim centres – Makkah, Kufa, Damascus, Cairo, and Sana'. Since then all texts have been identical, and handed down to us unaltered; and there is probably no other book in the world which has remained 12 centuries with so pure a text.

If non-Arabic-speaking Muslims wish to read the Qur'an translated into their own languages, it is best done with the original Arabic alongside. Muslim scholars all try to master Arabic, and those with no Arabic usually refer to several translations.

The art of calligraphy

Calligraphy means 'beautiful writing'. The early scribes concentrated on finding styles worthy of the words they were putting down. Master writers believed that a person's handwriting revealed their inner character and nature, so only a spiritually pure person should attempt the task.

The earliest scripts were the *Ma'il* (slanting) and the *Mashq* (extended), and the most famous are *Kufic* (from the Islamic centre at Kufa) and *Naskhi* (inscriptional). Eighth century Kufic has formal, simple lines easily drawn on parchment or inscribed on stone, but so angular and ornamented that only a practised eye can read it. The more cursive Naskhi style is easier to understand, and more easily done with pen on paper. It largely displaced the Kufic script and became the standard for most Qur'ans from the eleventh century onwards, and is the script used for virtually all printed Qur'ans today.

The first hand-written Qur'ans had no artwork, because the scribes believed it was wrong to make representations of heavenly (or even human) beings; and they did not wish people to pay attention to the decoration rather than the content of the verses. Later, the wealthy sultans commissioned lavish and colourful Qur'ans resplendent in gold, green, red and blue. A superb Qur'an in gold script on blue vellum survives almost intact from Kairouan in Tunisia where it was originally inscribed in the late ninth or early tenth century. The bulk of it is preserved in the National Library of Tunisia (a number of leaves removed from it are to be found in other public libraries and private collections).

The fate of the oldest Qur'ans

Leaves of the six special copies prepared under the official supervision of Uthman still exist. The one sent to Makkah was destroyed by fire in 683 CE, and those commissioned for Madinah and Kufa were also lost irretrievably.

One codex was found in Iraq by the conqueror Tamerlane who took it to his capital, Samarqand, where it remained from c.1485–1868 CE, and was then removed to St. Petersburg/Leningrad). Fifty facsimiles were prepared at the instigation of Czar Nicholas the Second in 1905, and the original sent to Uzbekistan. This is now kept in the Soviet State Library at Tashkent. It is incomplete, with only about one-third (some 250) of the original pages surviving, written in a bold *Hejazi* script, similar to Kufic script. It has eight to 12 lines of script to the page. Many pages are mutilated.

Critics often point out that there are many references to claims made in different parts of the Muslim world to possess not only one of Uthman's copies, but even his own copy stained with the blood of his assassination. In fact, the Tashkent text does appear to have the bloodstain, on Surah 2.137.

Another ancient manuscript is kept on public display in the Topkapi Museum in Istanbul, and another manuscript at the al-Hussein mosque in Cairo, the stack of leaves standing a staggering 50 centimetres high.

Modern technology has now taken over the task of the copyist; the Tashkent Qur'an has recently been photocopied.

How respect is shown to the Qur'an

The Qur'an is not just a book, but the Sacred Text. If Muslims have the space, their Qur'an may be kept in a special room which is kept clean and used only for prayer and reading the holy Text.

When a Qur'an is in the room, Muslims are expected to behave with reverence, so it would not be proper to act indecently, rudely, cruelly or selfishly. The Qur'an imparts an atmosphere of prayer – it is the silent reminder of the Muslim submission to Allah. If a TV or video is in that room any crude, violent or abusive programme content would not be suitable.

figure 3.2 Muslims start their studies at an early age

While the Qur'an is being recited aloud, Muslims should not speak, eat or drink, smoke, or make any distracting noise. Before touching the Qur'an, Muslims should be in a state of *wudu* (see page 67), or at least wash their hands. Muslim women would usually cover their heads as for prayer, and a woman who is menstruating or has recently given birth should not touch it.

Before beginning to read, Muslims 'prepare the heart' by consciously thinking about Allah and seeking refuge from Satan (Surah 16:98). They adopt a special position, so that the body is disciplined and alert, often sitting on the floor with the Qur'an on a special stand (called a *rehl* or *kursi*) in front of them. It is disrespectful to place the Qur'an on the floor.

Reading with heart, soul, mind and strength is known as *tilawah*, and the practice of correct pronunciation (usually learned in the mosque school or *madrassah*) is called *tajwid*. Many Muslims do not speak Arabic, and some initially learn how to recite the verses without understanding what they mean. However, as they progress in Islam they should also learn the meanings, and see how the messages apply to them and how they should alter their own lives.

figure 3.3 studying the Qur'an

When the reading is finished, the Qur'an is put away carefully. It should not be left casually on a table, where someone might put something down on top of it! Muslims are sometimes shocked and offended to see Qur'ans kept and handled in shops, libraries and classrooms.

Translations of the Qur'an into other languages are not regarded as being quite the same thing as the Qur'an itself, and most Muslims in countries where printed books are commonplace are used to the idea of translations being treated casually. It is perhaps important to realize, however, that a Muslim might be horrified rather than flattered by a non-Muslim, not in wudu, pulling a Qur'an out of his pocket to have a quick read in the pub!

Insulting the Qur'an

As the direct Word of God, Muslims react strongly when they see or feel that the Qur'an has been treated with insult or disrespect.

Muslims object to anything that contains God's name or revealed words to be misused, as in advertisements; one outrage was a design that looked strikingly similar to the Arabic name of God on the sole of a sports shoe. To be 'under the feet' has been a gross insult in the Middle East for centuries. Another design, tactfully withdrawn, was the Burger King logo for its ice cream cups.

Deteriorating or no-longer-usable worn-out Qur'ans are either buried or stored in a special room or 'grave' (like the Jewish *genizah*), as in the Sana' collection. Even newspapers in Muslim societies are disposed of carefully, in case they have the name of God or Qur'anic text in them. They may be buried, burnt or binned – but never left around to be used on wet floors or for other undignified purposes. Even a piece of jewellery inscribed with the name of God or Qur'anic text would be taken off before entering a toilet. In 2005 a soldier in the Guantanamo Bay prison camp reportedly flushed a Qur'an down a toilet after urinating on it, sparking off a huge outcry.

04

the sunnah - the Prophet's ﷺ way

ﷺ

In this chapter you will learn about:
- how Muslims find out about the Prophet's ﷺ way of life
- the hadith collections
- the meaning of sunnah, din and shari'ah
- the techniques for working out Islamic law.

'Show us the Straight Way, the way of those on whom You have bestowed Your grace, whose (portion) is not wrath, and who do not go astray.'

(Surah 1:6–7)

The life and example of the Prophet ﷺ is known as the *sunnah*. The *Shari'ah* is the general title for Islamic law. The *din* (pr. *deen*) is the complete Islamic way of life. The sunnah is known from a study of the hadiths, the sayings and teachings of the Prophet ﷺ, and narratives about him recorded by his friends and handed down to later generations.

Although the hadiths are not part of the Qur'an revelation, nevertheless they are regarded as vitally important for the full understanding of Islam. They often explain matters or give extra information about the matters ordained by Allah. Once, his wife Aishah was asked about the Prophet's ﷺ customs and way of life. She replied: 'His way of life IS the Qur'an.'

The Qur'an is roughly the same length as the New Testament. The teachings of Muhammad ﷺ himself, if all put together, would work out about the size of the Encyclopedia Britannica.

The hadith collections

The Prophet ﷺ actually disliked the writing down of his hadiths, lest anyone should mistake them for the Qur'anic revelations. Once the difference was quite clear, the Prophet ﷺ did not object. The Companion Abu Sa'id al-Khudri commented that what the Prophet ﷺ particularly objected to were hadiths being recorded on the same piece of parchment that had Qur'an on it.

The importance of checking

The Prophet's ﷺ disciples used to make a conscious effort to memorize his sayings accurately. The Companions used to sit in a circle to recount hadiths to each other from memory; sometimes as many as 60 people joined these circles.

The Prophet ﷺ gave a very stern warning to those who might be tempted to make things up or exaggerate: 'Whoever intentionally ascribes to me what I have not said, then let him occupy a place in Hell-fire.' (Bukhari)

The Companions were prepared to go to enormous lengths to check the hadiths. Jabir once undertook a month-long journey to Syria to hear a single hadith. Abu Ayyub once travelled to Egypt just to check the exact words of a hadith, and when he was satisfied set off home again without even entering the house for refreshment.

By the third century AH there was a vast amount of material in circulation, and unfortunately it is a well-known fact that many hadiths were pious fabrications. There is a record of one man being executed for inventing some 4,000 of them! The scholars developed very strict rules for deciding whether a hadith was *sahih* (authentic), *da'if* (weak), or *maudu* (doubtful). The chain of transmitters was always carefully examined. Out of tens of thousands scrutinized only a limited number were selected for the compilations and, of those selected, the scholars could only count on their own judgement, which was not infallible.

The two most important collections of hadiths are those of Imam Muhammad b. Isma'il al-Bukhari (d.870 CE), which is regarded as the most authentic (a collection of 7,563 hadiths, covering a vast range of subjects), and Muslim b. al-Hajjaj (d.875 CE) containing 7,422 hadiths. It is easier to read than Bukhari's collection because it arranges all the sayings relevant to one issue together. There are four other collections considered authentic – Ibn Majah (d.886 CE), Abu Dawud (d.888 CE), Tirmidhi (d.892 CE) and Nisa'i (d.915 CE), and all hadiths in them are accepted as being genuine by virtually all Muslims.

Weak and suspect hadiths

It is vital to realize that if a hadith is not in keeping with the words or principles of the Qur'an, it cannot be considered genuine. The Prophet ﷺ said: 'After me many hadiths will be related. Thus, when one is said to be a saying of mine, check it against the Qur'an. If it agrees with the Qur'an accept it, and if it disagrees with the Qur'an, reject it.' (*Kitab al-tawdeeh wat-talweeh* page 480).

Is keeping the sunnah compulsory?

The vast majority of Muslims would never go against the teachings of the Prophet ﷺ as recorded in the hadiths; but occasionally reformers or people wishing to 'update' Islam take the point of view that it is enough to study the Qur'an, and that if Allah had wished a thing to be known or done, He would have certainly included it in the Qur'an and not left it to chance.

The Prophet ﷺ himself was well aware that this would happen, and gave clear warning against it:

> 'I have indeed been given the Qur'an and something similar to it besides it. Yet, the time will come when a man leaving on his couch will say: "Follow the Qur'an only; what you find in it as halal, take as halal, and what you find in it as haram, take it as haram." But truly, what the Messenger of Allah has forbidden is like what Allah has forbidden.'

> (Abu Dawud and Darimi)

The Qur'an granted the Prophet ﷺ enormous authority:

> *'Take whatever the Messenger gives you, and keep away from what he forbids you.'*

> (Surah 59:7)

The Prophet ﷺ specifically stated:

> 'Behold, I have left among you two things; you will never go astray so long as you hold fast to them – the Book of Allah and my sunnah.'[2]

> (Hakim)

Fard and sunnah

Many Muslims are so devout that they take all the Prophet's ﷺ *sunnat* (recommendations) as *fard* (compulsory obligations of Islam). However, scholars do make a difference between the two on these grounds: if a fard is missed, then the Muslim has committed a sin for which he or she would be accountable, and if the fard is done, they have done good for which they will be rewarded; but on the other hand, if a Muslim does something sunnah, he or she will be rewarded for it, but there is no punishment if it is omitted. This is a very important difference.

---

[2]The Shi'ite version of this saying differs significantly. The two things mentioned are the Book of Allah and the Prophet's ﷺ descendants.

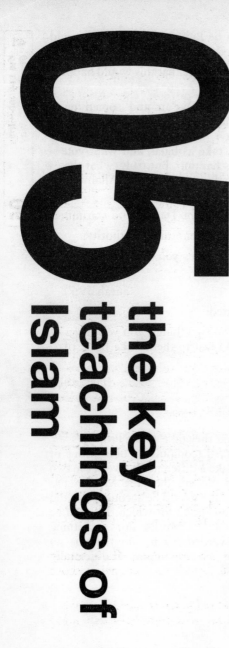

05

the key teachings of Islam

In this chapter you will learn about:
- Islamic theological terms
- the key beliefs of Islam:
  - the reality of the One Almighty God
  - the channel of prophecy
  - the judgement and life to come
- free-will and predestination.

Tawhid and shirk

There are three basic concepts in a Muslim's awareness of God – His One-ness, His Transcendence, and His Immanence.

God's Unity or One-ness is known as tawhid, 'There is no God but One'. Muslims reason that if God is the First Cause, Creator and Supreme Force in the universe, there can only be One by definition – it is impossible to have two 'supremes' or 'first causes'.

Nothing is remotely like God, and nothing can be compared to Him. Nothing shares His power, and He certainly does not have partners, or any kind of 'family'. The name al-lah is the name also used for God by Arab Christians. It means 'the Almighty', 'the Supreme'.

> 'He is Allah (the Supreme), the One. Allah is Eternal and Absolute. None is born of Him. He is Unborn. There is none like unto Him.'
>
> (Surah 112)

God is only referred to as 'He' because it is traditional. 'He' has no gender; this is why Muslims prefer to use the word 'Allah' rather than 'God', which has a female form, goddess. All the many names of God revealed in the Qur'an reflect qualities and not sexuality, for example, al-Badi (the One Who creates out of nothing); al-Batin (the One Who knows the latent and hidden properties of things); al-Muqit (the Controller).

Many times He is called Rabb, or Lord; but never once in the entire 23 years of revelations did He call Himself Abb, or Father. This cannot have been accidental. The word 'Father' has human and sexual connotations, and although Muslims are aware of God in an intimate and personal way, they think of Him as Creator rather than Father. To a Muslim, the concept of 'father' has dangerous implications that can lead into shirk (the division of the unity of God).

Allah, the Supreme knows and sees everything. He is totally 'other' from His created universe, outside time, eternal, without beginning or end.

> 'No vision can grasp Him, but His grasp is over all vision. He is above all comprehension, yet is acquainted with all things.'
>
> (Surah 6:103)

He is beyond the limits of the human mind. It is impossible for humans to imagine what He is like, except as He chooses to reveal it. Our senses always present a limited picture of reality; for example, we think we can touch and see solids, but the microscope reveals something completely different. Allah revealed that He is absolute Order, Justice, Mercy, Truth and Love, and many other concepts.

He is the Owner of everything; what humans think they own is allotted to them by God's will, a gift, and should be used in order to do His will, and must be given back to God in due course.

The love and compassion of Allah

God is not only Creator, He is also Judge, and the eternal fate of every living being lies in His 'hands'. Thankfully, the justice of Allah is not the same as that of human beings, who have incomplete knowledge, or who can be vengeful. God knows every thought and motive, every influence acting upon a person. The nature of Allah, repeated over and over again in the revelation, is Love and Compassion. (*Allah, ar-Rahman ar-Rahim.*)

His mercy is far greater than any humans have the right to expect, or that they show to each other.

> 'If God punished us according to what we deserve, He would leave on earth not one living thing.'

> (Surah 34:45; 16:61)

> 'O My servants, who have transgressed against their own souls! Do not despair of the mercy of God, for Allah forgives all sins. He is the Compassionate, the Merciful.'

> (Surah 39:53)

Many humans, of course, find this hard to accept, either because they are too proud, or too hard-hearted, or too despairing, or for many other reasons. Nevertheless, Allah assures us of His mercy constantly throughout the Qur'an and hadiths.

> 'O child of Adam – so long as you call upon Me and ask of Me I shall forgive you for what you have done . . . Were you to come to Me with sins as great as the earth itself, and were you then to face Me, ascribing no partner to Me, I would forgive you in equal measure.'

> (Tirmidhi, Ahmad)

Similarly, Muslims are expected to forgive those who sin against them, to treat them with gentleness and 'cover' their faults (Surah 3:159).

The unseen

The universe consists of that which is seen and understood by our five senses, and that which is unseen (known as *al-Ghayb*). What we see and understand is only the tip of the iceberg in the vastness of God's creation. The two most important non-physical created entities are angels and jinn.

Angels are the agents and servants of God, the means by which He governs the universe and the channels by which humans become aware of Him. They do not have free-will, but carry out God's wishes. They are sometimes seen by people in times of crisis; many sensitive people feel aware of their presence when they pray and meditate. They may take any shape or form.

Each human is assigned two special angels as guardians and 'recorders'; they activate a person's conscience, and note down every good and evil deed in each person's 'book', the record which they will see and understand, and on which they will be judged on the Day. All good deeds are recorded for ever, but if a person repents, the record of the evil deed is wiped out.

'Surely those who say "our Lord is Allah" and who follow the straight path, the angels descend upon them saying: "Fear not and do not be sad ... we are your protecting friends in this life and in the next."'

(Surah 41:30–1)

A few angels are named and have specific roles: Jibril (Gabriel) brings messages to the chosen ones, and is frequently referred to as the 'holy spirit' in the Qur'an; Mika'il (Michael), is the protector of holy places and life-sustainer in times of trouble; Azra'il takes away the souls of the dying; Israfil is the angel who calls the souls on Judgement Day; Munkar and Nakir are the questioners; Malik, the keeper of Hell; Ridwan, the keeper of Paradise.

Jinn are also non-physical beings, and they can be either good or evil, having free-will like humans. They are thought to inhabit unclean places, and can often frighten and confuse human beings by involving themselves in their lives and homes. Occasionally they attempt to possess human bodies and have to be exorcized. They are not always malevolent, however, and Surah 72 mentions jinn that were converted to Islam.

The Devil, (Shaytan or Iblis), is not a fallen angel in Islamic tradition, but the chief of the jinn. He became the origin of evil through pride, disobedience and rebellion when he refused God's command to honour the newly created humans because he thought he knew better than God. Out of jealousy, he became the enemy of all humans, determined to lead people's hearts and minds away from God. (See Surah 15:28–31; see also 2:36; 3:36; 4:117–120; 5:94; 7:200–1; 8:48; 15:17,34; 16:98–100; 22:52–3; 24:21; 35:6; 36:60.) Evil is never equal to Good.

Human beings

So far as we know, human beings are the highest physical creations of Allah, and possess both material and spiritual characteristics. Each being has a distinct individual soul (the *rouh*). It is the soul and not the body the soul lives in, that is the real person.

Adam and Eve, or evolution?

Muslims believe that human beings are all descended from an original soul created by God and then divided into male and female (Surah 4.1). As regards the theory of evolution, it is as yet unproven and remains no more than a theory, for which there is debatable evidence; apes were created in their own image, and still exist as apes, and so on. Many Muslims accept the notion of 'intelligent' or 'guided evolution', but believe that all scientific theories should be studied with an open mind, since today's 'facts' are often quickly out of date with new discoveries.

It is usually accepted that the first created humans were Adam ﷺ and Eve[3]. The Qur'an does indeed state that Adam ﷺ was created without parents, from 'clay', which may symbolize that human beings are made of or dependent upon humus. The tradition about the woman being created from Adam's ﷺ rib is not part of the Qur'an; the Prophet ﷺ referred to it with some humour when counseling male Companions not to try straightening them, as they would snap.

[3]A grave said to be Eve's exists in Jiddah, and Adam's ﷺ skull is said to be buried in Jerusalem.

The Qur'an also states that Allah chose a human, Adam ﷺ, and called him to be His *khalifah* or deputy on earth, responsible for the care of the planet (Surah 2.30–2). Humans have an allotted time-span of life on earth, over which they have no control. They are created with equal rights and are equally loved by God, but do not have equal talents or characteristics. Because they exercise free-will they can love and be kind, or hate and be destructive. Their worth in Islam is not measured in intelligence or status, but in submission to God and right living.

Tests

Life is not seen as random with no point, but as a period of training and testing for the life to come. We are allotted circumstances, talents, and so forth, and are tested in the use we make of them.

'We shall certainly test you with fear and hunger and with the loss of goods or lives or the fruits of your toil. But give encouragement to those who patiently persevere, and, when calamity befalls them, say: "We belong to Allah, and to Him do we return."'

(Surah 2:155–6)

Some are tested with poverty or ill health – will they become despairing, dishonest, or show patience and faith? Others are tested by being rich – what use will they make of their riches? Will they become selfish, greedy, or act with responsibility? It is pointless to bewail one's lot – all situations can be reversed in a second if God wills; the Muslims' duties are to accept, remain firm, patient and faithful, and seek to do God's will in whatever circumstances they find themselves.

Risalah – revelation

If the Muslim's duty is to serve God and do His will, it is God's duty to explain clearly what that will is, otherwise the individual cannot be held responsible for their choices (Surah 17:15). *Risalah* is the channel of communication from Allah. A prophet who merely taught and did not leave writings is a *nabi*, and one who left writings is a *rasul*.

No judgement without a prophet first

> 'At that time Allah will also ask: "O Assembly of Jinns and Humanity! Did not there come to you prophets from amongst you who proclaimed to you My revelations and warned you about the meeting of this Day?" They will reply: "Yes they did, we bear witness against our own souls." ... This testimony will be taken in order to prove that your Lord would not destroy towns without just cause while their residents were ignorant of the Reality.'
>
> (Surah 6. 130–1)

The chain of prophecy

Before the Blessed Muhammad ﷺ there was a whole chain of prophets, including the 26 named in the Qur'an, that were sent to people of all times and races with messages suitable to those who heard them. These include 23 celebrities known from the Bible; Noah (Nuh), Abraham (Ibrahim), Moses (Musa), John the Baptist (Yahya ibn Zakriyah), Jesus ('Isa), and many others. Only three are not named in the Bible – Hud, Salih and Shu'aib – though this last is believed to be the same as Jethro, Moses's father-in-law (may peace be upon all of them). The great leaders of other monotheistic faiths may have been amongst the thousands of unnamed prophets.

Holy books mentioned in the Qur'an

Four Divinely Revealed books are mentioned in the Qur'an; the *Sahifa* or scrolls dictated to Abraham ﷺ, the *Tawrat* (or Torah) revealed to Moses ﷺ, the *Zabur* (or Psalms) of David ﷺ, and the *Injil* (or Gospel) revealed to Jesus ﷺ. The first is completely lost, and Muslims believe that the others are not to be identified with the contents of today's Bible, which are compilations and editions written many years after the prophets lived.

Was Muhammad ﷺ the greatest prophet?

It is considered inappropriate to try to guess who were the best prophets, or to elevate any messenger above the human status.

> 'Say: "We believe in God and that which has been revealed
> to us, and (also) that which was revealed to Abraham
> (Ibrahim), Ismail (Isma'il), Isaac (Yizhaq), Jacob (Yaqub)
> and the tribes, and in that given to Moses (Musa), Jesus
> ('Isa), and (all) the prophets from their Lord. We make no
> distinction between any of them, and to God do we submit
> our will."'

(Surah 3:84)

All the prophets were messengers from the One and the same
God, a single 'chain' or prophecy, and all are to be respected and
believed. Jesus ﷺ was the most famous as a miracle worker;
Muhammad is regarded as the 'seal' of the prophets, and the *last*
messenger. Although many other great teachers have inspired
the world throughout history since then, there have been no
further prophets in the chain bringing direct revelation from
God. Muhammad said:

> 'My relationship to the other prophets before me is that of
> a man who has expertly and beautifully built a house,
> except for the placement of one brick in the corner. People
> pass by and wonder at its beauty, but say: "Would that this
> final brick be put in its place!" I am that brick, and I am
> the last of the prophets.'

(Bukhari 4.735)

Jesus ﷺ

Jesus ﷺ is regarded by Muslims as one of the greatest of all
prophets, the miracle worker. It is always made very clear in the
Qur'an that he was not to be thought of as Divine, a Son of God,
in the Christian sense. Muslims believe in his virgin birth, but that
this was a miracle of God in creating a child without a father, not
that it made the miraculous child in any way a part of God.

Muslims believe Jesus ﷺ was the Messiah (Ar. *Masih*), the
messenger to the tribes of Israel. The vast majority of his
recorded teachings would be accepted as Islamic (especially such
well-known passages as the Sermon on the Mount, the Lord's
Prayer, the parables of the Prodigal Son, the Sheep and the
Goats, etc.), which teach clearly that God always forgives the
genuine penitent, and that we will be judged on the efforts and
actions of our lives, a judgement tempered by Allah's grace
and mercy.

Basically, Muslims believe what Jesus ﷺ taught but not the later doctrines taught about him. They can never accept the Church Creeds as formulated around a Trinitarian theology during the three to four centuries after Jesus's ﷺ lifetime. Throughout the Qur'an there are verses reminding Muslims that to believe that God has partners or a family is shirk and a fundamental misunderstanding of the nature of God.

Jesus ﷺ the saviour?

The Qur'an indicates that Jesus ﷺ was not overcome by death, and this is taken to mean either that God rescued him from crucifixion, or that he physically survived the crucifixion, and then ascended alive into Heaven (Surah 4:157). Another possible interpretation was that by God's will, death could not kill him. Christian theories in the centuries before Islam included Docetism (that Jesus ﷺ was never fully human), or that God somehow substituted another to die in his place (for example, Simon of Cyrene, Judas Iscariot). These theories also exist in Muslim folklore, but not in the Qur'an.

Jesus's ﷺ function can never be seen by a Muslim as a redeemer or saviour, except in the sense that those who follow his teachings will be 'saved'. He cannot be a sacrifice to save people from their sins – for every person will be judged as an individual, and no one will bear the sins of another. He was a messenger of God and his life was dedicated to showing the way to God. Islam teaches that Jesus ﷺ the masih will return before the end of the world and the Day of Judgement.

Akhirah – life after death

Muslims believe that the human soul lives only once on earth, and after death faces a Day of Judgement, and an eventual fate in either Paradise or Hell (*Jannam* and *Jahannam*).

After death the body is buried, but the soul of the good person may experience expanded horizons without limit, while the bad person is cramped in the grave. On the Day, God will resurrect all people, and recreate their decomposed bodies, down to the details of their individual fingerprints (Surah 45:24; 75:1–4). None will escape this, for God will reconstruct them, no matter how they died or what happened to their bodies.

Heaven and Hell are frequently described in graphic physical terms; Heaven, or Paradise, being like a beautiful garden, where people become young again and enjoy untainted pleasures, and Hell being a terrible, scorching place of torment, sorrow and remorse. Although many Muslims take the descriptions literally, there are also clues in the Qur'an that they should rather be considered symbolically, since Heaven and Hell are not physical dimensions at all, and our future state lies beyond the scope of our limited human knowledge.

> *'In Heaven, I prepare for the righteous believers what no eye has ever seen, no ear has ever heard, and what the deepest mind could never imagine.'*

> (Hadith Qudsi, and Surah 32:17)

> *'We will not be prevented from changing your forms and creating you again in forms you know not.'*

> (Surah 56:60–1)

Islam teaches that God does not wish to send anyone to Hell, and they will only be obliged to go there if they insist on evil living without repentance, and treating the truth of God as a lie.

Some Muslims even interpret Hell as being rather like a hospital, where the cure may be painful and drastic, but in the end the patient is made whole. Most accept that the state will be eternal.

> *'Their status in Heaven or Hell may last for eternity – but this is subject to God's will and mercy.'*

> (Surah 11:106–8)

Muslims do not believe in reincarnation (souls living a series of lives in different bodies), but no person may suggest a limit for what God might choose to do. The notion of reincarnation is rejected as there is no textual evidence for it in the Qur'an or hadiths.

al-Qadr – pre-destination

Muslims believe that the entire universe is under God's control and direction, therefore nothing can take place without His ordaining it. There cannot be such a thing as a random or chance event (see Surah 35:2; 57:22). Muslims accept that things happen according to our destinies; one often hears the phrase 'It is written' (Ar. *maktub*).

Everything is known (even the number of hairs on your head or how many breaths you will take in your life), and everything that happens is an expression of His will, and has purpose and meaning. God alone is the source of benefit or harm, and to turn to anything else for protection or help is futile.

This idea of pre-destination is notoriously difficult to reconcile with the concept of free-will, but Islam should not be considered a fatalistic religion. The whole point of sending messengers from God to give revelations is to allow humans to use their free-will; the whole point of human life is a test, which would be totally pointless if God had pre-destined human choices.

'Indeed Allah declared He would not alter the condition of humans until they changed what was in themselves.'

(Surah 13:11, 8:53)

Fatalism renders people helpless and weakens their sense of responsibility, a criticism frequently made of Muslims who misunderstand the importance of revelation and free-will. No prophet ever taught fatalism.

Although everything in the universe is governed by natural law, human beings are not governed in the same way that the Sun and Moon are, for example. We are warned that we are under Law, and the breach of Law brings penalty. This applies on both the physical and moral levels; if we do not wish to be burned, we must keep our hands out of the fire. It makes no difference whether or not we knew in advance that fire would burn.

The Sun is the source of light, but if we choose to close the curtains, it will become dark for us. If we stay in the darkness too long, our eyesight will suffer. These misfortunes occur according to natural laws, the outcomes of which God knows in advance, but we choose how we will act, and are judged accordingly.

Muslims accept that every breath we take is a gift fom God, and He alone knows how many breaths he has allotted to us. Can a person cheat God's will and die at a time other than the one allotted? Muslims accept there is a difference between dying (which happens when God wills) and killing – which is governed by human free-will and natural law (see pages 240–1).

06

worship – ibadah

Ibadah comes from the word '*abad*', meaning a slave or servant. Ibadah is therefore service of Allah, or slavery to Him. Basically, it is what Muslims mean by 'worship'. However, for Muslims, worship is not something confined to special days or particular prayers, but it involves a conscious awareness of God throughout the day, every day, and a conscious desire to carry out His will in every sphere of activity.

The concepts of worship

Ihsan

Muslim worship really begins with the concept of *ihsan* or realization. It is perfectly possible for a human being to go through all sorts of forms of worship, prayer and other ritual without really being truly aware of the presence of God. Human nature being what it is, this rather barren worship can happen to anybody from time to time. However, ihsan implies that a person really is making a conscious effort to be 'in communication' with God.

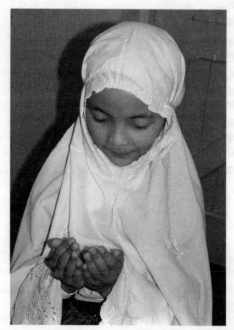

figure 6.1 'in communication with God' – this Muslim girl wears a prayer veil

There is a very famous hadith recorded by Caliph Umar that describes ihsan. One day the Prophet ﷺ was approached by a traveller in very white clothing, who sat down with him knee to knee, and asked him to tell him about Islam. This traveller was the angel Jibril, the very one who had revealed the messages of the Qur'an to the Prophet ﷺ. One of the direct questions he asked was for a definition of ihsan. The Prophet ﷺ replied that it meant you should worship God as though you could see Him, for He sees you even though you do not see Him.

Awareness of God (also known as *taqwa* or God-consciousness) leads to deepened consciousness of the importance and meaningfulness of the gift of human life, and the desire to make the very best of it while one has the chance.

Iman

The word *iman* means 'faith'. When the same traveller (Jibril) asked the Prophet ﷺ to define iman, he replied that it was to believe in God, His angels, His books, His prophets, and the Last Day, and the decreeing of both good and evil. We have already considered the implications of iman in the previous sections.

Amal

Amal means 'action'. Muslims see no point in academic beliefs or doctrines unless they are translated into action. The whole point of Islam is to submit to Allah and direct your life into carrying out His will to the utmost of your ability.

The concept of amal can actually be divided into two categories. The first is to obey the command of Allah in the practice of the five disciplines known as the 'Five Pillars', which will be described shortly. The second is to do one's best in every aspect of daily life and routine to follow the sunnah or practice of the Prophet ﷺ, or at least the principles behind the sunnah (if one is dealing with some aspect of modern society that was beyond the personal experience of the Prophet ﷺ) so that every single thing one does is for the greater glory of God. That way, the Muslim believes he or she will keep on the right path, and will find peace, satisfaction, justice and happiness.

56

worship – ibadah

06

Din (*pr. Deen*)

Putting faith and way of life together is known as the din, the total desire to commit to Islam.

Jihad

Jihad is often thought to mean military activity, and obviously it can have a military context, but this is not the true meaning of the word. The definition of jihad according to Qur'an and sunnah is a struggle or an effort that is exerted in order to attain some end or result, any kind of striving which involves either spiritual or personal effort, material resources, or lastly, military means.

A jihad or struggle in the cause of Allah (*fi sabi'l illah*) involves an unceasing effort to eliminate evil in the form of wrong beliefs, ideas, and values that are projected via thoughts, words and deeds – things like racism, abuse, selfishness, laziness, miserliness, aggression and oppression. It could also be a personal struggle involving some form of hard work or effort to accomplish something of value for Allah's sake – such as studying, teaching others, caring for others in trying circumstances, facing up to bullying, even trying to eliminate some harmful personal habit, such as smoking or obesity.

The Greater jihad

The true jihad is the battle against what Muslims call *dunya* (literally 'the lusts and degradations of worldliness'). The jihad against selfishness, ignorance and corruption is the 'inner' or 'major' jihad (*jihad al-akhbar*) because all evil arises from the desire of the *nafs* or human soul to put self before Allah. Ignorance, arrogance and lack of compassion lie at the root of all evil, are the causes of all corruption, and the sources of all suffering. The opposite of ignorance is knowledge (*ilm*) that gives rise to wisdom (*hiqmah*). This jihad is therefore an act of devotion with the same significance as the Five Pillars of Islam, so much so that it is often called the Sixth Pillar. 'Striving after (the jihad for) knowledge,' said the Prophet ﷺ, 'is the sacred duty of every man and woman' (Ibn Majah).

While the sacrifice of struggle of jihad 'with the sword' is a great act when it comes to defending Islamic values, or the innocent and defenceless from unjustified aggression, the jihad 'with the word' (*dawah*) to spread the teachings and values of Islam to the ignorant is far greater. It was the first command to the Prophet ﷺ, (i.e. the command '*Iqra*!' meaning 'recite' or 'tell them') and many verses of the Qur'an start with the word '*Qol*' – 'speak' or 'say to them'. The Prophet ﷺ faithfully obeyed this charge laid upon him until his life's end, transforming people into a devout and virtuous community.

Dunya

Dunya (literally, 'the world'), as creation of God, is not in itself an evil thing or place, but there are certain aspects of material existence which are directly opposed to God's will.

The Prophet ﷺ said:

> 'It is not poverty which I fear for you, but that you might begin to desire the world as others before you desired it, and it might destroy you as it destroyed them.'

> (Bukhari and Muslim)

The most basic wrong thing is obsession with self. The self is a creation of Allah, and something to be loved, cherished, cared for and respected. But when a person becomes selfish then they are putting their own base greeds and desires before right living, and love of self has become a form of shirk. People who are selfish are worshipping themselves rather than God; they are certainly putting themselves before their duties towards God, which are generally expressed in our love and concern towards others, whether people or animals.

Thus, dunya represents the lure of the world's luxuries and lusts that lead people away from the right way and influence them to become miserly, greedy, cruel, cowardly, arrogant, callous and so on. *Jihad* is the fight against this tendency.

> *'The life of the world is but a past-time and a game. Lo! Real life is the Home of the Hereafter, if you but knew it.'*

> (Surah 29:64)

The Prophet ﷺ taught:

> 'Riches are sweet, and a source of blessing to those who acquire them by the way; but those who seek them out of greed are like people who eat but are never full.'

> (Bukhari)

'Richness does not lie in an abundance of worldly goods, but true richness is the richness of the soul.'

(Muslim)

Ummah

The Prophet ﷺ was told by Allah as part of His revelation to say:

'O *humanity! I am the messenger of God to you all!'*

(Surah 7:158)

'Believers are one single brotherhood (ummah), so make peace and reconciliation between two contenders, and have reverence for Allah, that you may receive mercy.'

(Surah 49:10)

The faith of Islam is a universal faith, intended for all people. The worldwide community of Muslims is known as the ummah. It extends across all places and ethnic groupings. Believers belong to local ummahs, or Muslim communities, but the entire worldwide Muslim community follows the same faith, shares the same basic values, and has sworn allegiance to the will of Allah and obedience to the Prophet ﷺ. When Muslims travel around the world, they find they can mix very easily with other Muslims, even if they do not understand their language.

Ibadah

'Declare your jihad on thirteen enemies you cannot see – egoism, arrogance, conceit, selfishness, greed, lust, intolerance, anger, lying, cheating, gossiping and slandering. If you can master and destroy them, then you will be ready to fight the enemy you can see.'

(al-Ghazzali – note: the thirteenth 'enemy' is not listed)

Taking all these concepts together, ihsan, iman, amal and jihad make up the Muslim concept of ibadah; worship of Allah. This is why Islam is not just a matter of ritual, prayers or fasting or feasts; it is the conscious bringing of every moment of the day, every decision, every detail of one's thoughts and actions, into deliberate line with what one accepts as being the will of Allah.

07

the pillars
of Islam

In this chapter you will
learn about:
- shahadah – bearing witness
- salah – prayer
  - the call to prayer
  - ritual and personal prayer
  - the purposes of prayer
  - prayer leaders, or imams
  - preparation for prayer
  - the formal Muslim prayer.

Shahadah – bearing witness

The first 'pillar' of Islam is *shahadah* or bearing witness to the faith. It is a simple statement of creed that falls into two parts: that there is no God but Allah (The Almighty), and that Muhammad ﷺ is His genuine messenger. It comes from the word '*ash-shadu*' which means 'I declare' or 'I bear witness'.

In Arabic, the words are:

'Ash-shadu an la ilaha illallah wa Muhammadar-rasulullah.'

When people make this declaration and truly believe it in their hearts, then they have entered the faith. There is no ceremony like a Christian baptism; what counts is the conscious awareness and firm conviction that one genuinely does hold these two beliefs.

Sometimes a new Muslim will talk things over with an imam (teacher), or have a course of study sessions; once the new Muslim takes the decision to become Muslim (or realizes that he or she is Muslim), their first act is to declare the faith publicly, in front of two witnesses. From that moment of public witness, they have started on the path of submission to God. Some new Muslims, particularly white ones, like to have a certificate for occasions when proof might be needed. However, shahadah is not just a matter of reciting words; it is something that has to be believed with all one's heart, because following this declaration Muslims are intended to trust God with all their hearts, and hand over their lives to His service.

Making this decision can cause some pretty drastic changes. It involves far more than words; your whole life must back up what has been declared. Most people coming into Islam in the Western world have to change a great deal of their diet and lifestyle; they have to give up pork products, any animal products that are not *halal* (permitted), alcohol, entertainment based on the social giving of alcohol, immodest dress, and so forth. They also have to give up arrogance, selfishness, deceitfulness, lust and indecency and many other weaknesses of character.

The call to prayer

The shahadah is also used for the call to prayer five times per day. If the mosque has a tower, a man known as the *muezzin* or *mu'adhin* climbs up and calls aloud:

Allahu Akbar! (four times)
Ash-hadu an la ilaha illallah (twice)
Ash-hadu ana Muhammadar-rasulullah (twice)
Hayya ala-salah (twice)
Hayya ala-falah (twice)
Allahu Akbar (twice)
La ilaha illallah. (once)

In English, these words mean:

God is the Most Great!
I bear witness that there is no God but Allah.
I bear witness that Muhammad ﷺ is the Prophet of Allah.
Come to prayer!
Come to success (or salvation)!
God is the Most Great!
There is no God but Allah!

At the end of the first prayer of the day the phrase 'It is better to pray than to sleep!' is added – '*as-salatul khairum min an-naum.*'

This call to prayer is known as the *adhan*, and it gives Muslims time to get ready if they are going to attend at the mosque. Just before the actual start of the prayers, a second call to prayer is uttered before the congregation, known as the *iqamah*. It is the same as the adhan, except that the words '*qad qamatis salah*' – 'The prayer has begun' – are added before the final *Allahu Akbars*.

Other times that the shahadah is pronounced are at the birth of a new baby, first thing on waking and last thing before going to sleep at night and, if possible, they are the last words in the hearing of a dying person.

Salah – prayer

'*O you who believe! Be steadfast in prayer and regular in charity, and whatever good you send forth for your souls before you, you shall find it with God; for truly God sees all that you do.*'

(Surah 2:110)

Prayer is the second pillar of Islam. Prayer in general terms means being conscious of God and communicating with Him in some way or another, and Muslims try to maintain an attitude of prayer and be constantly aware of God throughout the day.

However, the prayer ritual of *salah* is somewhat different from the casual making of appeals to God of a personal nature. It is perhaps better translated in English as 'worship' rather than 'prayer'.

Salah is a ritual of movements and words (each full sequence of which is called a *rakah*), some of the words repeated as part of the regular routine, and others chosen from the Qur'an by the Muslim as he or she wishes. This prayer is one of the five duties laid down as fard, or 'compulsory', for a Muslim. Allah requires those who submit to carry out this prayer five times per day, at certain set times.

Prayer times

The five daily prayers are now known as fajr (the morning prayer between dawn and sunrise), zuhr (just after the height of the midday Sun), asr (during the afternoon when the shadows have lengthened), maghrib (just after sunset), and isha (during the hours of darkness).

The prayer times deliberately avoid the exact times delineated by sunrise, midday and sunset because of their pagan connotations of Sun worship. At those exact times, Muslims are actually ordered not to pray. However, the times are obviously related to the Sun's progress through the day, and since times of sunrise and sunset change according to the seasons and the country in which one lives, these days Muslims usually have timetables for each region showing the exact moments when the prayer times begin and end. (In the United Kingdom sunrise comes very early in summer months; Muslims are allowed to go back to bed after they have performed their fajr prayer!)

Since many Muslims go to the mosque to pray together, they also have timetables for congregational prayer, for obvious practical reasons. Many mosques set up clock faces showing these times, five for the daily prayers and one for the special Friday prayer.

Muslims regard it as preferable that men meet together in congregation to pray, but women are generally encouraged to pray in the home. However, there should be nothing to prevent women coming to congregation if they so wish, and it is not compulsory for men to attend every single prayer in the mosque if they prefer to pray elsewhere.

figure 7.1 young men praying together

Salat al-jama'ah

Only one congregational prayer in the mosque is regarded as compulsory, the midday prayer on Fridays – *salat al-jama'ah* – also known as *salat al-jumah*. The word *'jama'ah'* means 'congregation' or 'gathering', and the word *'jumah'* simply means Friday. All adult male Muslims are expected to attend, and are thought to have left Islam if they do not attend for more than three weeks. In Islamic countries all shops and businesses close during this time, so that men can go.

> *'O believers, when proclamation is made for prayer on the Day of Congregation, hasten to God's remembrance and leave business aside; that is better for you, did you but know.'*

> (Surah 62:9)

Even Muslim men who are negligent about the other daily prayers make an effort to gather at the mosque on Fridays. During the special service, the key features are the two *khutbahs* or sermons given by the imam. The Congregational Prayer itself consists of only two rakahs. After this, people can pray individually, and then go back to work. Having allowances made for Friday prayer is one of the difficulties confronting workers and students in non-Muslim countries where Friday is not a day off.

It is sometimes possible to make up a congregation in the workplace or school, but Muslims always consider it preferable to meet together in the full congregation at the mosque, wherever possible.

Individual devotion, not priests

In the age-old conflict between 'priestly' religion and personalized and accountable faith, Islam comes down solidly behind the latter. Historically, organized religion always seems to have been a battle between those who claim that only special priestly figures, with special knowledge of how to perform the ritual and carry out sacrifices accurately, are effective, and those who claim that such formalism is meaningless before a God who requires personal morality and devotion. (Some people in the Christian faith would no doubt see the historical conflict between the 'Romanism' of Roman Catholics and the 'Protest' of Protestants in the same terms.)

For many simple folk in pre-Islamic times, worship had become little more than a vast system of sacrifice, the value of which depended not so much upon the moral conduct of the individual worshipper as on the qualification of the officiating priest. Priests monopolized the number, length and terminology of prayers, the liturgies and dogma, and were largely responsible (even if unintentionally) for the notion that an individual could turn up to a congregation once a week to make up for the spiritual and moral deficiencies of the other six days.

There are no priests in Islam. No monopoly of spiritual knowledge or special holiness intervenes between believer and God. No sacrifice or ceremonial is needed to bring the anxious heart nearer to the Comforter. Each Muslim is his or her own priest, no individual being denied the possibility of drawing near to God through his or her own faith. Islam recognizes the dignity and responsibility of every individual human soul; each person faces God on a one-to-one basis, in worship which is a most heart-felt outpouring of devotion and humility before God.

The practice of the Prophet ﷺ has, however, attached certain rites and ceremonies to Muslim prayer, and this is the most obvious aspect of it to an observer; it should be pointed out in unmistakable terms that it is to the devotional state of the mind that the Searcher of the spirit looks. Prayer without the presence of the heart is to no avail; devotion without understanding is a useless empty formalism and brings no blessing. Mere external or physical purity does not imply true devotion, but rather a sense of pride and religious hypocrisy. It is purity of heart and mind, and humility of spirit that bring an individual close to God.

Imams

The person who stands before the congregation leading the prayer is not in any sense a priest, but simply a person who has volunteered to lead, someone who is respected, has good knowledge of Muslim faith, and who knows enough of the Qur'an to recite during the prayer. Most mosques have a regular imam these days, but this is not a compulsory requirement, and any Muslim may lead the prayer in his absence, or when the prayer is being carried out elsewhere, for example, in the home.

If men and women are praying together, the leader is always a man; it could even be a very young man – there are hadith showing how a seven-year-old boy led prayers during the Prophet's ﷺ lifetime. If women are praying together, one of the women leads from the middle of the row, and is in effect a female imam (see Female imams page 313). A male imam stands just in front of the other worshippers, who form lines behind. If there are only two worshippers, the imam stands on the left with the other worshipper on the right-hand side, just a few inches back.

The purpose of prayer

Muslim prayer is intended to purify the heart and bring about spiritual and moral growth. The aims are to bring people close to Allah; to bring a sense of peace and tranquillity; to encourage equality, unity and brotherhood; to develop gratitude and humility; to demonstrate obedience; to train in cleanliness, purity and punctuality; to develop discipline and will-power; to draw the mind away from personal worries, calm down passions, and master the baser instincts.

Preparation for prayer

Niyyah

The first part of prayer is *niyyah* or intention. By closing the mind to all worldly distractions (whether pleasant or unpleasant ones), the worshipper begins to make ready for prayer.

Although prayer can be said at any time in any place, the Muslim prepares for salah by making his or her own body physically clean, and by selecting a clean place in which to pray, if possible. If one prays in the desert or by the roadside, one is not able to dictate conditions, but in Muslim countries there are usually little areas marked out and set aside for prayer and kept in a clean condition. In the home, or at the mosque, prayer is usually said on a carpet. It may be an individual prayer-mat or, at the mosque, the floor is usually carpeted or covered with rush-matting, with lines marked out on it so that the worshippers may arrange themselves in orderly fashion.

Prayer-mats are usually small colourful rugs, decorated with abstract designs or depicting some holy mosque. They frequently show the Ka'bah or the mosque at Madinah where the Prophet ﷺ is buried. The only significant point about the design is that it should not depict living beings. Otherwise, any mat will do.

Clothing

Muslims should wear clean clothes for prayer, as far as possible. They remove their shoes, but it is not necessary to remove socks, stockings or tights. Men must be covered at least from waist to knee, and women must completely cover themselves, leaving only face and hands visible, and should not wear perfume. It is preferred if women do not wear make-up, and nail polish is not accepted as it prevents full wudu, although staining the nails with henna is acceptable.

figure 7.2 many people wear prayer-caps

It is not compulsory for men to cover their heads, but many wear a special prayer-cap, often of white lace.[4]

Wudu

There is a difference between everyday washing away of dirt and becoming purified for prayer. Purification (*taharah*) is a mental as well as a physical cleansing. Before prayer, Muslims perform the ritual wash known as wudu or *wuzu*, cleansing certain parts of the body in running water.

'O you who believe! When you rise up for prayer, wash your faces and your hands as far as the elbows, and wipe your heads and wash your feet to the ankles; and if you are under the obligation to perform a bath (i.e. ritually unclean after sex, menstruation or childbirth) then go through the complete wash; and if you are sick, or on a journey, or have come from the toilet or have been intimate with a woman, and you cannot find water, then take clean earth and wipe your faces and your hands with it. Allah does not wish to put you into difficulties, but He wishes to purify you that He may complete His favour on you.'

(Surah 5:6)

The Prophet ﷺ taught:

'Wash your hands up to the wrists three times; rinse your mouth three times with water thrown into your mouth with the right hand; sniff the water into the nostrils and blow it out three times; wash the entire face, including the forehead, three times; wipe the top of the head once with the inner surface of both hands together; wash your ears with your forefingers and wipe the back of the ears with your thumbs, and wipe the back of your neck once; wash the right foot and then the left foot up to the ankles three times; let the water run from your hands up to your elbows three times.'

The washing is always done in a quiet, prayerful manner, for it is in itself part of the act of worship. While washing, Muslims pray that they will be purified from the sins they have committed by hand or mouth, that they will be empowered to do good and refrain from evil, and that they should walk on the right path and not go astray.

'In the Turkish attempt to force secularization, men were ordered to wear 'Western' caps with a peak at the front. They solved the problem of not being able to put their foreheads to the earth during prayer by simply turning them back to front.

If water is not available, the worshipper can perform a dry wash known as *tayammum*, which simply involves touching clean earth and wiping over the face, hands and arms in an imitation wash.

Muslims are not required to make a fresh wudu before every prayer if they have remained 'in wudu' between times. Wudu is broken if a person has sexual intercourse, or if any discharge leaves the body (such as blood, seminal fluid, urine or faeces, or wind), or if the person has lost consciousness through sleep or other cause. Women who are menstruating, or are in the days after childbirth, cannot enter wudu and are excused from salah prayer at these times. A full bath, known as *ghusl*, is necessary after sexual intercourse, when menstruation has finished, and after contact with dead bodies.

If socks are worn, it is not considered necessary to wash the feet every time; so long as they are in wudu at the first wash, Muslims may simply wipe over the socks with wet hands the next time, although many Muslims regard this as laziness.

Qiblah

The *qiblah* is the direction faced during prayer. All Muslims, when they pray, turn to the direction of Makkah. They usually know its position in advance, but if they are in a strange place they can ask, work it out from the position of the sun, or use a small compass.

There is a consolidating effect in fixing a central spot around which to gather the religious feelings of Muslims throughout the world. Muslims do not believe that God somehow lives at Makkah, or in the Ka'bah sanctuary, or could be 'confined' to any temple made with human hands, much less that they are worshipping the famous black stone set in one of its corners. In the spiritual sense, the true qiblah means to turn the heart in the direction of God – and He, of course, cannot be located in any physical direction whatsoever.

The barrier

It is bad manners to pass in front of someone at prayer. If they are praying in the open, Muslims usually mark off the area of their prayer with a barrier, or *sutrah*, which separates them from any people or animals passing in front of them. The Prophet ﷺ used to stick his staff into the ground, just to the right of him, in case there might be any thought that he was in some way bowing down to it as one might bow down to an idol.

figure 7.3 the *Mihrab* and *Minbar*, Zagreb, Croatia

The practice of prayer

The series of movements and accompanying words is known as a rakah. These always follow a set pattern.

During the rakah there are eight separate acts of devotion. The first, after niyyah (conscious intention), is *takbir* or glorification, the deliberate shutting out of the world and its distractions, delights and miseries. Muslims stand to attention, and raise their hands to the level of their shoulders, and acknowledge the majesty of God. They say 'Allahu Akbar' – 'God is the Most High'.

Second, they place their right hand over the left on the chest, and say in Arabic 'Glory and praise be to You, O God; blessed is Your name and exalted is Your majesty. There is no God other than You. I come, seeking shelter from Satan, the rejected one.'

After this comes the recital of the first surah in the Qur'an, *Surah al-Fatihah* – the translation is:

> *'In the name of Allah, the Compassionate, the Merciful. All praise be to Allah (the Almighty), the Lord of the Universes, the Most Merciful, the Most Kind, Master of the Day of Judgement. You alone do we worship, and from You alone do we seek help. Show us the next step along the straight path of those earning Your favour. Keep us from the path of those earning Your anger, those who are going astray.'*

Next, another passage from the Qur'an is recited, the choice of the prayer-leader. It can be long or short, but the Prophet ﷺ recommended keeping recitals short for public prayers (where people in the congregation might be suffering discomfort, illness, coping with children, or have business to attend to), and whatever length you liked for private prayers.

A favourite short surah is *al-Ikhlas* (the One-ness):

'He is God the One; He is the Eternal Absolute; none is born of Him and neither is He born. There is none like unto Him.'

(Surah 112)

figure 7.4 Muslims carrying out *rakah*

Next comes *ruku*, the bowing. Men rest their hands on their knees and bow right over with a straight back; women do not bow quite so deeply. This bow is to show that they respect as well as love God. They repeat three times:

'Glory be to my Great Lord, and praise be to Him.'

The next state is *qiyam*, when they stand up again and acknowledge their awareness of the presence of God with the words:

'God always hears those who praise Him. O God, all praise be to You, O God greater than all else.'

Next comes the humblest of all positions, the *sujud* or *sajda*. Muslims prostrate themselves upon the ground, touching the ground with their hands, forehead, nose, knees and toes. Their fingers face qiblah, and their elbows are raised and not lying on the ground. They repeat three times:

'Glory be to my Lord, the Most High. God is greater than all else.'

Then they kneel up again in a sitting position known as *julus*, palms resting on the knees in a moment of silent prayer, before repeating sujud again.

There is a set number of rakahs for each prayer; fajr, the dawn prayer requires two, the zuhr and asr have four; maghrib has three and isha has four. At the end of the compulsory sequence they pray for all the brotherhood of the faithful, the congregation gathered there, and for the forgiveness of sins. When they pray for forgiveness, they place their right fist on right knee and extend the forefinger. The last action is to turn the head to right and left with the words:

'Asalaam aleikum wa rahmatullah' – 'Peace be with you, and the mercy of Allah.'

This is known as the *salaam*, and acknowledges not only the other worshippers, but also the attendant guardian angels. Some Muslims can be seen sighing, and wiping their hands over their faces to end their prayer session.

Prayers not done together

Sometimes you see Muslims praying on their own, or praying 'out of time' with the other Muslims there. This is because many Muslims pray extra non-compulsory rakahs before and after salah, at their own speed, following the practice of the

Prophet ﷺ. It is normal to pray two rakahs upon entering a mosque, before the congregation is ready. You always know when the compulsory prayer is ready to begin because someone will make another call to prayer (the iqamah) and everyone will line up behind a leader. When Muslims join the prayer-lines late, they usually make up the missed part of their prayer after the main prayer is finished. Many Muslims finish the set prayer, then change their position to indicate this, and then pray as many more rakahs as they like.

The *Tahajjud* prayer is an optional prayer that is supposed to be performed in the middle of the night. It can be performed anytime between isha and fajr.

Du'a – personal supplications

Private prayer requests are known as *du'a*. These may be said at any time. They include private thanksgivings for some blessing received (such as childbirth, passing exams, recovery from sickness and so on), requests for help, pleas for forgiveness or guidance.

figure 7.5 *du'a*, after *Salah* prayer

Tasbih (subhah)

Sometimes worshippers carry a string of 99 or 33 beads, and can be seen praying quietly while passing the beads through their fingers. These beads are called *tasbih* or *subhah*. They are divided into three sections by larger beads. While praying, the Muslim may say *Subhanallah* (Glory be to Allah), *Alhamdu lillah* (Thanks be to Allah), and *Allahu akbar* (God is Most Great) 33 times, as they pass the beads.

figure 7.6 Bosnian Imam with tasbih

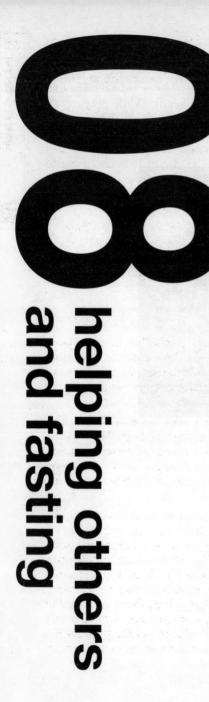

08

helping others and fasting

In this chapter you will learn about:
- zakah – the Muslim tax on income
- sadaqah – charity through compassion
- sawm – fasting
- Ramadan – the fasting month
- the rules and benefits of fasting.

Zakah – the religious tax

'By no means will you attain to righteousness until you spend (in the way of Allah) out of that which you cherish most.'

(Surah 3:91)

The third pillar of Islam is zakah from the word meaning 'to thrive, be wholesome, purify'. Virtually every time Allah asked for the practice of regular prayer to be said by believers, He also asked for Muslims to give material help to those less fortunate than themselves. The Qur'an actually specifies the categories of those people who should be helped by this giving:

'Alms are for the poor and the needy, and (to pay) those employed to administer the funds; for those whose hearts have been (recently) reconciled (to Truth); for those in bondage, and in debt; in the cause of God; and for the wayfarer; (Thus is it) ordained by God, full of knowledge and wisdom.'

(Surah 9:60)

Muslims regard everything in the universe as belonging to God, including all the things humans usually count as their own possessions or earnings. If all our belongings are only loans in trust by God, then when anything is sacrificed for the sake of God it is only being given back to its rightful Owner.

God alone has the choice of who is to be born rich or poor; therefore all Muslims have a duty towards others. The wealthy have an obligation to give; it is not a matter of personal choice. Muslims living in hope of an eternal future know there is no point in clinging foolishly to possessions, or even worse, letting them become your masters.

Muslims have a duty to look after themselves and their families and dependants; but after that is taken care of, Allah requires that they should look at their surplus money, capital or goods, and give up one fortieth of it (or 2.5 per cent) to God's service, asking neither recompense nor thanks (Surah 26:109). This is a reasonable amount and is is not usually a massive sacrifice. However, if the person is extremely wealthy, they can afford to give more. Alms are due only when the property amounts to a certain value, and has been in the possession of the person for a whole year. Alms are not due on cattle employed in agriculture, or used for the carrying of burdens.

Basically, Islam is against the idea of hoarding. All of earth's commodities, including cash, should be in use, or in flow. Any time an individual hoards something, this is disapproved of in Islam, because it is a selfish misuse of that commodity, and depriving others who might be able to put it to use.

Paying zakah therefore allows wealth to circulate more fairly in society, and by paying it the individual purifies himself or herself and at the same time purifies his or her wealth. It helps the Muslim to fight greed, and the recipient to fight jealousy, envy and hatred.

It is not only the poor who are helped by receiving zakah; it is also a means of helping rich people to carry out their responsibility towards others honourably, since Muslims believe that the rich person is only so by the grace of God, and his or her riches are only given in trust to them, to be used properly and not in a miserly fashion.

People giving zakah normally do it anonymously, so as not to cause embarrassment. The only time giving is done with publicity, is if that would help and encourage others to give also (see Surah 2:271). The Qur'an disapproves of people who make a show of their giving:

> 'Don't nullify your charity by reminders of your generosity, or by holding it against those you give it to – like those who give their wealth only to be seen by others . . . They are like hard, barren rock on which is little soil. Heavy rain falls on it and leaves it just a bare stone.'

(Surah 2:264)

There is no authority to force any Muslim to pay this; it is entirely up to the conscience of the individual whether or not he or she pays it; nobody checks, and it is not a state tax even in Muslim societies – although the Muslim authorities will collect and distribute moneys when required. Therefore, zakah is very much a test of sincerity, as well as unselfishness. Being willing to pay it shows that your heart is clean of the love of money and the desire to cling to it. It shows that you are prepared to use your money for the service of humanity, and the promoting of good and justice in the world.

> 'He is not a believer who eats his fill while his neighbour remains hungry by his side.'

(Muslim)

Sadaqah – charity

Giving zakah is not to be confused with the sort of charity giving that is called forth by public response to tragic catastrophes in the news today. That is quite a different sort of charity, known in Islam as *sadaqah* or 'righteousness'. Zakah is a regular, sacrificial giving that depends on motives quite different from sympathy and charity. Sadaqah indicates the sincerity (*siddiq*) of the almsgiver's religious belief, a choice of his/her own free will. Without that free choice it is not considered an act of merit.

'Every good act is charity,' said the Prophet ﷺ. 'Smiling upon your brother is charity; urging others to do good is charity, helping the blind is charity, removing stones, thorns and other obstructions from the road is charity, giving water to the thirsty is charity.'

Sawm – fasting

'O believers, you must fast so that you may learn self-restraint. Fasting is prescribed for you during a fixed number of days, so that you may safeguard yourselves against moral and spiritual ills.'

(Surah 2:183–4)

The fourth pillar of Islam is to keep the fast during the ninth month of the Muslim year, *Ramadan*. Many Muslims fast at other times too, and some fast one day every week.

Ramadan is a very special time for Muslims, for it was during this month that Allah chose to call Muhammad ﷺ to be a prophet, and sent down the first revelations of the Qur'an. Therefore, Ramadan is seen as the most significant of months, a time of spiritual and physical discipline, and a time for making extra effort to spread love, peace and reconciliation.

Muslim fasting involves deliberately cultivating a peaceful and prayerful attitude of mind, and undergoing the physical discipline of giving up all food, liquid, smoking and sexual intercourse during the hours of first light of dawn to sunset for the entire month. Nobody starves to death, for all these things are allowed after sunset, until the first light of the next day's dawn when a black thread can be distinguished from a white one.

It is not just a question of going without food; that is only one aspect of it, and indeed, it is not the most important aspect. Allah pointed out that if a person could not give up evil ways, violence, greed, lust, anger and malicious thoughts, He had no need of their giving up food and drink. It would be meaningless.

'There are many who fast all day and pray all night, but they gain nothing but hunger and sleeplessness.'

(Abu Dawud)

Breaking the moral codes of Islam break the fast just as much as eating or drinking. If a person breaks the fast by accident in a moment's forgetfulness, that day is still credited to them.

Ramadan and the seasons

As Muslims keep a lunar calendar, the Ramadan month travels through the secular calendar, coming ten or 11 days earlier each year. This means that when Ramadan falls during the winter months the fast is fairly easy, because the daylight hours are short. However, in the summer months the reverse is the case, and the fast is very strenuous indeed.

In the United Kingdom, for example, the fast on 1 July starts at 2.55 a.m. and finishes at 9.40 p.m. causing considerable deprivation and suffering. Muslims are often asked what happens in places like the Arctic Circle, the land of the 'midnight sun'. In those places, Muslims either follow the same hours as the nearest Muslims outside the polar zones, or follow the practice of Makkah, which is 6 a.m. to 6 p.m. fast. The object of the fast is not to make people suffer, but it is intended to make them realize what it is like to go without, and to share just for a little while the deprivations of the poor, so that a more sympathetic attitude is engendered.

Tarawih prayers

Most Muslims read through the entire Qur'an in Ramadan, and many go to the mosque every evening that month for around two hours of special extra prayers known as *tarawih* during which the whole text is read through. These voluntary prayers consist of either eight extra rakahs after the compulsory isha prayer (if Muslims are following the sunnah of the Prophet ﷺ), or 20 extra rakahs (the practice started by Caliph Umar).

Many mosques invite special huffaz (people who know the Qur'an by heart) to help lead these special prayers. Many are not trained imams, but pious visitors from 'back home' where the tradition of becoming a hafiz is still strong.

Laylat ul-Qadr

No Muslim knows for certain which is the night of the Descent of the Qur'an, but traditionally it is celebrated on the 27th Ramadan. Scholars admit, however, that it could have been any one of the odd nights during the last ten days of Ramadan. A large number of Muslims spend this entire night in the mosque, reading the Qur'an and praying together. Indeed, the mosque is usually completely packed. Muslims believe that if they spend the whole of this night in prayer and meditation, they will be granted the blessings as if they had prayed for a thousand nights.

People excused from fasting

Any person who would undergo real suffering if made to fast is excused from doing it. This applies to people who need to be nourished, such as small children and old people, and expectant and nursing mothers. Any invalids or people whose condition would be made worse by fasting are also excused, and so are menstruating women, soldiers in battle, people on long journeys, and the mentally ill – if they cannot understand the religious reasons behind the fast. All the people in these latter categories should, however, try to make up for the fasts they have missed as soon as it becomes practicable to do so. If this is impossible, then they should donate to charity the equivalent cost of two meals for each fast-day they have missed, if they can afford it.

Children generally start fasting when they are quite young, perhaps just missing a dinner; they are expected to be able to take an adult role when they are around 12 years old.

A time of joy

The fast is not dreaded by Muslims, but looked forward to as a time of great joy, family celebration, entertaining of guests, and reconciliation. It is a very special month, and has a very special atmosphere for the Muslims who keep it.

When the fast starts very early in the morning, it is quite normal for Muslims to stay up during the previous night, and then go to bed after they have prayed the dawn prayer and started their fast. In Muslim countries they are sometimes woken up by a drummer, or someone firing a cannon. In the family, it is often the mother who is up and awake first, who has the job of rousing her family and getting them to take the *suhur* or early breakfast before dawn. Light nourishing foods are generally eaten at this meal, and spicy things (which make people feel thirsty) are avoided.

I'tikaf

Some Muslims withdraw altogether from ordinary life and go into retreat for the last ten days of Ramadan to devote their entire time to prayer and reading the Qur'an. Men sometimes live and sleep in the mosque in order to do this, and women withdraw from normal life at home. They can only do this if they are supported by other family members who can prepare their food and so on, so the whole family feels involved.

Breaking the fast

Although fasting makes people feel very tired and quite weak, food is prepared very carefully during Ramadan, an extra sacrifice on the part of those preparing it, who must be very tempted to eat a little. If anyone forgets, and takes a taste of something while cooking, this is not counted as breaking the fast so long as it was not done deliberately. If one sees someone doing this, it is not good manners to comment on it, or draw it to their attention. The fault is 'covered'.

As the time draws near, people feel excited, hungry, proud of their achievement. They wait for the time to end the fast, which is sometimes signalled on TV or radio, or by the call from the minaret. As soon as the sun sets, they break their fast usually with a sweet drink and some fruit, frequently a few dates because this was the habit of the Prophet ﷺ. It is not sensible to fall upon a heavy meal and devour it without giving the stomach a little preparation first; people who do this are often sick, and regret it.

After the little meal, known as *iftar* (breakfast), the maghrib or evening prayer is said, and only then will the Muslims eat the main meal. This can be quite a feast, as friends and relatives are often invited, and any poor people or strangers welcomed and included if possible. Many mosques run a communal kitchen paid for by donated money, where people may eat for free. Those who are single, lonely and needy are particularly encouraged to come, and it is quite a party atmosphere.

figure 8.1 sharing food together

Ramadan manners

It is considered to be very bad-mannered to eat or drink or smoke in front of a person who is fasting. In some Muslim countries people would be arrested if they did this, and even kept locked up until the fasting month was over. Some tourists in Muslim countries feel they should still be catered for, even though the people are fasting, and this can cause problems. Tourists are usually aware of Ramadan, and often choose not to go to Muslim countries in that month. However, those that enter the religious spirit often find the experience and camaraderie wonderful.

General problems

People who do not fast, or who think that the Muslim fast is not particularly strenuous because they can eat at night, often do not realize the effects it can have. The first week is often the worst, until the body gets used to the new regime. Symptoms may include headaches, dizziness, nausea, light-headedness and faintness. It is especially difficult for Muslims who are addicted smokers, because they have to give up their cigarettes as well as food and drink (in fact, it is a very good time to try to kick the habit!). By the fourth week, some fasters are considerably weakened, and have little or no energy. Muslims frequently need to take rest and lie down, and because of the broken nights and little sleep, they try to catch up on some sleep during the day if possible. Muslim children at school should be excused heavy activity, such as PE, if they cannot cope with it. They are grateful when schools provide somewhere they can pray and rest, away from those munching through lunch. Other Muslims reap considerable physical benefit from the discipline and self-denial.

Why are they spitting?

Some Muslims take an extreme point of view, refusing even to swallow the saliva already in their mouths, and spit it out into cloths or handkerchiefs. Some will not clean their teeth or take showers in case they swallow some water, and they may refuse to have medicine or injections during the fast time. In fact it is allowed to swallow saliva already within the body, and if a person would be harmed by not taking medicine they are excused fasting – all sick people are, and there is little point in actually making a person ill by deprivation of medical aid.

Benefits of fasting

Muslims maintain that there are numerous benefits to be gained from fasting. Some maintain it is a healthy time anyway, as the stomach is rested and Muslims eat more fruit and less spices than they might do normally. However, the main benefits are spiritual and mental. First, it is excellent discipline and training in self-control. The Muslim becomes master of his or her own body and appetites.

There is a wonderful feeling of community and togetherness. Muslims are sharing an experience, and they are also sharing their food together at night. It is a particularly lovely feeling when a wealthy person can sit down with needy people, feed them and eat with them. The fast makes people appreciate what things they do have, particularly the blessings of food and drink.

People who come from affluent societies gain at least a little knowledge of what it is like to do without. It makes them more sympathetic and understanding, and generous when they are in the position to be.

figure 8.2 Eid Mubarrak: muslims greeting one another after the Feast Prayer

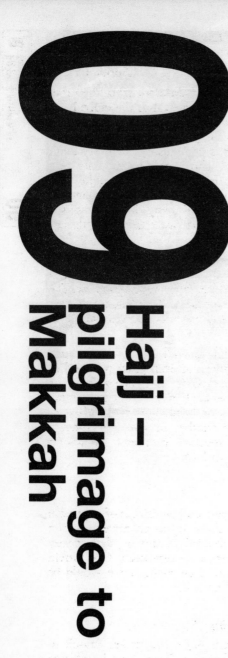

09

Hajj – pilgrimage to Makkah

In this chapter you will learn about:
- the background of Hajj
- the state consecration (ihram)
- the rituals of Hajj.

> *'It is the duty of all believers towards God to come to the House a pilgrim, if able to make their way there.'*

(Surah 3:91)

The fifth pillar of Islam is somewhat different from the other four, in that it involves a complete upheaval of the individual's life for the space of a few days. The Hajj (which means 'to set out with a definite purpose') is the pilgrimage to Makkah, the 'Mother-town' of Islam, and it is compulsory for every adult Muslim who can afford it, and who is able to go, once in a lifetime. If any Muslim cannot afford to go, or if it would cause hardship to their dependants, they are excused from making the journey. Some Muslims make the Hajj many times, but this is not encouraged nowadays because the vast number of pilgrims is causing considerable difficulties.

Anyone who wishes to make their pilgrimage more than once is encouraged to go at some time other than the Hajj time, when the pilgrimage is known as the Lesser Pilgrimage, or *umrah*. The true Hajj takes place at a specific time in the Muslim calendar, in the month of *Dhu'l Hijjah*, two months and ten days after Ramadan.

Making the Hajj used to be a considerable sacrifice and effort, some people travelling for months and even years overland to reach Makkah. Sometimes people save for a lifetime to make the trip, and when at last they have enough money, they are too old or infirm to go. Any Muslims who cannot make the Hajj are encouraged to pay instead for another person. Sometimes a family or community will club together in order to be able to send one representative on their behalf.

Niyyah

As always in Islam, the real worship and sacrifice is of a spiritual nature rather than the physical show. If, for example, a person who had saved up for Hajj decided to donate that money instead to some unfortunate person in dire need, God would accept the niyyah or intention of their Hajj, and it would be counted for them as if they had done it.

People excused from Hajj

Pilgrims have to be Muslim (it is not a tourist attraction), of sound mind and of the age of reason. They must be able to understand the religious significance of the experience. Children might be taken along with the family, but it does not count as their own Hajj until they have reached adulthood. Pilgrims have to have enough money to pay for the trip and keep up all their duty payments towards their dependants. If any person gained money to pay for the Hajj by dishonest means, their Hajj would be invalid.

Pilgrims should also realize that they have to be reasonably fit to cope with the strenuous conditions. In view of the numbers and circumstances, many people do pass away while on Hajj – through accident, sickness or old age. Those who leave for Hajj do it knowing they may never return.

The sacred place

Makkah is regarded by Muslims as a specially holy place, and no non-Muslim is allowed to enter it. It is *haram*, which means both 'sacred' and 'forbidden'. When travellers come to Makkah by road, they will arrive at places where their passports will be checked, to make sure that they are genuine Muslim pilgrims and not just curious tourists.

Background to the Hajj

The Hajj pilgrimage celebrates three particular events in Muslim history. The first is the reunion and forgiveness of Adam 卐 and Eve (unlike the doctrine of an original sin inherited from their descendants), the second is the Prophet Ibrahim's 卐 sacrifice of his son Isma'il 卐, and the third is the life of obedience of the Prophet Muhammad 卐.

Adam 卐 and Eve

According to the Qur'an, when Adam 卐 and Eve – the original human couple created from the division of the original soul – gave in to the temptation of Satan, they were cast out of Paradise and obliged to wander the earth in grief, hardship and pain. Not only had they lost God, they had also lost each other, and they were in great confusion and terrible unhappiness. But God had not abandoned them – He watched over them, waiting for the moment when they would turn back to Him and exchange their defiance for the desire for forgiveness. The moment they came to their senses and realized what they had done, God forgave them, and they were reunited on the plain of

Arafat, where there is a small hill, Mount Arafat, also known as Jabal ar-Rahman, the Mount of Mercy.

Muslims believe that for any pilgrim to be on that Mount of Mercy on the ninth Dhu'l Hijjah brings total forgiveness of all one's past sins, and enables life to begin again. The stand there is called the *Wuquf*.

The Ka'bah

Nearby, they built a simple shrine in gratitude – the area known as the Ka'bah sanctuary. This is now the sacred shrine of Islam, the qiblah towards which all Muslims turn in prayer five times per day. The word 'Ka'bah' means 'cube', and it gets this name from the fact that it is a simple, cube-shaped building, some 15 metres high, built of stone blocks. According to Muslim belief, since the first shrine of the Ka'bah (also known as al-Bait al-Haram – the Holy House) was built by the first human, it is therefore the first shrine for the worship of God on earth.

Ibrahim ﷺ and Isma'il ﷺ

Ibrahim ﷺ was known as the Friend of God (al-Khalil). He had vowed to sacrifice everything in his life to God, although his parents had been idol worshippers from Ur in Iraq. He was a most humble and devout man, even though he was the wealthy owner of vast herds of sheep and goats. He lived peacefully with his childless wife Sarah and a second wife, an Egyptian woman called Hagar (or Hajarah) who had given birth to his son Isma'il ﷺ.

The famous story of Ibrahim's ﷺ sacrifice of his son is quite different from that presented in the Bible (Genesis 22:1–14, where Abraham's ﷺ obedience to God was tested by God asking him to sacrifice his son Isaac ﷺ).

The Qur'an reveals that Ibrahim ﷺ dreamed that God wanted him to sacrifice his son Isma'il ﷺ (Surah 37.102). He told Isma'il ﷺ of it, and the boy agreed that he should do whatever he believed to be God's will.

Tradition added details that heightened the drama. Ibrahim ﷺ, his wife Hajarah and son Isma'il ﷺ were all visited by a stranger who was Satan in disguise, who tried to persuade them that they were being misled. Only the devil would ask Ibrahim ﷺ to do such a wicked thing. They all resisted this thought, still believing it was God's will. In the end, all three of them took up stones and threw them at the unwelcome stranger, driving him away.

Isma'il ⌖ was so determined to submit to the will of God that he made his father place him face down, so that he should not be overcome with grief when he saw his face. However, Ibrahim ⌖ had been mistaken and the sacrifice of his son was not God's will. At the last moment God told Ibrahim ⌖ he had long since fulfilled the purpose of that dream, i.e. to show his obedience (37:105). A ram was sacrificed instead, and became the origin of the 'tremendous sacrifice' of *Eid ul-Adha* at the end of Hajj.

The reward of Ibrahim ⌖ was that his barren wife Sarah at last gave birth to a son of her own – Isaac ⌖ (Surah 37:100–13).

Later, Sarah's jealousy on behalf of her son caused the family to split up and Ibrahim ⌖ left Hajarah and Isma'il ⌖ to God's care beside the ancient shrine. Here Hajarah was tested again, for although the place was on a caravan route no water-carrying caravans came by, and they begant to suffer severe thirst. When Isma'il ⌖ was on the point of death the angel Jibril (Gabriel) appeared and opened a spring – the well now called Zamzam.

Later the family was reunited and Ibrahim ⌖ and Isma'il ⌖ together rebuilt the sanctuary now known as the Ka'bah. For the last 4,000 years or so the Ka'bah has always been reconstructed on the same foundations, and the faithful have always gone there on pilgrimage.

The maqam Ibrahim ⌖

In the courtyard of the mosque is a stone known as the *maqam Ibrahim* ⌖, which marks the spot where he used to stand to direct building operations.

The graves of Isma'il ⌖ and Hajarah

The semi-circular enclosure in front of the Ka'bah marks the traditional site of the graves of Hajarah and Isma'il ⌖. Ibrahim ⌖ himself, his wife Sarah, his son Isaac ⌖ and Isaac's wife Rebekah, and Isaac's ⌖ son Jacob and his wife Leah are all buried at Hebron in Palestine. Jacob's ⌖ other wife Rachel is buried just outside Bethlehem.

The rites of Hajj

It is compulsory for each pilgrim to do four things on his or her Hajj. The first is to enter the state of *ihram* and put on ihram clothing; the second is to perform the circling of the Ka'bah (*tawaf*); the third is to make the stand at Arafat (*wuquf*); and the fourth is to circle the Ka'bah again, after returning from Arafat. When the pilgrim has done all these four things, he may take the title *hajji* (a female pilgrim is a *hajjah*).

Ihram

Ihram literally means 'consecration', to be haram (forbidden to or separated from the world) and it is a special state of holiness, expressed by three things: the complete purification of the body with full bath; the casting aside of normal garments in order to wear special clothes; and the keeping of the ihram rules of conduct.

Women may wear any plain, loose, full-length clothing and a head veil, so that every part of them is covered except the face, hands and feet. They often choose to wear white. Men have to put on two simple pieces of unsewn white cloth, one wrapped around their waist which reaches to their ankles, and one thrown over the left shoulder. They wear nothing else (see figure 1.2 on page 14). The object of ihram garments is both purity and equality, single-mindedness and self-sacrifice. Clothing frequently indicates rank, special career or high office; in *ihram*, no matter how wealthy the pilgrim or how highly born, everyone is dressed the same in these simple unsewn clothes, and they stand before God as equals.

The places where it becomes obligatory to put on these garments are known as *miqat*, around 4 km from the Ka'bah shrine. These days many pilgrims put on ihram even before they board their planes.

Rules of ihram

Once Muslims pass miqat, they say two rakahs, and they have entered the state of ihram. From this moment they must not do anything dishonest or arrogant, but behave like true servants of Allah. Normal marital relations are set aside, and all flirtatious thoughts about the opposite sex are forbidden. One may not get engaged, or marry, on Hajj. To express confidence and the atmosphere of purity, and to show that all lustful thoughts have been put aside, women should not cover their faces. If any pilgrim had sexual intercourse while on Hajj, their Hajj would not be valid.

Men must not wear jewellery or rings, and women may wear wedding rings only. No one may use perfume or scented soap (unscented soap is on sale for pilgrims). Men must leave their heads uncovered to express their humility, but they are allowed to carry umbrellas to shelter from the sun. To express simplicity, everyone must go barefoot or in sandals that leave the toes and heels bare.

To express non-interference with nature, no one must cut hair or fingernails. To curb aggression and feel unity with God's creatures, no blood must be shed by killing animals, except fleas, bedbugs, snakes and scorpions. To develop mercy, no hunting is allowed. To feel love for nature, no plants may be uprooted or trees cut down. Muslims strive to keep their minds at peace, and not lose their tempers, quarrel, or get exasperated by difficulties. They have to turn their minds completely to the will of Allah.

Talbiyah

On arrival at Makkah, Muslims start reciting the *talbiyah* prayer, a deeply moving experience as each individual among the thousands and thousands of pilgrims cries to Allah that he or she has arrived, in His service.

The translation is:

> 'At Your command, here I am, O God, here I am! At Your command I am here, O Thou without equal, here I am! Thine is the kingdom and the praise and the glory, O Thou without equal, God Alone!'

This is the pilgrim's personal answer to the divine call to come. Some pilgrims are overcome with emotion at this point. Some shout out joyfully, and others weep. As they enter Makkah, they pray this prayer:

> 'O God, this sanctuary is Your sacred place, and this city is Your city, and this slave is Your slave. I have come to You from a distant land, carrying all my sins and misdeeds, as an afflicted person seeking Your help and dreading Your punishment. I beg You to accept me, and grant me complete forgiveness, and give me permission to enter Your vast Garden of Delight.'

Tawaf

The first thing all pilgrims are required to do on arriving at the Ka'bah is to encircle it seven times in an anticlockwise direction. (They try to run for the first three circuits if they are able.) They do this, no matter what time of day or night they arrive. If they can reach the black stone (*al-hujr al-aswad*), they will touch or kiss it, or raise their hands in salute if they cannot get near. Invalids and old people are carried on specially constructed stretcher-chairs. An example of the prayers prayed is this one, used on the fourth circuit:

> 'O God, Who knows the innermost secrets of our hearts; lead us out of the darkness into the light!'

At the end of the circling, they go to the Station of Ibrahim ﷺ to pray two rakahs.

al hujr al-aswad

This is the black stone set in one corner of the Ka'bah. It was said to have been sent down from heaven, and is probably a meteorite. There are numerous traditions about it, one being that it was originally white in colour but it turned black in sorrow at the world's sin (in reality, shiny as it entered the Earth's atmosphere, and black now).

figure 9.1 the black stone in the Ka'bah

It now has a silver surround, but it is still open to the touch. The deep hollow in the middle has been worn away by the millions of pilgrims who have touched and kissed it. It is not, however, an object to be worshipped.

Al-Kiswah

Al Kiswah is the black cloth that covers the Ka'bah shrine. It is traditionally made afresh each year in Cairo by male embroiderers. Verses from the Qur'an are embroidered around it, in gold thread. It is draped over the Ka'bah like a veil and, like the women's veils, is lifted up during the Hajj. At the end of Hajj it is taken down and cut up into small pieces, which become souvenirs or gifts for special pilgrims. Pieces are sent to mosques throughout the world, and many Muslims frame their piece and hang it on the wall as a reminder.

figure 9.2 the black cloth over the Ka'bah

Inside the Ka'bah

People rarely go inside the Ka'bah through the huge door. It has remained empty ever since the Prophet ﷺ cleansed it of its

360 idols. Inside, there are no *mihrabs*, since the Ka'bah itself is the 'centre of the world' and all Muslims pray towards it. It is decorated simply, with texts from the Qur'an on the walls.

Sa'i

The *Sa'i* is the ritual of running or walking briskly seven times between the two small hills of Safa and Marwah (now a passageway enclosed within the Ka'bah shrine). Any invalids, old people, or those who cannot walk have a special protected wheelchair path down the middle. This ritual is in commemoration of the desperate trail of Isma'il's ﷺ mother, Hajarah, between these two viewpoints, when looking for caravans carrying water. It symbolizes the soul's desperate search for that which gives true life.

The well of Zamzam represents the truth that when all seems lost, God is still present, with healing and life for the soul. The well is still there in a chamber under the courtyard. Pilgrims drink some of the water, and might even collect some in little bottles (these can also be bought as souvenirs). Some pilgrims dip their ihram cloths in the water intending to keep them and use them as their shrouds, when they die.

When Muslims have done both tawaf and sa'i, they have completed umrah, the lesser pilgrimage. After this, male pilgrims either shave their heads, or at least cut their hair, and women cut off an inch or so of their hair. After this, they are allowed to put on their normal clothes again.

Mina

On the eighth day of Dhu'l Hijjah, the pilgrims take a full bath and put on ihram again, and proceed to the valley of Mina some 10 km away. This used to be a walk into the desert, but now the town of Makkah reaches virtually as far as Mina, and there are special walkways to make it easier for the huge crowds. It was in the underground walkway that there was a horrific accident with hundreds being suffocated and crushed a few years ago.

There are a few hotels in Mina, but most pilgrims stay in a huge city of tents. Some pilgrims now miss out Mina and take modern transport straight to Arafat, because of the sheer numbers involved.

Wuquf

On the ninth day, all the pilgrims have to reach the plain of Arafat (24 km east of Makkah) and make their stand before God on or surrounding the Mount of Mercy. They have to be there between noon and dusk. Some arrive in good time, but others come rushing up from Mina, having made their dawn prayer there. If they do not arrive for the Standing in time, their Hajj is invalid.

This is really the most important part of the pilgrimage. The pilgrims must stand in the sweltering heat, bare-headed (for men), thinking about God and praying for His mercy. It is a time of great mystical and emotional power, and there is a tremendous sense of release – being totally wrapped in love, totally 'washed', totally cleansed.

It is an amazing sight to see over 2 million pilgrims perform the zuhr and asr prayers here, especially the moments of prostration and total silence as they bow before Allah.

Muzdalifah

By sunset, the pilgrims begin to head back to Muzdalifah, between Arafat and Mina. There they say the maghrib and isha prayers, and collect small pebbles. They arrive back at Mina by the morning of the tenth Dhu'l Hijjah.

Stoning the Jamrahs

Next comes the ritual of casting their pebbles at Satan, in remembrance of the temptations of Ibrahim ﷺ and his family. There are three pillars set up at representative places, known as *jamrahs*, and pebbles are hurled at each one. While doing this, pilgrims rededicate themselves to Allah and promise to do their utmost to drive any devils out of themselves. Muslims are reminded, incidentally, to be careful when hurling these pebbles, so that no one gets hurt.

These days police are in attendance to keep an eye on over-enthusiastic pilgrims, and recently large walls have been added to give much larger targets. Despite the recent improvements and precautions over 350 pilgrims were crushed to death there in the Hajj of 2006. A four-level approach-way is planned for 2007, and ultimately it will reach ten levels. Some scholars feel it would be better to make this ritual symbolic only.

The sacrifice

After all this, on the tenth Dhu'l Hijjah, the pilgrims who can afford it buy a sheep, goat or young camel, to make their animal sacrifice. This is a three-day festival to commemorate Ibrahim's ﷺ willingness to offer his son's life, but Allah making the substitution of a ram at the last moment.

The animals provide a huge amount of meat to be consumed, so not every person does this. Some pay a cash equivalent. The sacrificer may use two-thirds of the meat for himself and those with him, and a third of it is given away to those too poor to buy their own animal. After the sacrifice the meat is roasted and eaten. The vast number of animals slaughtered presented quite a problem until the Saudi authorities stepped in to organize the disposal of the carcasses. It is impossible for all the meat to be eaten, even if it is shared, so modern technology freezes and processes all the excess meat for distribution further afield.

This is the festival known as Eid ul-Adha, the major festival (see page 105), and at the same time as the slaughter, Muslims all over the world are making their own sacrifices to keep the feast.

Final rites

After this festival, male pilgrims can again shave their heads or shorten their hair, and females trim their hair again. This is done by someone not in ihram. When they return to Makkah they make the final tawaf, and then the pilgrimage is complete.

Muslim 'tourism'

Most pilgrims also take the chance to visit sites in the neighbourhood connected with the Prophet ﷺ, and may also visit Madinah, where the Prophet ﷺ is buried in what used to be Aishah's room (the *hujurah*), along with his friends, Abu Bakr and Umar. Nearby is the cemetery of al-Baqi where many of his family and the early Companions are buried. Here one notices the extreme simplicity of the tombs, which are simply mounds of small stones. There had been grander mausoleums there in the past, but after being preserved for centuries they were destroyed by the strict Islamic Wahhabi sect in the reign of King Abd al-Aziz al-Saud, which disapproved of hero-worship or saint cults.

Pilgrims might also climb the hill Jabal Nur to see the cave where the Prophet ﷺ received his first vision, and Jabal Thawr where he hid from the Makkans. They might perhaps also visit some of the famous battlefields and mosques. The Masjid at-Tawqa, built when the Prophet ﷺ first entered Madinah, is interesting for having two mihrabs, one facing Jerusalem.

The Prophet ﷺ said:

> 'He who comes for Hajj and does not visit me is a miser. One that comes to my grave and gives me salaam, I say salaam to that person in reply.'

10 jihad

In this chapter you will
learn about:
- the meaning of jihad
- no compulsion or
  persecution
- the rules of military jihad.

Jihad is one of the most misunderstood of all aspects of Islam. Most non-Muslims take it to mean military action for the purpose of forcing other people to become Muslims, but this is totally against the principle of Islam, which defends individual liberties. The fact that various persons claiming to be Muslim have acted incorrectly, some even to the extent of horrifying brutality, does not alter this fact, any more than one could judge Christianity by the atrocities of the Klu Klux Klan in the USA.

Islamic jihad in fact insists that oppression for the sake of religion is wrong. Religion should never become an oppressor. People should never be forced to accept things that they do not believe. The whole essence and reason for jihad is to be prepared to sacrifice one's own self in order to fight against tyranny and oppression, to bring freedom and justice and a just peace.

No compulsion in religion

It is impossible to force anyone to believe or love anything. It is hopeless to expect conversions without education. Muslims are required to present the evidence, show the results and consequences of actions, present the proof – then leave it to people to believe or not. It is their choice. In any case, faith is not complete when it is followed blindly or accepted unquestioningly.

> 'If it had been the Lord's will for all who are on earth to believe, they would have believed! How do you, therefore think you can compel people to believe against their will? No soul can believe except by the will of Allah, and He Himself places doubt (or obscurity) in the minds of those who do not wish to understand.'

(Surah 10:99–100)
See also Surah 18.29 and Surah 28.56.

Human beings need to build faith on well-grounded convictions beyond any reasonable doubt. The attempts of those who try to force a belief on someone are really ridiculous and can only work through tyranny and aggression. The way of dawah in Islam is to make as clear as possible the evidence and proof – but every person must be allowed to believe or disbelieve what they want.

Persecuting non-believers

Nowhere does Allah give permission to force or kill people who refuse to accept the message. On the contrary, believers are asked to be patient with those who do not believe:

'Bear with patience what they say, and when they leave give a courteous farewell.'

(Surah 73:10)

'Deal gently with disbelievers; give them enough time (to change their minds).'

(Surah 86:17)

Duty to warn, not enforce

All Muslims are required to do is give the message:

'The delivery of the message is the duty for you, and the judgement is the duty for Us.'

(Surah 13.40)

Allah is the Judge. It is for Him to decide, in ultimate terms, what the fate will be of those who reject the message, and not any zealot militia. It is up to Muslims to show that everything in the message is good, and promotes goodness and happiness and progress and peace, and that Allah never asked anyone to promote anything that was evil or harmful, or hurtful verbally, physically, mentally or morally. The message was and is all good.

Military jihad

The much-used term 'holy war' is actually not found anywhere in the Qur'an. War with its awful devastation and suffering and death can never be a good thing (except in the circumstances to be mentioned shortly), and Allah denies Muslims the right to ever inflict suffering in order to take power, food, land or anything else, by force. One meaning of the word 'Islam' is 'peace'. The greeting used by all Muslims when they meet each other is *'salaam aleikum'* – 'May peace be with you.'

Whenever a tyrant is successful, even if there is no actual fighting there is no peace, because:

• there is no security

- people feel dishonoured and ashamed in allowing the situation to continue
- people feel frustrated and helpless, and unable to do anything about it
- people feel ashamed because they think they have acted in a cowardly manner.

In fact, the Prophet ﷺ stated quite clearly that:

'If anyone walks with an oppressor to strengthen him, knowing that he is an oppressor, he has gone forth from Islam.'

(Bukhari, Muslim)

Islam cannot acquiesce in wrongdoing, and this is where personal and political decisions could be interpreted differently – who is the oppressor and who the oppressed? It is regarded as weak and irresponsible cowardice to ignore tyranny, or to fail to try to root it out.

'If God did not check certain people by using others, surely many monasteries, churches, synagogues and mosques would all have been pulled down. God will aid those who fight for Him.'

(Surah 22:39–40)

Jihad with the use of weapons is only to be resorted to by Muslims as a means of necessary defence against aggressors who have first attacked believers, or tyrants who have abused and corrupted others. However, once attacked, injustice would soon be triumphant in the world if good people were not prepared to risk their lives, and even sacrifice their lives, for a righteous cause.

Like Christianity, Islam permits fighting in self-defence, in defence of religion, or on the part of those who have been expelled forcibly from their homes. War is the last resort, and jihad subject to the rigorous conditions laid down by the sacred law, rules of combat that include prohibitions against harming civilians or destroying crops, trees and livestock, as far as is humanly possible.

Rules for jihad

Jihad, therefore, does not mean every single battle fought by any Middle-Eastern soldier, who may be anything from a Marxist to a member of a private bodyguard, and not a martyr for God. Many battles have nothing whatever to do with Islam.

Islam placed legal restrictions upon the conduct of war. In general, Muslim armies may not kill women, children, seniors, hermits, pacifists, peasants or slaves unless they are combatants. Vegetation and property should not be destroyed, water holes not be poisoned, and flame-throwers should not be used unless out of necessity, and even then only to a limited extent.

Torture, mutilation and murder of hostages are forbidden under all circumstances. One of the Prophet's ﷺ worst enemies, Suhayl, was captured – a man who had a cleft lower lip. Umar threatened to knock out his two front teeth, stating: 'Then his tongue will flop out, and he will never be able to speak against you again!' The Prophet ﷺ was not pleased. 'I will certainly not mutilate him,' he replied, 'for if I did, surely Allah would mutilate me, even though I am His Messenger. Think – it may be that one day he will make a stand for which you will not be able to find fault with him.' (Ibn Kathir 2.324) Suhayl did indeed convert and became a Muslim hero. The Prophet's ﷺ forward-looking and generous attitude is an important *sunnah* for those zealots who regard non-Muslim territories as Dar al-Harb (House of War), full of enemies who need conquering. The Prophet ﷺ on the contrary, saw such territories as Dar al-Dawah (House of Missionary Preaching), full of potential converts.

A jihad should be declared only:

- in defence of the cause of Allah, not for conquest
- to restore peace and freedom of worship
- for freedom from tyranny
- when led by a spiritual leader
- until the enemy lays down arms.

Jihad does not include:

- wars of aggression or ambition
- border disputes or either national or tribal squabbles
- the intent to conquer and suppress, colonize, exploit, etc.
- forcing people into accepting a faith they do not believe
- acts of terrorism, suicide bombings, etc. (see suicide bombings page 301).

National jihad has to be commanded by a leader who is accepted as a spiritual guide and supreme judge, who can assess the need, the cause, and give right guidance to oppose a clear unjust oppressor; someone not governed by personal ambition.

Sometimes after starting jihad in the correct spirit, a human leader then becomes ambitious. In this case, the qualification for leadership is lost and the community has the right to demand a change of his ways or his abdication, or even his death if he refuses to give way.

When to cease the jihad

All the following texts are direct orders to Muslims from the Qur'an:

'The reward for an injury is an equal injury back; but if a person forgives instead, and makes reconciliation, he will be rewarded by God.'

(Surah 42:40)

'If two sides quarrel, make peace between them. But if one trespasses beyond bounds against the other, then fight against the one that transgresses until it complies with the law of God; and when it complies, then make peace between them with justice, and be fair.'

(Surah 49:9)

'Goodness and evil cannot be equal. Repay evil with what is better, then he who was your enemy will become your intimate friend.'

(Surah 41:34)

The physical fighting is only allowed until the enemy seeks peace terms, and then it must cease.

'Fight them until there is no more persecution, and religion is for God. But if they desist, then let there be no more hostility – except against those who continue to do wrong.'

(Surah 2:193)

'If they seek peace, then you seek peace. And trust in God – for He is the One that hears and knows all things.'

(Surah 8:61)

The highest sacrifice

When all else fails, the highest sacrifice people can make is obviously of their actual lives. The Prophet Jesus ﷺ said: 'Greater love has no man than this – that a man lay down his life for his friends.' (St John's Gospel 15:13) He was talking about sacrificing his own life for the sake of those who followed him, because he loved God more than he loved himself. In Islam, people who are prepared to die because they love God more than their own lives are called *shahid*. By dying in Allah's cause they bear the ultimate witness to their faith in the existence of God and the Life to Come. Some believe and love God so much they do not even regard it as a sacrifice – but to those helped or protected by them no sacrifice could be higher, or more admired.

11

festivals and special days

The Muslim word for a festival is *id* or *eid*, from the Arab word meaning 'returning at regular intervals'. The fact that they do occur in a regular cycle is important, for it gives a repeated opportunity for renewal, to forgive enemies, put right quarrels, do things you ought to have done but have perhaps put off or forgotten, and contact people you have not seen for a long time.

Although there are several special times in the Islamic calendar, there are really only two religious festivals. These are *Eid ul-Fitr*, the feast that breaks the fast at the end of the Ramadan month, and Eid ul-Adha, the feast of sacrifice that takes place during the hajj. Eid ul-Adha is the major festival, and Eid ul-Fitr the minor festival.

Both of these feasts are times of celebration and joy, at the express command of Allah as revealed in the Qur'an, when family and friends get together and the local community feels a strong sense of fellowship with the whole Muslim world.

The aims of Eid

The aims of Eid are basically to praise and thank God for His many blessings, in particular those connected with the background of the feast, and to enjoy oneself and appreciate God's blessings.

The second basic aim is unity, to arouse a heightened feeling of ummah or one community. At Eid, Muslims are requested to bring loved ones to memory, particularly those who cannot be present because they live in far distant parts of the world. One should also think lovingly of all the members of the family of Islam, not just those in one's own family – whether known or unknown, rich or poor. Equally important are loved ones who have died. Eid is a time to think about them, and say prayers for their souls.

The duties of Eid

There are several aspects to Muslim duty at Eid, all geared towards the aims of unity, peace and brotherhood. Blessings must be shared and a conscious effort made to see that no one is left lonely or depressed. The rich must share what they have (any animals sacrificed for Eid must be shared, with at least a third going to the less fortunate) and the poor must be welcomed. The lonely must not be left alone, but invited to join in either with a family or at the mosque. (Muslims have a particular responsibility to look after orphans and see that they are being loved and cared for.)

People who are not usually particularly zealous in their religion make new resolutions and put in extra effort. Those who are involved in quarrels or feuds must settle them if they are to keep the spirit of Eid.

Eid ul-Fitr

Although Eid-ul-Fitr is known as the minor festival, many young Muslims enjoy it more than the 'major' one, coming as it does at the end of the month-long fast of Ramadan. It is also known as *Sheker Bairam* (Turkish for 'sweet festival'), *Eid Ramadan* and *Eid ul-Sagheer* (the 'little festival'). It is little because it lasts for three days, whereas Eid ul-Adha lasts for four.

Preparations for the feast begin well in advance, as the amount of food required to feed many guests turning up for meals requires much shopping and advance cooking, usually in gargantuan quantities. Sometimes Muslim shops are so busy that they stay open all night for a few days beforehand.

Many families make decorations and hang them up, or use the tinsel trimmings Christians use at Christmas. These can now be bought all over the Muslim world, and really have nothing to do with Christmas at all – they are just glittering signs of joy. Sometimes families take the opportunity to spruce up the entire house with a fresh coat of paint, or new curtains or cushion covers.

Gifts or sweets are prepared, and cards made or bought and sent out to relatives and friends. These cards usually show famous mosques, or flowers, or designs, and carry the message Eid Mubarak ('Happy, or blessed, Feast-time').

Special contributions are collected for the poor, the *zakat ul-fitr*. This is not the same as the annual *zakah*, but is charity bestowed as an act of purification for the giver. Zakat ul-fitr is the equivalent of a good meal from each adult member of the family, and should be paid well before the Eid day to ensure that the poor are able to take part in the celebrations, and perhaps to buy some new clothes.

Non-Muslims may notice that post offices and banks are rather more full than usual; this is because so many Muslims whose roots lie elsewhere send money to the country of their origin, to help known poor people, or to add to a particular fund. Many use the opportunity to send their annual *zakah* at the same time.

The announcement

The Eid depends on the sighting of the new moon, and this has caused some confusion in countries where the night sky is not always clear. If the new moon is sighted during the evening of the 29th day of the month, that night becomes the first of the new month, but if the moon is not sighted some Muslims fast an extra day to be on the safe side. In the United Kingdom, it has not been uncommon for Eid to be celebrated on three different days, as various communities decide their date of Eid from different sources – a source of irritation to those involved in planning such things as school diaries in advance. Many Muslims have also become irritated by these differences, and feel that scientific calculations should be used to make the whole matter beyond dispute.

Traditionally, the fast is broken by the call to prayer from the mosque, or by the firing of cannons and guns, or the beating of a drum. In Indonesia, for example, the drummers are known as *al-musaharati* and they also wake the faithful before every dawn during Ramadan. The time is also announced on radio and TV in Islamic societies, and mosques get the news by radio, telex and telephone (if one can get through, the switchboards are so jammed at this time!).

Breaking the fast

As soon as the signal comes, there is a release of emotion and much hugging and greeting, handshaking and kissing. The fast is traditionally broken with something very simple, as was the practice of the Prophet ﷺ – usually dates or other fruit, and fruit drinks or milk. After this simple food and drink, the family leaves the table to make the maghrib prayer. The big meal comes later.

In Muslim societies people are so excited and full of the urge to congratulate each other on completing a successful fast that they go out into the streets in party mood to wish each other 'Eid Mubarak'. Visitors go round to call on friends and family, trying to make sure that no one is forgotten.

The Eid day

In Muslim countries there is no work or school on Eid days – everybody has a three-day holiday. In the United Kingdom, Muslim children are granted a day off school, and sympathy from employers towards their Muslim employees is increasing. Others have to content themselves with making the early *salat ul-fitr* prayer, an hour after sunrise, and then getting on with their jobs as usual, looking forward to a good feast in the evening. Salat ul-fitr consists of two rakahs with extra takbirs (saying of 'Allahu Akbar') and a sermon, usually about giving in charity. There is no call to prayer. Other Eid prayers take place in congregation between sunrise and noon.

Each person going to Eid prayer must first take a full bath or shower, and then dress in new or best clothes. They take a quick breakfast, and hurry to the Eid congregation, which may be a huge gathering in the largest mosque in the area, or the principal mosque of the city, known as the *Jami'a Mosque*. Streets become so crowded that surrounding roads are cleared of traffic so that people overflowing from the mosque can pray. In many places there are open fields called *Eid gahs* which are used for the festival prayers.

Sometimes the Eid prayer takes place in a park or playing field, or even a car park – any large open space where a very big crowd can gather. The congregation may consist of thousands of people, because women and children are also encouraged to attend, and traditionally mosques try to gather together to make as large an ummah as possible.

After the prayer, everyone greets each other with 'Eid Mubarak' and hugs and kisses, and then the round of visits to friends and family begins. Children get lots of presents and pocket money.

At midday there is a large dinner – the first meal eaten during the day for over a month! It may have to be in several sittings if large numbers of guests arrive. Needless to say, the female members of the family will have put a great deal of effort into preparation of these huge meals. Luckily, the Middle Eastern style of cookery lends itself to these large feasts, and it is fairly easy to expand the food to fit the numbers that turn up.

During the afternoon, families often visit the cemetery to remember their beloved dead, and sit by their graves for a while. The day ends with more visiting and entertaining, going on late into the night.

figure 11.1 enjoying a feast

Eid ul-Adha

This is the major festival, lasting four days, and is celebrated
at the end of the Hajj. It commemorates the obedience of the
Prophet Ibrahim ﷺ when he was called upon to sacrifice his son
Isma'il ﷺ, and his triumph over the temptations of the devil.

Every Muslim takes part in this feast, not only the ones on Hajj.
Everyone thinks about the pilgrims who have gone on Hajj, and
joins with them in spirit, particularly any who have gone from
their own family or community. In Muslim countries, the Hajj
is reported on TV for everyone to see.

Eid ul-Adha is a serious occasion, symbolizing the submission of
each individual Muslim, and the renewal of total commitment
to Allah. The mind is concentrated on the idea of sacrifice and
self-sacrifice, symbolized by the actual sacrificing of a sheep,
goat, cow or camel.

The animal sacrifice

In Muslim countries this does not usually present a problem as
many Muslim men will have been trained in how to slaughter an
animal according to the principles of Islam. People in the West
are often horrified at the thought of animal slaughter, and
regard it as cruelty and a barbaric practice. They are confusing
Islamic slaughter with the ancient worshippers of idols who

used to consider that their gods needed the ritual sacrifice of blood to give them strength, and so on. This has nothing to do with Islam.

> 'Neither the flesh of the animals of your sacrifice nor their blood reaches Allah – it is your righteousness that reaches him.'

(Surah 22:37)

The creature is not slain in any way as a propitiatory sacrifice to God, but as meat for a communal feast. Any person who eats meat should be aware that the meat was once a living animal that was slaughtered specifically so that they could eat. In fact, the Islamic principles of slaughter are to slay the creature in the kindest possible way, with the least amount of pain, and without putting the animal to fear or distress. There is sometimes controversy amongst non-Muslims over whether or not halal (or 'permitted') killing is cruel or kind; Muslims maintain that it is the kindest possible method, ordained by God Himself, and that is why they do it. They do not regard killing an animal by electrocution, or by firing a bolt into its brain (normal United Kingdom slaughter house practices) to be kind methods at all.

Muslim slaying should be done with a very sharp knife across the jugular vein, so that the animal loses consciousness immediately. Prayers are said throughout the proceedings. Killing the animal in this way causes the least pain or distress, and the blood drains away easily.

In the United Kingdom, people must have a special licence to slaughter animals, and it is not permitted for Muslims to slaughter their own on their own premises. Licence-holders have to go to the slaughterhouse to sacrifice there on behalf of the community. When newspapers sometimes print 'horror stories' of Muslims slaughtering sheep or goats in their backyards, it is usually newcomers who are unaware of the rules or facilities provided.

Dates

Months in the Islamic calendar are calculated according to a lunar year, therefore each month has 29 days, 12 hours and 44 minutes; the Islamic year is shorter than the solar year by 11 days. The odd 44 minutes of the lunar month means that some years will have 355 days instead of 354. (In a stretch of 30 years, there would be 11 of these 'leap' years.) Therefore, the Islamic festival days are not seasonal, like Christian festivals, and cannot have fixed dates. Each festival comes 11 days earlier each year.

Islamic months and their special days

The Islamic months are *Muharram*, *Safar*, *Rabi'ul-Awwal (al Ula)*, *Rabi ath-Thani (al-Akhir)*, *Jumada al Awwad (al Ula)*, *Jumada ath-Thani (al-Akhir)*, *Rajab*, *Shaban*, Ramadan, *Shawwal*, *Dhu'l Qidah*, and Dhu'l Hijjah. There are no special days in Safar, Rabi al-Akhir, Jumada al-Ula, Jumada al-Akhir or Dhu'l Qidah.

Muharram

Muharram is the first month of the Muslim calendar. New Year's Day is declared after the sighting of the new moon. The Muslim year commemorates the Hijrah, the departure of the Prophet ﷺ to Madinah, the moment that marked the turning point for Islam and the beginning of the spread of Islam which took place in the month Rabi'ul Awwal, but Caliph Umar took the start of year 1 AH back to Muharram. Muslims date all their years from this year, and call them AH – after the Hijrah.

On New Year's Day (Muharram 1) Muslims have to 'migrate' from their past to their future, putting old sins and failings behind them and making a fresh start with new year resolutions.

Ashura

The tenth of Muharram, known as *Ashura*, was already a time of fasting before Islam, according to the Jewish tradition. It was originally the Jewish Day of Atonement, when the High Priest of that faith made sacrifices for the sins of the nation.

In Muslim tradition, this day celebrates a number of major events: the creation of the seven heavens, the land and sea; the birth of Adam ﷺ; the day when Nuh (Noah) ﷺ left the Ark after the flood to begin a new life on earth; the birth of the Prophet Ibrahim ﷺ and the day on which he was supposed to sacrifice Isma'il ﷺ; the day on which the Prophet Ayyub (Job) ﷺ was released from his suffering; the day on which Allah saved Musa (Moses) ﷺ from the cruel Pharaoh; the day on which the Prophet Isa (Jesus) ﷺ was born, and the Day on which the Day of Judgement is expected. Fasting is not obligatory for Muslims on this day, but most do keep a day's fast. The Prophet ﷺ praised the excellence of fasting on this day.

It is a particularly special day for Shi'ite Muslims (see page 28) for it marks the day when the Prophet's ﷺ heroic grandson, Hussain, was martyred at Karbala in the year 61 AH. Shi'ites mourn for the first ten days of Muharram, wearing black mourning clothes. On the tenth day, they perform dramatic processions led by a white horse, with floats called *tazias* depicting scenes of the events, and plays portraying the events of the suffering and death of Hussain. Some of the more fervent even beat themselves with chains and cut their heads with swords, to share in a small way the sufferings of Hussain.

Milad an-Nabi

12 Rabi'ul-Awwal is traditionally celebrated as the birthday of the Prophet ﷺ (probably originally 20 August, 570 CE). There is some controversy among Muslims as to whether this day should be celebrated or not; some purists feeling it wrong to celebrate a human being, no matter how much loved and respected. Others feel it is wrong not to commemorate the birth of such a great Prophet ﷺ.

> 'God and His angels send blessings on the Prophet. O ye that believe! Send blessings on him, and salute him with all respect.'

(Surah 33:57)

The Prophet's ﷺ birthday was not observed in the early years of Islam, but was introduced by the Abbasid Caliphs of Baghdad and made popular by the Sufis in the tenth century CE. There has always been opposition to it, because it is an innovation, and it is forbidden by strict sects such as the Wahhabi Muslims of Arabia and the Deobandis of India.

However, it now has an important socio-religious function in many communities as an opportunity to remind young and old Muslims alike of what the Prophet ﷺ taught and what lessons can be learnt from his life and sunnah. It is an occasion to generate love and reverence in Muslim hearts, and to send blessings on the soul of the Prophet ﷺ. Celebrations might include a procession in places with strong Sufic influence, and there are marches and meetings in Malaya. It is a public holiday in Pakistan. However, Milad an-Nabi is usually only celebrated with special meetings at the mosque to hear sermons about the Prophet's ﷺ life, mission, character, sufferings and successes.

Laylat ul-Isra wal-Miraj

27 Rajab is traditionally recognized as Laylat ul-Miraj, the commemoration of the Prophet's ﷺ night journey and ascent to Heaven (see page 10), three years before the migration to Madinah. The Prophet ﷺ travelled with the Angel Jibril on a winged animal known as a buraq from Makkah to Jerusalem, and was then allowed to see both Paradise and Hell before passing on through various heavens to the final heaven where there was the Presence of God. At that point, where he had attained the highest spiritual state attainable by humans, neither he nor the angel could go any further.

The main feature of this experience was the institution of the five daily prayers.

> 'Glory to God Who did take His servant for a journey by night from the sacred mosque to the farthest mosque whose precincts We did bless – in order that We might show him some of Our signs.'

> (Surah 17:1)

Many Muslims will spend the entire night reading the Qur'an and praying. In some countries the mosques are illuminated for this night. Others reject all this as innovation.

Laylat ul-Bara'at

Laylat ul-Bara'at is the 'Night of Blessing', or the 'Night of the Decree', celebrated on 14 Shaban. It is the night of the full moon before the start of Ramadan, and it was at this time that the Prophet ﷺ used to begin his preparations for Ramadan by passing whole nights in prayer. Many Muslims also celebrate this night by staying awake in prayer all night. They usually visit the graves of their relatives on 15 Shaban, and pray for the good of the departed souls.

Muslims believe that every year on this night God makes His order known to the angels as to who will live and who will die, what will be the means of livelihood for each individual for that year, and whose sins will be forgiven and who will be condemned.

Sometimes a special meal is eaten, and candles are lit. Sweets are made, and sweets and loaves distributed among the poor. Many Muslims fast for two days. Others reject all this as innovation.

Laylat ul-Qadr

27 Ramadan is traditionally recognized as Laylat ul-Qadr, the Night of Power, on which the Prophet ﷺ received his first revelation of the Qur'an.

> 'We have indeed revealed this (message) in the Night of Power. Who will tell you what the Night of Power is? The Night of Power is better than a thousand months. Therein came down the angels and the Spirit (meaning Jibril) by God's permission, on every errand: Peace! This until the rise of the morning!'

(Surah 97:1–5)

In fact, the date is not known for certain, and Muslims may celebrate this night on any of the odd nights during the last ten days of Ramadan. Most keep the night of the 27th as an all-night of prayer at the mosque.

figure 11.2 Kurdish Muslims celebrating Laylat ul-Bara'at

'When the Night of Power comes, Jibril descends with a company of angels who grant blessings to everyone who is standing or sitting and remembering the Most Gracious and Glorious Allah.'

(Tirmidhi)

Some Muslims make a religious 'retreat' (*i'tikaf*) for the whole of the last ten days of Ramadan.

12

mosques

In this chapter you will
learn about:
- places where Muslims pray
- the functions of a community
  mosque
- the major features outside
  and inside a mosque
- how to behave in a mosque.

figure 12.1 Dar al-Islam mosque, Abiquiu, New Mexico, USA

The Muslim place of prayer is known as a *masjid* or mosque. Masjid means literally a 'place of prostration' (Ar. Sujud), in other words, a place where someone bows down. This place of prayer does not have to be a special building – any clean place will do. Indeed, the Prophet ﷺ said:

> 'The whole world has been made a place of prayer, pure and clean.'

> (Muslim)

> 'Wherever the hour of prayer overtakes you, you shall perform it. That place is a mosque.'

> (Bukhari)

Simple mosques

In Muslim countries it is quite normal to see people praying by the roadside when it is time for prayer. It is also normal for little areas to be set aside for prayer at places like railway stations, often just a rectangular area facing the direction of Makkah, marked out by a few stones, perhaps under a tree, sometimes with a wooden board or a mat to kneel on. You might also see an arrow erected somewhere like a weather-vane, showing the direction of Makkah to the stranger. If possible, there will be a water supply near at hand, for the ritual washing, although *tayammum* (dry washing) is acceptable for the traveller.

Great or historic mosques

The two most important mosques in Islam are the Great Mosque in Makkah and the Prophet's ﷺ Mosque in Madinah. The al-Aqsa Mosque in Jerusalem is usually accepted as the third most revered mosque in Islam, but many countries have a chief mosque, or a special place, which is often spoken of as 'the third most holy site in Islam'. This is because Muslims who cannot go on Hajj often go to their country's special mosque at Hajj time.

The functions of a community mosque

Communal prayer

The mosque serves several functions. First and foremost, it is the place where Muslims gather to pray together. Mosques in the West began with groups of Muslims gathering together in somebody's house; then using properties bought specifically so that they could function as mosques. Nowadays, most Muslim communities in the West are wealthy enough to afford purpose-built centres with prayer halls, and increasing numbers of major beautiful buildings are appearing in most big cities.

The mosque is a very important part of the social life of the Muslim community, and its size and facilities depend on the wealth of its communities or sponsors. Modern mosques run homework clubs, women's activities and youth clubs, and may have IT facilities, computers, crèches and kitchens. Once the prayers are over, Muslims often stay on, chatting to their friends, and using facilities provided for activities such as table tennis and snooker.

Women's facilities

Initially, lack of funds and space has often meant that mosques have concentrated on facilities for men, but this is gradually being remedied. The sunnah is for women and small children to pray in lines behind the men in the same prayer-space, but in many mosques they have a segregated space such as a balcony or a separate room. (See Islamic feminism, and women imams on pages 310–13).

Relaxation and company

Sometimes Muslims feel quite lonely in a non-Muslim community, so the mosque gives them a chance to meet and relax with people who speak their native language.

The imam can use the premises if he wishes to meet people, discuss problems in the community, or help people with problems concerning their families (or, perhaps, immigration queries).

Education

Most mosques have a collection of books for study, sometimes sufficient to qualify being called a library. Muslims often invite visiting speakers and use the mosque for lectures and talks, or to discuss problems of Muslim law. The mosque also fulfils an important function as the school (or madrassah) where people can study the Arabic language, the Qur'an and various Islamic subjects.

The madrassah

All Muslims are expected to learn as much of the Qur'an as they are able, and for many this is a difficult business as Arabic is not their natural language. Boys and girls usually start these Islamic studies at the age of five, and continue until they are 15 or so. It is quite possible to go on being a student for the rest of your life.

Classes to learn Arabic, and to study the meaning of the Qur'an (known as *tafsir*) are held every day, children usually going straight after school and studying for around two hours, five nights per week. Some schools even demand weekend work, too. Adults study at later times.

There are mosque exams every year, and few children fail them. Many youngsters and new converts are also urged to study for the GCSE in Religious Studies when there is an Islamic option. Teachers are not usually specially teacher-trained, but are willing and knowledgeable volunteers. Discipline is considered important, the duty of an adult towards a child, and adults are allowed to use corporal punishment; however, it is virtually never needed because Muslim children are respectful to their elders and behave politely.

Social functions

The mosque can be hired out for all sorts of functions – meetings, parties for weddings and festival days, birthdays, circumcision parties, or welcome home parties, celebrating the passing of an important exam. These are all joyful functions, and usually involve huge meals. Most mosques will have a good kitchen area as part of the complex, and perhaps a special function room. Some even run a café for the public.

Hospital and hospitality

Sometimes people sleep overnight in a mosque, either on the carpeted floor of the prayer hall or in specially provided facilities. The oldest traditions reveal that many mosques also did service as primitive hospitals, feeding centres, and 'rest-room' facilities. Many still do.

Farewells to the dead

Less happy gatherings are those to mourn the dead and pay the last respects to friends and relatives before burial. The mosque may have an ablutions room where it is possible to administer the last washing to the deceased before shrouding them.

Imams

The imam is the leader of the mosque, but there is no suggestion of priesthood; every Muslim stands before God responsible for himself or herself. However, whenever two or more Muslims come together to pray, the one with the most knowledge, or the eldest, leads the prayer.

The imam also usually has the job of *khatib*, that is, he delivers the khutbah or double sermon at the Friday congregation, and probably organizes Islamic studies for the young people. After the first sermon, the imam will sit down for a few moments, and then give the second. Then the Friday prayer of two rakahs follows, and after this people pray individually.

Any person respected by the mosque members, who has studied Qur'an and hadith, has good knowledge of the faith, and is known for his piety and common-sense can be elected imam for the community. In the United Kingdom, each mosque elects its own imam. Some imams have become famous teachers, and have rallied the faithful in times of persecution and war.

The year 2005 saw the Government propose a 'Britishness test' for foreign-born imams, after concern was expressed that some could speak little English and had hardly any knowledge of western societies. The idea has been welcomed by many Muslim mosques, since community members frequently did not understand the sermons in either Arabic or the ethnic languages of the original immigrants. This has now been watered down to a test on life in Britain, including its constitution, legal system, customs and religious life, if they apply to settle after four years or seek citizenship after being in the country for five years.

It is hoped that future imams will be chosen who have good understanding of Muslims brought up in the West, and will perhaps be encouraged to take part in the civic life of the community, including mixing with other faiths, as part of a drive to improve community cohesion and end ghettoization. There are now several training courses for imams, with certification.

The major features outside a mosque

Muslims can convert any sort of building into a mosque – many old churches and houses, warehouses and even a fire station, have been put to this use by the growing communities. Mosques do not always look like mosques. None of the traditional features is compulsory.

It is advisable to have good car-parking facilities and, where possible, toilet facilities that are quite separate from the carpeted prayer-hall, for reasons of hygiene and to prevent wetness – from the Muslim practice of washing after toilet.

Dome and Minaret

Where the mosque is purpose-built, the two most typical features are the dome and the minaret. The dome is an architectural device giving the impression of space and calm when one goes inside; it also helps acoustically. It is also a feature that reminds Muslims of their origins in the Middle East.

The minaret is a tall tower where the man who summons the faithful to prayer (known as the muezzin or mu'adhin) gives the call known as the adhan. Throughout the Muslim world this stirring cry is given five times per day, but in non-Muslim societies it is frequently not sounded, so as not to upset and disturb those who would not be sympathetic.

Symbol of Islam

Atop the dome or the minaret one can usually see the symbol of Islam, a crescent moon. Sometimes there is also a five-pointed star which reminds Muslims of the five 'pillars' or obligatory duties of their faith; the moon reminds them of God the Creator, and the lunar calendar which governs Islamic festivals and special days.

The major features inside the mosque

Clocks

A series of clocks usually shows the prayer times each day – prayer times are flexible when praying on your own, but have to keep to a strict timetable for a congregation to come together. The clocks will show the five *salat* and the Friday prayer.

Washing facilities

It is not necessary to perform wudu at the mosque, and many Muslims prefer to do it at home before going. In the mosque, men and women usually have separate facilities for toilet and ablutions, where there is running water.

The toilets frequently have both the flushing style, and the hole in the ground type as well, for people who are most used to coping with this sort of design. There will be several pairs of slip-ons lying around for people with bare feet to borrow. There is always water available for washing in a Muslim toilet, but there might not be toilet paper. There will either be a pipe that will automatically wash you if you are in the right position, or it is traditional to use a *loti*, rather like a jug with a curved spout. (Use the left hand. The right hand is used for eating, and all 'honourable' purposes.) Outside the actual toilet there will be wash-basins and towels.

The most common arrangement for wudu ablutions is for a row of taps to be set in the wall over a drain, with stools arranged for people to sit on while they wash their feet. People coming to pray often leave the water to dry by itself and do not use towels.

Decoration in the mosque

The most noticeable thing straight away is the lack of furniture or decoration in the prayer room. There are no chairs or pews for people to sit on. Everyone sits on the floor. There are no pictorial decorations or statues, because representation of this sort is forbidden in Islam as it encourages idolatry. You will never see any representation of God, angels, or the Prophets. However, this does not mean that mosques are dull places. Many are extremely beautiful, with richly coloured carpets, different marbles for columns and surfaces, intricately patterned and colourful tiles, carved woodwork, stained glass, beautiful chandeliers, gold-painted ceilings, ornamental calligraphy on texts from the Qur'an, and so forth.

The carpet in the prayer hall is generally marked out with lines or regular patterns, so that when the prayer lines form, people know where to stand and how much space to occupy. Some massive carpets like the one at Regent's Park Mosque in London have patterns like individual prayer-mats. However, when a large congregation comes together for prayer, they form up very close together, shoulder to shoulder, and often literally toe-to-toe, with their toes touching those of the next person.

The qiblah and mihrab

The wall facing Makkah is known as the qiblah wall, and set in this wall is a specially decorated niche or alcove known as the mihrab. This is not in any way an altar, although it looks to a Christian rather like an altar area with the altar-table taken away. It simply points the direction of the Ka'bah, and concentrates the Muslim's mind upon Allah.

The prayer leader stands in front of the mihrab, which is sometimes known as the 'niche of lights', the symbol for the Divine Presence in the heart. Some mihrabs incorporate a shell-shape; the shell symbolizes the 'ear of the heart', and the pearl within is the 'Divine Word'.

When Muslims have taken over existing buildings and converted them into mosques the qiblah may seem to be in a very odd place, not at all a focal point – but it always indicates the direction of Makkah.

figure 12.2 the *minbar*

The minbar

On the right side of the mihrab is the *minbar*, the platform from which the imam gives the khutbah sermons. These can be very simple, or highly ornate. The simplest ones are usually just a couple of carpeted steps with a small platform at the top. Ornate minbars can consist of a high flight of stairs, beautifully carved and decorated.

What to do when entering a mosque

When visiting a mosque, one should be suitably dressed. For men, this involves being clean, smart and tidy. Muslim men would not go into a mosque with shirt hanging open, or wearing shorts. For women, it is polite if they are sensitive to Muslim custom and cover the arms and legs, and wear a scarf or veil over their hair. Muslim women's dress is always modest – transparent, over-tight or too short clothing would be out of place, as would too much make-up and any perfume.

Both men and women should bear in mind that they will have to take off their shoes, and will probably be asked to sit down on the floor, difficult and embarrassing with dirty feet/socks and short, tight skirts.

There will probably be two entrances at the mosque, one for men and one for women. In many mosques men and women pray in separate areas, and how this is arranged depends on the design. Sometimes the women have a balcony, or they might pray behind a curtain at the back.

On entering the mosque, both men and women take off their shoes and place them in the rack or on the shelves provided. (If it is a very big meeting, it is sensible to keep your shoes with you in a carrier bag to avoid an irritating scramble after the prayer.) In mosques where there are a lot of tourists, there may be someone employed to look after the shoes, but they are normally quite safe.

It is not necessary to take off socks, stockings or tights, but polite visitors will make sure their socks are clean and not smelly or full of holes. Muslims, who may wash their feet five times per day, are often somewhat shocked by the state of non-Muslim feet! It is impolite to soil carpets with dirt trodden in from outside, or with sticky, smelly feet.

How to behave in the mosque

Quiet, respectful behaviour is expected at all times. It is considered very bad manners to talk loudly or shout to someone or call out, to smoke, or to interrupt the devotions of people who might be already praying or reading the Qur'an. It is also 'not good form' for an individual to perform personal recitations of the Qur'an too loudly, and thus disturb others, unless the others are happy with that.

Muslims should not continue any meetings or activities in the hall up to the last moment before prayer-time, so that the hall is not ready, or people arriving for prayer feel they are disturbing them. It is good manners in Islam to pray two rakahs before the salah prayer to 'greet the mosque'.

The mosque in the home

All Muslims pray at home sometimes; most Muslim women pray at home every time. Therefore many Muslims have a special place set aside, perhaps an entire room, which is kept clean and ready at all times, and is usually carpeted so that people can kneel in comfort. Many Muslims use little individual prayer-mats to kneel on as well as the carpet, but this is not compulsory. The prayer-mat is simply an aid to providing a clean place.

A non-Muslim visitor might find it strange that an almost empty room is regarded as the most important place in the home, but it is the heart of the Muslim home, the place of prayer.

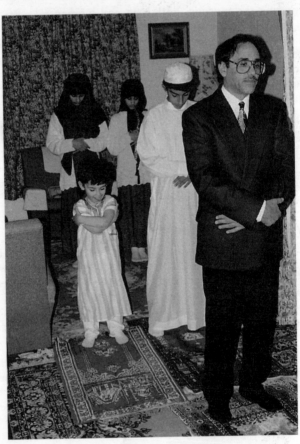

figure 12.3 Muslims set aside a special place to pray at home

13

Islamic human rights and ethics

Many people seem to spend a great deal of their time and effort demanding their rights, and are frequently discontented whatever they receive. In Islam, rights are not an end in themselves, but the means to fulfil the duties of life. The human being who is worthwhile contributes to life and shares in the service of humanity, alleviating human suffering and working hard to take care of those in his or her charge. The true Muslim is interested in the economic and scientific advancement of humanity, as well as moral and spiritual well-being.

Moral awareness

It is moral awareness and participation in the good of society that makes a human being different from an animal, and was the aim of Allah in ordaining humans as His khalifahs on the planet.

> *'Do you think that We created you for nothing, or that you would not return (and give account)?'*

(Surah 23:115)

Humans are granted the right to life in order to use it in the production of good works and deeds. They have free-will to behave as they choose, but when they choose to submit to the will of God, they strive to pass their lives in the best way possible.

Consciousness of these duties drives the Muslim to strive to uphold the rights of the oppressed by strengthening the legal and social foundations of society and by countering those who trample on the rights and dignity of others. Any so-called Islamic government that has itself become a tyrant has departed from the principles of Islam, no matter how self-righteous it might claim to be.

The basic human rights

All human beings are the creations of God, and loved by Him. Therefore there are certain basic rights which should be shared by the whole of humanity, whether people are Muslim or not. All have the right to be fed, clothed, educated and cared for by the society which governs their existence. Every society contains people whose disabilities prevent them from working, or who are too sick or too weak to earn sufficient wages to secure a decent life. There are children who have lost parents, wives who have lost husbands, old people who are no longer able to care for themselves. Any society with the least respect for human dignity would not allow such people to be left neglected and uncared for.

Islamic obligations

Islam makes it obligatory for the wealthy and able-bodied to support the less fortunate. No society should victimize or terrorize its weak members, or deprive people of liberty for no reason. No society should try to 'brainwash' its members, or attempt to force them to believe things against their natural will, ability or awareness.

These human rights have all been granted by God Himself, and not by any ruler or government, and it is the duty of Muslims to protect these rights actively. Failure to do so results in the loss of these rights, and leads to *tughyan* – tyranny and suffering.

'He will not enter Paradise whose neighbour is not secure from his wrongful conduct.'

(Muslim)

'None of you is a true believer until you wish for your brother what you wish for yourself.'

(Bukhari and Muslim)

Specific human rights in Islam

In Islam, human rights include the following specific areas:

- The right to life.
- The right to equality.
- The right to freedom.
- The right to freedom of opinion.
- The right to emigration and refuge, to remove oneself from oppression.
- The right to work and provide for oneself and one's family.
- The right to justice.
- The right to equality before the Law.
- The right to protect one's honour.
- The right to social welfare and the basic necessities of life.
- The right to marriage.
- The right to privacy, and security of private life.
- The right to dignity, and not to be abused or ridiculed.

- The right to education.
- The right to protest against tyranny.
- The right to freedom of expression.
- The right to freedom of conscience and conviction.
- The right to protect religious sentiments.
- The right to participate in affairs of state.
- The right to rise above the level of animal life.

There are numerous passages in the Qur'an and hadith expressing people's rights.

> *'Why should you not fight in the cause of Allah and of those who, being weak, are ill-treated and oppressed? Men, women and children, whose cry is: "Our Lord, rescue us from this town whose people are oppressors, and raise for us one who will protect and help us!"'*

(Surah 4:75)

> 'How are rights neglected? When sins are committed openly, and no one prevents the sinners from wrongdoing.'

(Targhib)

> 'He who amongst you sees something abominable should modify it with the help of his hand; and if he has not the strength to do that, then he should do it by word of mouth; and if he has not the strength enough for that, then he should at least (abhor it) from his heart.'

(Muslim)

The useful guide of the conscience

The conscience is the guide to the Muslim, and should always be listened to, for it brings the stirrings of Allah's will. The Prophet ﷺ accounted a person a believer 'when your deed pleases you and your evil deed grieves you'. He was then asked what sin was, and replied: 'When a thing disturbs your heart, give it up.' (Hadith Ahmad).

Moreover, the Prophet ﷺ had no time for hypocrisy. He said:

> 'Look at your own faults. This will prevent you from finding faults with others. Never be in search of the faults of others. It is sinful on your part to detect those faults in others which exist in you.'

(Abu Dawud)

In Islam, the conscience is used to determine the huge range of actions that are not specifically ruled to be halal (allowed) or haram (forbidden). Sometimes a matter might fall into several categories, depending on the circumstances, and how your conscience feels about it.

Islamic ethics

'God does not look upon your bodies and appearances; He looks upon your hearts and deeds.'

(Bayhaqi)

The aim of Islam is to promote certain values specifically, and deliberately try to reduce or stamp out others. Surah 25.63–76 gives us:

'True servants of the Compassionate (Allah) are those who walk on the earth in humility and when the ignorant people address them, they say: "Peace"; who pass the night kneeling and standing in prayer before their Lord; who say: "O our Lord! Ward off the punishment of hell from us..."; who, when they spend, are neither extravagant nor stingy, but keep the balance between those two extremes; who do not invoke any other god besides Allah, nor kill any soul which Allah has made sacred, except for a just cause, nor commit fornication...; who do not bear witness to falsehood, and, if they ever pass by futility, pass with dignity; who, when reminded about the revelations of their Lord, do not turn a blind eye and a deaf ear to them; who pray: "O our Lord! Make our spouses and our children to be the comfort of our eyes, and make us leaders of the righteous." Such are the ones who will be rewarded with the lofty places in paradise for their patience, wherein they shall be welcomed with greetings and salutations. They shall live forever in that excellent dwelling and excellent resting place!'

The key values in Islam:

The key values in Islam are:

Faith

'You should worship God as if you are seeing Him, for He sees you even if you do not see Him.'

(Muslim)

Justice

'*O believers, be seekers after justice, witnesses for God, even though it be against yourselves or your parents and kinsmen.*'

(Surah 4:133)

Forgiveness

'Be forgiving and control yourself in the face of provocation; give justice to the person who was unfair and unjust to you; give to someone even though he did not give to you when you were in need, and keep fellowship with the one who did not reciprocate your concern.'

(Bukhari)

Compassion

'He who has no compassion for our little ones … is not one of us.'

(Muslim)

Mercy

'*Hold tight to the rope of God, and never let it go. Remember that God showed mercy to you and blessed you while you were still enemies. Remember how He united your hearts together in love, so that by His grace you became brothers.*'

(Surah 3:103)

Sincerity

'God does not accept belief if it is not expressed in deeds; and He does not accept your deeds unless they conform to your beliefs.'

(Muslim)

Truth

'Always speak the truth, even if it is bitter.'

(Bayhaqi)

Generosity

'*The truly virtuous person . . . gives food, for the love of Him, to the needy, the orphan, the captive, (saying): "We feed you only for the sake of Allah; we desire no recompense from you and no thanks."*'

(Surah 76:7–10)

'An ignorant person who is generous is dearer to God than a worshipper who is miserly.'

(Tirmidhi)

Humility

'Those who are humble for the sake of Allah will be exalted by Allah, for though they consider themselves lowly they are great in the eyes of others; but those who are proud will be debased by Allah, for though they consider themselves great they are lowly in the eyes of others to such an extent that they might be of less value than a dog or a pig.'

(Bayhaqi)

Tolerance

'Let there be no coercion in religion.'

(Surah 2:256)

'To you be your religion, and to me, mine.'

(Surah 109.6)

Modesty

'Modesty and faith are joined closely together; if either of them is lost, the other goes also.'

(Muslim, Bayhaqi)

Chastity

'The fornicators who fornicate are not believers so long as they commit it.'

(Ahmad)

Patience and fortitude

'Nobody can be given a blessing better and greater than patience.'

(Bukhari)

Responsibility

'Every one of you is a shepherd, and will be questioned about the well-being of their flock.'

(Muslim)

Courage

'*Fight in the cause of Allah those who fight you, but do not go beyond the limits . . . for tyranny and oppression are worse than murder.*'

(Surah 2:190)

The key things that are abhorred:

The key things that are abhorred are:

Hypocrisy

'*Woe to those who pray but are unmindful of their prayer, or pray only to be seen by people.*'

(Surah 107:6–7)

Cheating

'The truthful and trusty merchant is associated with the prophets, the upright and the martyrs.'

(Tirmidhi, Darimi)

Backbiting and suspicion

'*O believers, avoid suspicion, for suspicion is a sin. And do not spy or backbite one another.*'

(Surah 49:12)

Lying

'If you do not give up telling lies, God will have no need of you giving up food and drink (in fasting).'

(Abu Dawud)

Pride

'*Do not turn your face away from people in scorn, and do not walk about in the earth exultantly; God loves not the proud and boastful. Be modest in your walk and lower your voice; the most hideous of voices is that of the ass!*'

(Luqman, in Surah 31:19)

Envy

'In the worshipper's heart, faith and envy cannot dwell together.'

(Nisa'i)

'Beware of envy, for it eats up goodness as fire eats up fuel.'

(Abu Dawud)

Anger

'Truly, anger spoils faith just as bitter aloes spoil honey.'

(Ahmad)

'Allah holds back His punishment from him who holds back his anger.'

(Bayhaqi)

Divisiveness

'This is My straight path, so follow it, and do not follow other paths which will separate you from this path.'

(Surah 6:153)

Excess and extremism

'O people of the Book! Do not exceed in your religion the bounds, trespassing beyond the truth.'

(Surah 5:77)

'O believers, do not make unlawful those good things which Allah has made lawful for you, and commit no excess. God loves not those given to excess.'

(Surah 5:87)

Summary

These ethical values are shared with all serious followers of many religions – they are universal values. Islamic ethics could be summarized by this one verse from the Qur'an and this one famous hadith:

'Goodness and Evil cannot be equal. Repay evil with what is better, then he who was your enemy will become your intimate friend.'

(Surah 41:34)

'You shall not enter Paradise until you have faith, and you cannot have faith until you love one another. Have compassion on those you can see, and He Whom you cannot see will have compassion on you.'

(Muslim)

14

women in Islam

In this chapter you will learn about:
- the equality of male and female in Islam
- Muslim women's issues.

'For Muslim men and women, for believing men and women . . . for men and women who are patient and constant, who humble themselves, who give in charity, who fast, who guard their chastity, who engage in the praise of Allah – for them Allah has prepared forgiveness and a great reward.'

(Surah 33:35)

This particular verse was the answer from Allah given in direct response to the Prophet's ﷺ wife Umm Salamah, who asked him one day why the Qur'an revelations never specifically mentioned women.

In Arabic, the word *insan* (man) means 'a human being', 'person', or 'male and female' without a particular gender identification, and thus every instruction given to Muslims in the Qur'an refers to both male and female believers alike unless it clearly specifies otherwise. They have been given the same religious duties and will be judged according to exactly the same criteria. If a verse is intended for men only or women only, this is made clear.

Equally erroneous is the common translation of *Bani Adam* into 'sons of Adam' or 'men' instead of a more accurate term 'children of Adam' or 'people'.

From the same soul

Muslim doctrine holds that women are not in any way inferior beings to men, but were created originally from the same single soul.

'O humanity! Have reverence for your Lord, the One who created you from a single soul (nafs) and from that soul He created its mate, and through them He spread countless men and women.'

(Surah 4:1)

Women's rights

Muslim women are granted equal, but different, rights in Islam as well as equal responsibilities. Allah gave them the burdens of menstruation and childbirth, and therefore certain privileges and allowances are made for them, such as being excused from salah prayers and fasting while menstruating.

A woman in Islamic law is equal to her male counterpart, just as liable for her actions as a male. Her testimony is demanded and valid in court, her opinions are sought and acted upon, just as the Prophet ﷺ consulted his wives. She has the same duty as a man to become educated and a useful member of the community. To seek knowledge is the duty of every Muslim.

The Qur'an clearly shows Allah's intention to liberate women from injustice by giving them rights not previously enjoyed. Some examples include rights of ownership, decision-making in marriage, divorce and so on. Both Muslim men and women were/are expected by God to *'enjoin the doing of what is right and forbid the doing of what is wrong'* (Surah 9:71) in all spheres of life, and to act as His viceregents in ensuring justice, freedom and equality for all. Yet Muslim women have varying roles, rights and obligations depending on the particular society in which they live. In many Muslim countries women have fewer rights than men with regard to marriage, divorce, civil rights, legal status, dress code, professional lives and education (see Islamic Feminism page 308).

Women and education

Muslim women were/are commanded by Allah to seek education from cradle to grave and from any source available. When Muslim women and girls are refused education this is the very opposite of what the Prophet ﷺ taught. He appreciated forthright women who were not frightened to speak out, or discuss and debate matters. He appreciated women who were educated and had knowledge, who were also kind and compassionate, and hard-working and hospitable. Certainly some Muslim women live in societies that do not stretch to education for girls, but happily, many Muslim women are among the most highly qualified professionals in the world.

In some places Muslim females are not allowed to be taught by men, yet all the women of Madinah were taught by the Prophet ﷺ himself; and moreover, even before his demise, men were also being taught by intellectual women – such as Umm Waraqah, Umm Darda, Shifa bint Abdullah, and the Prophet's ﷺ beloved Aishah, despite her youth.

These days many homes cannot afford the luxury of a housewife. Parents may think of their male offspring as future breadwinners, but ignore the fact that all too often men are unemployed and the females are the breadwinners. Girls are persuading their parents that there is a desperate need for Muslim women to acquire a good education using modern methods and tomorrow's technology, and to achieve useful qualifications.

Educated Muslim women are a necessity. It is highly preferable in Islam for women to be treated by female nurses and doctors, dentists and midwives, and taught by female teachers, and counselled by female lawyers – therefore Muslim women need to train. Muslim women's services are needed – as tailors, bakers, librarians, chemists, engineers, nurses, secretaries, teachers, police, those who work with the mentally ill, marriage counsellors, ambulance drivers, doctors, dentists, midwives, lawyers and so on. One has only to think of the Indian Muslim women fleeing Idi Amin's Uganda who now staff our National Health Service.

The right of access to the mosques

In the Prophet's ﷺ day, women went regularly to the mosque to pray with the men, despite the attempts of some of those men to keep them away. The Prophet's ﷺ wife Aishah reported: 'I used to set out towards the mosque and observe prayer along with Allah's Messenger ; and I was in the row of women nearest the row of men.' (Muslim). The Prophet's ﷺ order to menfolk reluctant to encourage their wives to attend the mosque was: 'Do not forbid the mosques to the women of Allah.' (Bukhari 11.12) 'When a woman asks one of you to go to the mosque, grant this to her.' (Nisa'i 2.32)

Some small mosques are men-only prayer-clubs, even turning away travelling Muslim women who arrive looking for a place to pray – when they should function as useful community centres with all sorts of facilities, and not only allow womenfolk to pray there, but to utilize their talents in the general running of the place. These places drive up-and-coming Muslim women to despair, and will no doubt find more and more people voting with their feet, leaving them to their community of like-minded souls, and joining other more progressive communities.

Women and work

There is no Islamic injunction against women going out to work, so long as that work is compatible with Islamic principles, and does not threaten the security and well-being of the home. The Prophet's ﷺ first wife, Khadijah, was a highly successful business woman, who was the Prophet's ﷺ employer before she became his wife. Several of his later wives also earned their own incomes.

Having a wife who does not work is usually a luxury of the wealthy. All over the world Muslim women work, and may be the breadwinners. Muslim women can get just as bored at home as non-Muslim women, and are just as entitled to employ household staff so that they can take other employment themselves – but many Muslim women do not wish to do this, or to leave the raising of their children to others.

In fact, Islam puts a big burden of responsibility upon the husband, for Allah granted Muslim women the right to be provided for, and not to be obliged or forced to go out to earn money if they do not wish to. Even if the woman happens to be more wealthy than her husband, he has the duty to keep her, and should not rely on her for support.

It is true that some of the world's poorest women are Muslims, but then so are some of the most fabulously wealthy.

Inheritance

At the time of the Prophet ﷺ, giving a woman any inheritance was a radical departure from Arab practice. (Indeed, it was a radical notion in much of the West as well until the twentieth century.) Prior to the Quranic injunction, women not only did not inherit from their relatives, but women themselves were bequeathed as if they were property to be distributed at the death of a husband, father, or brother.

By giving women the right to inherit, Islam changed the status of women in an unprecedented fashion. Moreover, this right was God-given and not aquired as a result of political pressure.

It is interesting that inheritance rights were not granted to women in England until the Married Women's Property Act in the mid-nineteenth century.

Strict laws govern the shares of property and money Muslims may leave to others. The Qur'an lays down that a son would inherit double the share of a daughter, which makes daughters sound inferior. Where the society is tribal and patriarchal, and where women generally have no financial security other than that provided by men, the reason men are granted larger shares is because they are expected to provide for their womenfolk and the entire household, whereas women's bequests are theirs to keep, and they are not obliged to share them.

The injunction that a male receives a share equal to that of two females applies only to the inheritance of children from their parents. Parents who inherit from a deceased offspring each inherit equally.

In matters of witness

In matters where their witness would be just as valid as a man's, the witness of one woman is quite sufficient and accepted as the same as a man's. All the Qur'an references except Surah 2:282 apply equally to women as to men – this verse is the exception to the general rule that the testimony of a woman is equal to that of a man.

In modern society, where both women and men are well versed in business and financial matters, there is no special danger of a woman forgetting or misunderstanding a transaction. The *Shari'ah* generally accepts that two female witnesses are advisable in cases where women have little knowledge and no expertise of the subject, and could be cheated.

Seclusion of women

Seclusion of women was originally nothing to do with Islam but an aspect of social class, both for security and snobbery. Wealthy people were able to afford privacy. These days it is largely Muslim societies where the practice still persists, but extreme seclusion for all women was never asked for by Allah or the Prophet ﷺ, and the hadiths are full of descriptions of active, courageous and hospitable women out and about, entertaining, nursing, or on the battlefield.

The urge for Muslims to seclude women arose from a narrow interpretation of the following verses addressed specifically to the Prophet's ﷺ wives:

'O wives of the Prophet! You are not like ordinary women. If you fear Allah, don't be too casual in your speech, lest someone with an unsteadfast heart should be moved with desire . . . live quietly in your houses, and don't make a worldly display as in the times of ignorance; establish regular prayer and give regular charity, and obey Allah and His Apostle.'

(Surah 33:32–3)

If devout Muslim women choose to regard this as binding upon themselves from the desire to emulate the Prophet's ﷺ wives, all well and good, and they have the right to it, but if they are forced into it, this is an abuse of Islam.

In a village community, a woman can often have considerable freedom, since most of the villagers will be her own relatives, and therefore *mahrem*. The Prophet's ﷺ wives lived eyeball to eyeball with the public, and must have appreciated being able to retreat from it. This is obviously not the same thing as being *forced* to stay indoors. The privilege of seclusion indicates distinct and superior rank in societies where much of life was lived 'on the street'. If a wife wanted to be totally secluded, and to live inside the home, she would normally require servants to perform the numerous errands.

Purdah

Many Muslim men from the Asian subcontinent and various Arab countries, will not allow their womenfolk to mix at all with males outside the family circle. This practice is declining as, all over the world, Muslim women are receiving education and taking up employment.

Purdah implies complete segregation of men from women, and in many Muslim societies the women have a separate and private part of the house (or even tent), and may use separate entrances. Most mosques have separate entrances for men and women, because the women pray at the back, but they usually rejoin their menfolk afterwards.

There is no text requiring women to be hidden away at all times, although in many cultures Muslim women are very shy of strangers, and many accept seclusion as one form of piety. In today's world, you can see Muslim women in public in every country and culture, content that in their modest dress and behaviour they are fulfilling any requirement of Islam.

Exploitation of women

The Prophet ﷺ was alert to unfortunate women being exploited in work situations, and commented on the injustices done to women workers in this way:

> 'Allah will definitely enforce the settlement of the dues of those entitled to receive them on the Day of Judgement; even the wrong done to the hornless goat (i.e. the female) by the horned goat (i.e. the male) will be redressed!'
>
> (Muslim)

Any woman working to increase the financial income of her family should have the same rights as a male worker, and should not be taken advantage of, or subjected to any form of harassment (especially not sexual harassment). She also has the right to fair wages, and decent conditions of work. If a so-called Muslim employer is using women more or less as slave-labour, it is an abuse and he or she is flying in the face of Islamic principles and will ultimately be called to account for it.

The right to be protected

Women's honour is highly regarded in Islam, and a woman of any age has the right to be treated according to her position; as a protected virgin, a respected wife and partner, an honoured mother or grandmother.

Islam takes note of the physical differences between the sexes; it does not assume that men and women are 'the same'. Thoughtful allowances should be made to protect women and make them comfortable. Men do not have to endure menstruation, pregnancy, childbirth and suckling children. A Muslim woman has the right to be cared for at times of physical pain and discomfort. Men are not usually harassed because of their attractiveness, or forced to accept sex in order to 'get on', or not lose a job.

In many cultures women have been and still are subjected to all sorts of abuses and restrictions from their menfolk. It is not Islam that causes abuse or oppression of women, but chauvinism and the mingling of Islamic teachings with tribal customs and traditions.

Feminists are calling for re-evaluation of attitudes and practices that, although done in the name of Islam, are actually the result of strong cultural influence, some even contrary to the basic messages found in Qur'an and *sunnah*. They seek to revive the equality bestowed on women in the religion's early years by re-reading the Qur'an, putting the verses in context, and disentangling them from tribal practices.

A woman forbidden from driving a car in Riyadh will cheerfully take the wheel when abroad, confident that her country's bizarre law has nothing to do with Islam. A woman forbidden education or the chance to work in Afghanistan might have been a high Court Judge in pre-Taliban days.

Forced marriages may still take place in certain Indian, Pakistani and Bangladeshi communities, but would be anathema to Muslim women from other backgrounds. Female genital mutilation is still practised in certain pockets of Africa and Egypt, but is viewed as an inconceivable horror by the vast majority of Muslims (see page 313).

If the rule or practice does not apply to every single Muslim woman, then it is not an Islamic requirement.

15

Islamic dress

**In this chapter you will
learn about:**
- rules of modest Muslim dress
- hijab veiling.

People who have travelled about the world will be very aware that there are all sorts of styles and garments that qualify as Islamic dress. Basically, the principles are modesty and cleanliness. What people actually wear is very much governed by the society in which they live, but Islamic garments are always modest and, if possible, clean.

Men's clothing

There are few particular rules for men's wear, except for pilgrims in ihram, and when it comes to the time of prayer. At prayer times, even in the most primitive conditions, men must be covered at least from navel to knee. In ihram male clothing consists of two unsewn sheets of white cloth and nothing else. Otherwise, the only rulings are that men should not wear garments made of silk, unless they have a skin disorder that requires it, and should not wear jewellery other than a wedding ring, which should be made of silver and not gold. Women are allowed to wear gold and other jewellery.

Hijab

Hijab means veiling, covering or concealing, and indicates modesty both in dress and behaviour, an expression of piety for all Muslim women. Discussion only arises over the extent of the cover. Muslim women are not expected to wish to display their sexual attributes in public. That is something reserved for their husbands, for whom they should make themselves as beautiful and attractive as possible.

Some Western women may regard Muslim women's dress as dull, and restrictive – but this is not how Muslim women see it. They prefer to dress in beautiful clothing which is graceful but modest, and regard revealing and sexually provocative clothing as pandering to the lowest instinct of the male, and encouraging men to look on women as sex objects rather than equal and independent characters. Women going about in public dressed to stir up male lust are regarded as 'offering the goods' and 'asking for trouble'.

Islam does not require women to wear black veils, nor to hide their faces, but to cover their bodies from the neck to the wrist and foot. This can be done with long robes, dresses and skirts, long shirts and trousers, and so on. Muslim women do not wear

Malaysian and Dutch hijab

Arabic hijab

Iranian hijab

figure 15.1 different types of hijab

garments that show the outline of their private parts. Various cultures have different standards of modesty; in some Muslim societies colours are more muted than others, head-veils less decorative, and so on. The majority cover their heads, and the extreme extent is to cover faces, and to wear socks and gloves also.

'Every religion has a characteristic, and the characteristic of Islam is modesty.'

(Ibn Majah)

Veiling

The Qur'an 'verse of the hijab' was sent specifically to the Prophet's ﷺ wives and referred to a curtain that allowed them to have some privacy in their small houses. It was not an item of clothing:

'Believers, do not enter the Prophet's house ... unless asked. And if you are invited ... do not linger. And when you ask something from the Prophet's wives, do so from behind a veil (hijab). This will assure the purity of your hearts as well as theirs.'

(Surah 33.53)

The verse giving the command for women's clothing is:

'Believing women should lower their gaze and guard their modesty; they should not display their ornaments (i.e. private parts) except as is normal (i.e. socially acceptable). They should draw their veils over their bosoms and not display their beauty except to their close male relatives.'

(Surah 24:30–1; the surah then lists these relatives)

The Qur'an order is to cover their bosoms, but the verse does imply that they were already wearing a veil. However, a different view is that the veil was more like the Asian doppata, and the thrust of the verse was to cover their female curves with it rather than their heads. Certainly Muslim women were no longer to show cleavage nor should they breast-feed in public, as many pre-Muslim ladies did, but should be modest. They were expected to cover any flimsy feminine garments with an outergarment (jilbab) when going outside the home.

There is considerable disagreement over what is meant by 'ornaments', ranging from not being a show-off with expensive jewellery, to defining it as anything that draws attention to a woman, in the most extreme view including even a woman's voice.

Covering the head

The one item of clothing that usually marks out Muslim women is the head veil, of any material and in any style, that hides the hair from public view. This was the sunnah of the Prophet's ﷺ wives, and the Prophet ﷺ himself said on one occasion that nothing of a female past the age of puberty should be seen except her face and hands. Muslim women usually do cover their heads with some kind of scarf or veil.

The fact that millions of Muslim women dress modestly but do not cover their heads does not alter the fact that it is a sunnah. Those who do wear some sort of head-cover regard this as part of their discipline of piety, and where there is a resurgence of Islamic faith, women are choosing to wear a scarf in increasing numbers.

Head veiling for Muslim women today is complex and varies from place to place. In Saudi Arabia and Afghanistan state law obliges women to dress in this fashion, but that is not the case in Egypt, Morocco or most other Middle Eastern countries. In Tunisia and Turkey the veil is prohibited in governmental buildings like courts, universities, schools, town halls, etc. In Turkey, it is a source of controversy, as it is banned in various places, but both secular feminists and pious Muslim women march for the right of freedom to wear it. In many Western minds the 'cover' is an indication of oppression – an assumption that possibly derives from the West's past experience of its own history of repressive religious states and societies. Last century many Islamic feminists demanded the right to cast aside their veils, but today Islamic feminists demand the right to not face discrimination if they choose to wear them.

Covering the face

There is no text in the Qur'an requiring Muslim women to veil their faces. A face veil was considered a status symbol in pre-Islamic Arabia and other countries, a form of social snobbery preventing the common masses from looking at ladies of high rank. This is not the Muslim attitude.

The face veil (*niqab* or *khimar*) was indeed worn by some Muslim women at the time of the Prophet ﷺ, but there are dozens of hadiths where it is obvious that Muslim women's faces could be seen. Aishah commented that she did not wear it at all times, but drew her veil across her face when she did not wish to talk to strangers.

The face veil did not become widespread for several generations – until conservatives became ascendant. In some parts of the world today Muslim women veil their faces leaving only their eyes visible; sometimes they even cover their eyes. Elsewhere devout Muslim women do not veil at all and regard face veiling as odd, or attention-seeking.

No coercion

There is no stipulation in the Qur'an or hadiths that any particular styles of garment are in any way compulsory, and any strictly pious male feeling that it is right for him to try to force a woman in matters of religion is ironically going against the true spirit of Islam. Some Muslim women have resisted the traditional hijab of their cultural communities because it is so hot, cumbersome, and the pugnacious attitude of males to their women who do not wear it has put them in revolt.

It is particularly important to emphasize these things in societies where groups of extremist sectarians have gained the upper hand over moderate Muslims, because there is a danger in those circumstances of men becoming so obsessive and overzealous about women's clothing that it leads to repression and even cruelty.

Style and tact

Muslim women may wear any type of clothing provided it is not attention-seeking by being either too revealing, transparent, too brash, too tight or too short, and so on. Some wear dark, plain clothes, and others prefer brilliant colours decorated with embroidery or beadwork. The clothing does not have to be dull – Aishah was particularly fond of red and yellow.

Many forms of trousers are acceptable for women, Asian women in particular favouring the *shalwar-qameez* outfits of a long shirt, with baggy trousers beneath. These can be as colourful or decorative as individuals desire, but they should be modest. Tight trousers are not approved of. Many Muslim women wear Western-style trousers, with an over-shirt or blouse long enough to be acceptable.

Veiling the eyes

> 'Instruct believing men to lower their gaze and guard their modesty; that is more chaste for them. Surely Allah is well aware of their actions.'
>
> (Surah 24.30)

Muslim men are supposed to look away, and not leer, and to control any feelings of arousal. The Prophet ﷺ excused the first such look, but not the second. Both men and women were expected to 'veil their eyes' or 'lower their gaze' and not be brazen or attempt to raise feelings in others by intimate eye contact.

Some clothing presents women as 'naked even though they are clothed', and their only object must be to stir the passions of men and tempt them, which is neither fair, nor kind, nor sensible.

figure 15.2 Bosnian girls, modestly dressed

Transparent blouses or sleeves are not approved of, and it is worth noting that many Western blouses, even those with long sleeves, are thin enough to reveal the underwear beneath. This is not approved of in Islam.

Tourist women who wear shorts, bikinis, flimsy tops, and tight T-shirts in Muslim areas are regarded as tactless, and possible temptresses. Some Muslims might forget their manners, and the tactless visitors find themselves being tutted, or hissed at or pinched as they pass, or they might be ignored in embarassment.

True Islamic motives

A woman's standards of behaviour and dress should never be from pressure of others, but simply because she herself has the desire to please Allah, and submit to Him, even in the matter of her clothing. In fact, in certain societies, some Muslim women have taken to wearing hijab in spite of opposition from their husbands, or secular governments.

It is important to remember that people are not judged by their clothing, but for their characters and the quality of their lives. A fully-covered woman might be proud, hard-hearted, cruel or selfish. A less-covered woman might have more natural modesty. Allah knows best.

16

Islamic diet

In this chapter you will learn about:
- Islamic food laws
- reasons for not eating pork
- what happens if no halal food is available.

In Islam, foods are either halal or haram. That which is halal is allowed, and that which is haram is forbidden. This is not a matter of likes and dislikes, but of discipline and submission to God's will. As in every other walk of life, Allah gave instructions to guide believers, and even the need to eat is under discipline. Allah created all the goodness of the earth and its produce for humanity to utilize, but requested certain restrictions.

'O believers! Eat of the good things that We have provided for you, and be grateful to God if it is Him you worship. He has only forbidden you meat of an animal that dies of itself, and blood, and the flesh of pigs, and that on which any other name has been invoked besides that of God.'

(Surah 2:172)

'The strangled, the beast beaten down, the beast that died by falling, the beast gored, and that devoured by beasts of prey . . . and anything sacrificed to idols.'

(Surah 5:4)

Pork

First, no Muslim should ever eat the flesh of the pig, or any pork product. This does not mean a Muslim convert simply giving up sausages, bacon, ham and pork pies. It also means checking whether or not a product includes animal fat, for that fat might well have come from a pig.

In the East, the pig is regarded as a very unclean animal, with good reason, for it eats excrement. In some places it is deliberately used to gobble up excrement. Therefore, no Muslim would contemplate eating it, for it is simply regarded as disgusting. To put a piece of pork on a Muslim's plate would have the same effect as putting excrement on their plate; some Muslims would be physically sick.

Many Muslims are quite frightened when they come to the West, because they know that the populace is fed on pork. They believe it is the cause of all sorts of ailments and allergies, and there is increasing medical evidence that this may very well be so. In the East, pork meat is certainly riddled with minute worms and eating it causes all sorts of horrible disorders.

Other meats

Other meats, such as chicken, beef, lamb, and goat, are all allowed for Muslims, provided they have been slaughtered by the halal method, which is to cut the jugular vein with a very sharp knife, accompanied by prayer. Pronouncing the name of God is a rite to call attention to the fact that they are not taking life thoughtlessly, but with the permission of God for food.

Muslims believe that to cut the throat is not only the kindest method of killing an animal, but also that it is beneficial for the person who will eat the meat. Blood congeals in animals that are stunned, electrocuted, shot, clubbed or gassed, whereas to cut the jugular vein allows the beast to lose consciousness immediately and the blood to rush out freely. Muslims leave the animal carcass to bleed completely.

Muslims are not allowed to eat the meat of any creature which has died of itself, or been strangled, or clubbed to death, or savaged or gored by other animals. By analogy, birds of prey, animals with claws and fangs, rodents, reptiles and insects, with the exception of locusts, are also haram.

Halal shops

For this reason, Muslims in the United Kingdom usually buy all their meat from halal butchers, or special Muslim shops, not regarding the meat in ordinary butchers' shops to be acceptable. In Muslim countries all meat would be slaughtered by the halal method, so there would not be any problem of finding a supplier. As the Jews follow the same rules of slaughter for their kosher meat, Muslims are allowed to eat meat from Jewish shops, if they wish.

Some Muslims take the point of view that since one of the last revealed verses of the Qur'an says that both Jewish and Christian food was lawful for Muslims, then Muslims who live in Christian countries should be allowed to eat commercial meat (apart from pork), so long as they pronounce the name of God on it at the time of eating (Surah 5l6). However, many Muslims would rather do without meat than do this; nowadays halal shops are becoming more common, so the problems are lessened.

Other foods

All fish, fruits and vegetables are halal, and all grains and seeds. However, Muslims should still check packets for ingredients, for many biscuits, cakes, ice creams and soups contain the fat of animals or animal gelatine. Unless it is kosher or of vegetable origin the gelatine found in many desserts, creams, cake fillings, sweets, commercial yoghurts, and other foods is usually made from animal hide trimmings, including those of the pig.

Waste

Muslims believe that food should never be wasted. If anything is left over, it should be given away to the needy, or fed to the birds or the animals that come into the garden.

When no halal food is available

'If a person is forced because there is no other choice, neither craving nor transgressing, there is no sin committed. Indeed, Allah is forgiving, merciful.'

(Surah 2:173, 5:4)

In cases of absolute necessity, Muslims may eat what there is available, but no Muslim should eat the haram food eagerly, or become accustomed to it, or use this principle as an excuse to enjoy it under the pretext of necessity.

17

work and wealth

In this chapter you will
learn about:

- the importance of work
- work forbidden to Muslims
- the duties of employers and
  employees
- exploitation (riba) condemned.

The economic principles of Islam are to build up a just society in which people behave responsibly and honestly, and are enabled to find honourable employment that is not exploitative, corrupt, pornographic or based on cheating and swindling.

Earning for the family is still the responsibility of the Muslim man in most Islamic societies, although there is no ruling in Islam to prevent women from going out to honourable work, so long as they dress and behave modestly.

The importance of work

It is considered very important that a person does work, and does not stay idle or become a burden to others. It is considered very dishonourable to be a parasite on society, unless, of course, one is unable to work through illness or other handicap. Begging is strongly disapproved of, unless there is no other alternative and it is a case of extreme necessity.

> 'Receiving charity is permissible for three sorts of people only; one who is in grinding poverty, one who is seriously in debt, or one who is responsible for a debt and finds it difficult to pay.'
>
> (Abu Dawud)

Even people who have to be supported by others because of their devotion to religion are disapproved of:

> 'Some people once brought a hermit (religious recluse) to meet the Prophet ﷺ. "Who is he?" he asked. They replied that he was a man who had devoted himself to worship. The Prophet ﷺ then said: "Who feeds him?" "We all do," they said. "Then all of you are better than he," said the Prophet ﷺ.'
>
> (Bukhari, Muslim)

On the other hand, any work one does for anybody else (providing it is acceptable in Islam) is counted as if it was done for Allah.

Lawful and unlawful work

Islam makes a difference between lawful and unlawful methods of earning a living.

> 'No body which has been nourished with what is unlawful shall enter Paradise.'
>
> (Ahmad, Darmi and Bayhaqi)

Basically, if someone's means of earning a living hurts another, or results in another's loss, it is haram (forbidden). If it is fair and beneficial, then it is halal (allowed). Obviously, any form of making money that involves dishonesty, deceit or fraud, bribery, robbery, hoarding in order to take advantage of hardship, exploitation, artificial creation of shortages, or anything to do with alcohol, gambling or lotteries, sexual degradation or immoral practices, is forbidden to Muslims.

> 'People make long prayers to Allah although their food and their clothes are unlawfully acquired. How can the prayer of such people be accepted?'
>
> (Muslim and Tirmidhi)

The dignity of the menial worker

The Prophet ﷺ taught that there was no room in Islam for snobbery. There was no disgrace or humiliation in doing menial work, or work that was 'looked down on' by those better off. The only shame was in depending on others for hand-outs when you were capable of helping yourself. Communities need rubbish collectors just as much as professors. Nobody need regard any useful employment as being beneath them, and Islam gave dignity to many professions previously considered lowly and degrading. The toilet cleaner has as much dignity and worth in the eyes of Allah as the manager of a business empire. What counts is his or her faith, honesty, and attitude towards the work he or she is doing.

Slavery

Seizing people outisde of warfare, kidnap, and forced bondage are all criminal offences in Islam, subject to hadd punishment (see page 254, hirabah). Slavery as such was not specifically prohibited in Islam as for many people it was a way of avoiding debt and penury, but the Prophet ﷺ set the sunnah of welfare for slaves, and helping them gain freedom.

- Slaves were to be treated as family members, and fed and clothed well.
- Releasing or buying freedom for slaves was one of the best deeds a Muslim could do (many regarded their 'owners' as benefactors and refused to leave when freed).
- Children were not to be split up from their mothers.
- Slaves acquired as prisoners of war were to be treated kindly and ransomed if possible.

• Forced sexual intimacy with slaves was forbidden, and Muslims were encouraged to marry them and give them status.

The Prophet ﷺ said, 'He who has a slave-girl and teaches her good manners and improves her education and then manumits and marries her, will get a double reward.' (Bukhari).

Child labour

Throughout history children have always worked, and the Prophet ﷺ himself worked as a child, and was employed from the age of 12. The abolition of child labour is one key aim for today's reformers. In many Third World nations working children are deprived of education and a right to their youth. Often, the harsh truth is that when companies stop using children it does not change the economic conditions that had them working in the first place, or the local cultural standards that accept and expect child labour. Muslim reformers agree with other Human Rights agencies that this is a problem to be urgently addressed.

Collective responsibilities

Muslim economy regards certain crafts and industries as essential to the community, those known as *fard kifayah* or 'collective obligations'. Every Muslim community should try to include people to meet the needs of education, medicine, science and technology, politics and community welfare, and clothing, utensil and agricultural industries. All productive resources should be brought into use as far as possible, and not left idle or wasted, including unemployed manpower, unused land, and water or mineral resources.

The duty of employees and employers

Employed people have a duty to their employers, as well as to those they support, so they should not cheat on hours for which payment is claimed, or be lazy, or encourage any practice in the workplace which cheats the employer in some way. They should not waste money irresponsibly, or fritter it away on worthless and wasteful things. Extravagance and waste are strongly discouraged in Islam. Employers should treat their employees with justice and kindness, and should pay them fairly, without undue delay.

'Give the worker his wages before his sweat dries.'

(Ibn Majah)

Workers should be protected adequately from danger in the workplace and not exploited or made to work unreasonable hours, or worked to exhaustion in appalling conditions, with no opportunity to take rest or refreshment.

'An employer should not ask an employee to do anything beyond his capacity. If that which the master demands is necessary, the master himself should lend a helping hand to the servant.'

(Bukhari)

Riba – exploitation and interest on loans

Making interest on loaned money (*riba*) is regarded as a despicable, capitalizing on another person's misfortune or need, and is totally forbidden by the Qur'an. Charging interest makes rich people richer and the poor poorer, since they are forced into more debt and dependency. This is why Muslim societies establish their own Islamic Banks, which have worked out honourable ways of utilizing deposited money without the system of giving or taking interest on money, according to the complicated *Shari'ah* laws.' *Allah has permitted trade but forbidden usury; those who cease the practice after hearing our Lord's command will be pardoned for their past sins . . . but those who repeat the offence will be companions of the fire.'*

(Surah 2:278)

Riba means any unjustified advantage in trade dealings, a much wider meaning than the simple notion of taking 'interest' on one's money in the bank. In Islam, in order to be honourable, money has to be used as a facility and not a commodity, or the owners of money gain an unfair advantage over the producers or traders. They could wait until the merchandise lost value (as in food crops and other perishables) and force merchants to sell at a low price; or they could buy up commodities and hoard them until they increase in value. These practices are forbidden in Islam; wealth should be in circulation and not hoarded away for the private benefit of a few. To regulate this, Islamic governments impose a tax on all money which is not spent in circulation.

Islamic banks

The payment or receipt of interest is the cornerstone of modern conventional banking. Specifically, Islamic banks keep separate so that they can maintain the principles of not mixing their funds in any way that would compromise Shari'ah Law. They are supervised by Islamic scholars who act as a Shari'ah supervisory committee, and have the responsibility of approving all services, activities and investments, and will undertake regular audits to ensure everything is *Shari'ah* compliant.

Islamic modes of financing are based strictly on the following principles:

- transactions must be free of riba (interest, exploitation)
- haram (Islamically illegal) goods and services cannot be produced or consumed
- activities or transactions involving *gharar* (speculation, chance) must be avoided
- *zakat* (the compulsory Islamic tax) must be paid.

So, if a person borrows funds in order to create a business and it makes a profit, the lender has a share in that profit. But if it makes a loss, the lender also shares the loss, and does not carry on making a profit by charging interest on the funds loaned, as in non-Muslim banking systems.

Many mainstream banks are now considering how to make themselves 'Muslim-friendly'. In fact, customers are attracted by Islamic banking and in the next decade conventional banks may lose 30–40 per cent of their customers to Islamic banks or those that conform to Islamic regulations. Several top conventional banks have already designed commercial mortgage equivalents for use by Muslims. For example, Lloyds TSB already offers Islamic banking in many branches and the HSBC Amanah range of products includes the Home Tafakul policy, the first of its kind to be nationally available.

8

sex

In this chapter you will
learn about:
- aspects of sexuality including
  celibacy and homosexuality
- sex within marriage
- the duties of Muslim
  husbands and wives.

Sex is regarded in Islam as the gift of Allah that gives the human being, in a small way, the experience of the bliss of Paradise, in advance. It is a basic and fundamental urge in human beings, and in the search for sexual fulfilment people can give each other great joy and happiness, but it can also give enormous scope for great despair, hurt, and embarrassment.

Youngsters usually discover they have a rampant urge for sex when their hormones get going at puberty. Many Muslim societies have preferred to see youngsters married at the onset of puberty, rather than risk illicit relationships and unwanted pregnancies. This way they can gratify their desires as much as they like, but within the marriage relationship.

Celibacy

Since sex is a creation and gift of Allah, Muslims cannot regard it as evil and unclean, or that it should be resisted and suppressed. People who choose to be celibate for religious reasons are not approved of in Islam; that would be seen to be a form of ingratitude towards Allah which might lead to a dangerously stressed, repressed or perverted personality. 'Sa'id b. Abu Waqqas recorded that when Uthman b. Mazun decided to live in celibacy, Allah's Messenger forbade him to do so.' (Muslim)

Promiscuity

On the other hand, the gratification of sexual urges without moral considerations is also regarded as an abuse of Allah's intention; Islam seeks for sexual desires to be satisfied, but that the individual and the family are protected from dangerous consequences.

The practice of marriage is seen as the 'fortress' that protects people from being lured into immoral ways by their passionate urges. Sexual promiscuity is usually referred to in Islam as *zinah*, whether it refers to fornication (sex before marriage) or adultery (sex outside marriage after marriage).

The dangers of sexual freedom

Not only does Islam prohibit sexual activity before marriage, it does not approve any kind of privacy between unrelated people of the opposite sex past the age of puberty who are not married to each other, in order to avoid temptation.

The Prophet ﷺ knew that it was natural for men to see women and be stirred physically; that is why Allah requested that men and women should not seek to be alone together, that they should not tempt each other by seductive clothing or ways or looks; and that if a man happened to feel a sexual urge for someone other than his wife while out, he should:

> '...go straight to his wife and have intercourse with her, for that would take care of what he had felt.'

> (Muslim, Abu Dawud)

Homosexuality

> 'Of all the creatures in the world, will you approach males and abandon those whom God created for you as mates?'

> (Surah 26:165)

This topic presents a problem for Muslims living in the West where homosexuality has become not only acceptable in law, but is increasingly socially acceptable. Recently non-Muslim homosexuals have been permitted to marry openly and raise children.

There is a need to look into the possible genetic origin of homosexuality, as it makes a difference to Islamic logic if a person is born homosexual or simply decides to become one as a matter of personal preference, perhaps through distaste for or some psychological fear of the opposite sex. A homosexual might argue that they can hardly be held to blame if Allah created them that way; but a jurist would claim that Allah would not forbid anything He had created.

In Islam, if a person is born homosexual, this is not regarded as simply being just another version of 'normal' but as a disadvantage and a test, much the same as being born blind or deaf. Very likely the same percentage of Muslims are born homosexual as the rest of the population. The individual can hardly be blamed for it, and indeed has done nothing wrong, but has a physical difference that has to be coped with, a matter for sympathetic understanding and tolerance, and perhaps the attention of genetic research.

Persons of the same sex having sexual relations was forbidden by Allah in the Qur'an and in a revelation to the Prophet Moses ﷺ. (Leviticus 18:22, 20:13, the story of Lot ﷺ and the people of Sodom):

> 'You satisfy your lust with men (homosexual) instead of women. Indeed you are a nation that has transgressed beyond bounds.'

(Surah 7:81)

The Prophet ﷺ also declared that women should not wear male clothing and vice versa; neither should people imitate the opposite sex in their ways of speaking, walking or moving.

Muslim attitudes towards homosexuals vary according to the behaviour of the individuals concerned. God's law requires *all* sexuality with another person to be within the marriage relationship. This is a very hard test for many people, of both sexes, for all sorts of reasons, homosexuality being only one of them. Those who can control themselves and live within Islamic law are greatly to be commended for the sacrifice and control. 'Sleeping around' is as forbidden to homosexuals as it is to heterosexuals.

Private sexual behaviour is a matter for individual consciences, and no person has the right to hound or victimize another for what is done in private between consenting adults. If a Muslim homosexual chooses to take a same-sex partner, it is a matter between his/her own conscience and the Almighty, and will be judged in the Life to Come. Allah knows best if this sin is worse than taking forbidden substances in private, or choosing to be spiteful or cruel. He is the Judge, and knows all the circumstances.

Any sexual behaviour in public, including heterosexual (even between married couples), is distasteful to Muslims, who are expected to behave with dignity and control their sexual urges. Illicit public sexual behaviour (zinah) is a punishable offence (see page 256). Enticing children into the practice is not only sinful, but criminal.

In many Islamic societies men hold hands, and kiss each other in greeting – but this is a cultural expression of friendship and nothing whatsoever to do with homosexuality.

Modern alternatives to marriage

The modern notion that it is acceptable for single-sex couples to be 'married' is dismissed. Even worse is the suggestion that they might deliberately arrange to have children by some means and bring them up. Whereas any person volunteering to take care of an orphan or a child in distress is highly recommended, the suggestion that homosexuals might deliberately engineer some way of having babies is regarded as an abuse of that child's human rights by:

- depriving the child of its rights to a normal family upbringing
- affecting the child mentally and emotionally.

Sex within marriage

The Prophet ﷺ said:

> 'When a husband and wife share intimacy it is rewarded, and a blessing from Allah; just as it would be punished if they had indulged in illicit sex.'

(Muslim)

> 'Having sexual intercourse with one's wife is sadaqah (loving charity).'

(Abu Dawud)

Sexual intimacy becomes sadaqah if performed for the happiness and satisfaction of the spouse before one's own gratification. It is encouraged and blessed between loving spouses so long as what is done does not hurt, abuse, exploit or denigrate one's partner. In an Islamic marriage, neither partner should ever try to force the other one to do anything which is distasteful or unpleasant or painful to them. Marital rape should never take place, or abuse of the wife.

The Prophet ﷺ was a shy man who discouraged nudity, and Aishah recorded that in ten years of marriage they had never seen each other naked. Nudity between spouses was not forbidden in the Qur'an, however, and although it may amaze the young, many people past their first flush of youth are quite grateful for a little cover, including the cover of darkness!

The duty to please

Since Muslims should only have sex with their marriage partner, both partners have a duty not only to be faithful, but to honour and satisfy the needs of their spouses. If either side neglects this duty for no good reason, it is bound to cause suffering, depression, and lead to the breakdown of the relationship, and it is considered grounds for divorce.

> 'By Him in Whose hand is my life, when a man calls his wife to his bed and she does not respond, the One in Heaven is displeased with her until her husband is pleased with her.'

> (Muslim)

Obviously, there come times when there are good reasons for refraining from sexual intimacy, such causes as illness, menstruation, exhaustion, grief and so on. Only an extremely selfish person would try to insist at these times. Pleasant wooing is a different matter, of course.

The Prophet ﷺ was very concerned about male sexual selfishness, which was as commonplace in his society as it frequently is in many others. He urged his male followers to respect their wives and cherish them. They were not to fling themselves upon their women as if they were no more than animals, or just satisfying their own urges and then leave their women disappointed and frustrated, while they dropped off to sleep.

> 'A Muslim man should not satisfy his need of her until he has satisfied her need of him.'

> (al-Ghazzali)

Discretion

Marital relationships should be discreet, and intimate details not divulged to any outsiders which would be hurtful and embarrassing to the partner concerned. However, the rule of necessity does allow private discussion with medical personnel.

> 'The most wicked of people is the man who goes to his wife, and she comes to him, and he then divulges her secret.'

> (Muslim, Abu Dawud)

Sexual education

Muslims do not feel that instruction from strangers (whose own personal morals they do not know) is a good thing, hence there is much resistance to sexual education programmes in schools.

However, wives and husbands have a duty to make their marriage as happy as possible and, therefore, although Muslim youngsters are not exposed to the sexual experimentation now common in the West, it is their duty to know how to please their partners, and to strive to do this with the same Islamic dedication that they strive to do their best for Allah in any other sphere of life.

19

drugs, alcohol and other substances

In this chapter you will
learn about:
• the Muslim attitude towards
  alcohol, drugs, qat and
  tobacco.

Any substance which intoxicates is known in Arabic as *khamr*, and is forbidden to Muslims. The word '*khamara*' means 'veiled, covered or concealed'.

> 'Allah has cursed khamr, those who produce it, those for whom it is produced, those who drink it, those who serve it, those who carry it, those it is carried to, those who sell it and those who buy it.'

> (Tirmidhi)

Alcohol

At the time of the Prophet ﷺ alcohol was consumed in large quantities, and its antisocial effects were very well known. Allah's prohibition, interestingly enough, took human weakness into account, and was given in stages over quite a long period of time. First, it was pointed out that good and evil could come from the same thing; both nourishing and harmful products can actually come from the date palm or the vine.

The second revelation pointed out that the harm of khamr far outweighed the good, but it was still not forbidden. People were left to form their own judgements (Surah 2:218). Next came the request that Muslims should not be intoxicated when they come to prayer:

> '*O believers! Do not come to prayer with a befogged mind, but come when you can fully understand all that you are saying.*'

> (Surah 4:43)

Finally came the order, the complete prohibition:

> '*O believers! Intoxicants, gambling and trying to foretell the future are the lures of Satan; if you wish to prosper, you must keep away from these things. It is Satan's plan to stir up enmity and hatred in your midst with them.*'

> (Surah 93–94)

The effect of the prohibition

As news of the revelation spread like wildfire, the Muslims poured away any alcohol they were drinking and got rid of their stores; no 100 per cent Muslim has touched alcohol ever since. Obviously, one can find plenty of weak Muslims who do drink.

Some argue that drinking in moderation is not harmful, but this is not really acceptable.

There is no penalty laid down in the Qur'an for drinking, but a flogging was the mildest punishment laid down for slander and abuse, and since alcohol often makes people abusive and slanderous, flogging is sometimes ordered for publicly offensive drunk behaviour. It is not part of Shari'ah law to pry into private dwellings or spy on people, but any antisocial, threatening or dangerous behaviour caused by alcohol that is witnessed is always dealt with.

Alcohol in medicine

The Prophet ﷺ disapproved of the use of alcohol in medicine, even when it formed the base or preservative in the medicine. Muslims should consult the pharmacist before taking medicine. If there is no alternative, the alcohol base would be allowed.

Drugs

The plant world is full of substances which affect the human body and mind, and nowadays the medical profession manufactures artificial substances also, to give similar effects. Their use to provide cures for illness is not forbidden in Islam. However, many drugs, such as marijuana, cocaine, opium, nicotine, etc. – powerful intoxicants which affect the human mind – are all classed as khamr. They are frequently misused in a harmful way, totally in opposition to the spirit of Islam.

Drugs are used to escape from the pains and distresses of life, or to indulge in exciting fantasy experience and artificially induced euphoria. Those who experiment often find themselves on the downward spiral to crime, physical decline, insensitivity and depravity. The Muslim general principle against drugs misuse is the same as for alcohol – Allah owns our bodies, and anything which harms or injures them is haram.

Qat

Qat (*Catha edulis*) is a plant which produces alkaloid stimulants with a similar effect to strong coffee or tea, and chewing qat is a habit of many Yemenis, Somalis, Ethiopians and other peoples. In the Yemen up to 75 per cent of adults do it each afternoon for a period lasting at least five hours, and spend a considerable amount of their cash income on it.

There is debate over whether it ought to be more strongly disapproved. Complaints have been made in the UK of young Somali Muslims being in a 'permanent state of intoxication', and that it can become an addiction. Taken in moderation, the chief forms of abuse would probably be the length of time devoted to the chewing session, or chewing in an unhealthy environment (excessive smoking, limited aeration) or excessive expenditure on the substance.

Smoking

Millions of Muslims smoke. However, it is obvious that if one extends the principle of not doing harm to oneself or others, then smoking can never be an approved exercise. Non-smokers have the right to breathe clean air, unpolluted by others. Muslims, if they must smoke, should do so with discretion and not damage other people's lungs, furnishings, or set a bad example to the young, or encourage those who have given up to start again. By analogy with the rules for other harmful substances, it is really haram even if not declared so.

20

friendship and hospitality

Muslims are not supposed to abstain from the world in order to find 'religious purity'. They are part of the world, and must live out their faith in their communities. They belong to an ummah, or community of believers. They serve Allah, who they cannot see, by their service and love to others, who they can see. The Prophet ﷺ set the example, living in the midst of his followers and showing them how to live by his personal example, his *sunnah*.

The ummah

The unity of believers was one of the Prophet's ﷺ top priorities; on accepting Islam one's 'brothers' and 'sisters' were no longer just members of one's own family, but all believers in the 'family' of Islam, one ummah or set of people (one community). Each individual was part of the whole, each person important and cherished. Believers were to love each other, and support each other, and take care of each other in times of need.

> 'If any single part of the body aches, the whole body feels the effects of it and rushes to its relief.'
>
> (Muslim)

> 'Believers are like parts of a building; each part supports the others.'
>
> (Muslim)

Non-Muslims often cannot understand why Muslims in one part of the world get so worked up over what they regard as injustices done to Muslims in other parts of the world; they do not understand the deep feelings of ummah Muslims have for each other, or the duty of support they feel towards each other. Muslims feel passionately about injustices done to other Muslims thousands of miles away.

No monasticism

Islam disapproves of monasticism, and encourages people to mix and co-operate.

> 'Muslims who live in the midst of society and bear with patience the afflictions that come to them are better than those who shun society and cannot bear any wrong done to them.'
>
> (Abu Dawud)

Friendship

'Do not nurse hatred or jealousy or enmity, but be friends of each other and servants of Allah. Believers should not go for more than three days without checking on their friends.'

(Muslim)

'The better of the two is the one who is first to give greeting.'

(Muslim)

Friends are treasures to be cherished, respected, cared for, and loyally defended. Generosity, concern, and loyalty are expected – it is not unusual for Muslims to lend their cars, houses, or finances to each other.

Those to avoid

Friendships are a vital part of life, and highly influential in moulding the individual's mind and attitude. Muslims, therefore, consider it very important to choose their friends wisely. If friendship is based on love of Allah and commitment to the faith, Muslims believe it will be blessed. On the other hand, they are warned against becoming too friendly with people who may try to influence them away from Islam.

'Believers should not take unbelievers for their friends and helpers rather than believers; if you do that, there will be no help from Allah except to caution you, that you may guard yourselves from (their influence).'

(Surah 3.28)

Muslims are very serious about their religion, so they usually avoid people who take faith as a joke, belittle it, or deliberately agitate against it.

'Leave alone those who take religion to be mere play and amusement, and are deceived by the life of this world; proclaim to them this truth – that every soul delivers itself to ruin by its own acts.'

(Surah 6:70)

Is friendship with Jews and Christians forbidden to Muslims?

Not at all. All people are created by God and loved by Him. Moreover, people of any race are all separate individuals, and to think otherwise is racism.

Sometimes an unlearned Muslim might take a verse out of context and use as if it condoned racism:

'O believers! Take neither Jews nor Christians as your protecting friends (wali): they are only protecting friends of one another. Whoever of you disobeys this commandment will be counted as one of them.'

(Surah 5.15)

This surah was revealed to deal with specific problems that arose from the Treaty of Hudaybiyah when Muslims were allowed permission to fight such Jews and Christians as broke their sworn treaty of loyalty to the Islamic State of Madinah, as well as any other enemies who attacked them (Surah 9.29–31). It did not constitute an injunction against the normal friendly relations between Muslims and such Jews and Christians as were well-disposed towards Muslims. The term *wali* has several shades of meaning – ally, friend, helper, protector, etc. Later in the same surah Allah revealed:

'Rest assure that the believers (Muslims), the Jews, the Sabians and the Christians – whoever believes in Allah and the Last Day and does righteous deeds – will have nothing to fear or to regret.'

(Surah 5.69, also 2.62)

No racial superiority

No race of people should ever consider itself better than any other; all people are of equal value, irrespective of faith, language, race, belief and so forth.

'No Arab has superiority over a non-Arab; a white has no superiority over a black, nor a black over a white, except in piety and good deeds.'

(from the Prophet's ﷺ Last Sermon)

Good friendship

Having a good friend is a wonderful gift of God, and a treasure worth protecting. Muslims should make a deliberate effort to be good and loyal friends themselves, friends who are worth having, unselfish and considerate. Muslims are encouraged to keep in close touch with their friends, not neglecting them for more than a few days, and to be aware of their needs and distresses. If people practise sympathy, tolerance, unselfishness and genuine concern for each other, they will be actively carrying out the will of God.

Muslims are also expected to avoid gossip and backbiting, hurtful jokes, embarrassing remarks, snobbery, or fault-finding.

'Beware of suspicion, for suspicion is a great falsehood. Do not search for faults in each other, do not spy on each other, nor yearn after that which others possess, nor envy, nor entertain malice nor indifference; do not turn away from one another, but be servants of Allah, brothers (and sisters) to one another as you have been ordered.'

(Muslim)

'Whoever believes in Allah and the Last Day should speak good or be silent.'

(Muwatta)

figure 20.1 Islam extends across all places and ethnic groupings

'Don't sever ties of kinship, don't bear enmity against one another, don't nurse aversion for one another, and don't feel envy against the other. Live as fellow brothers and sisters, as Allah has commanded you.'

(Muslim)

Hospitality

Muslims are expected to view the guest as a gift from God, and to enjoy entertaining and giving food and gifts. Visitors to a Muslim house expect to be offered food and drink and, if necessary, facilities to wash, rest and pray. Many Muslims keep facilities ready at all times. If guests admire something, they will often find themselves urged to take it. Muslims expect to give for the sake of Allah, their only reward being to please Him, and to expect nothing in return.

For their part, guests are also expected to be considerate and bear in mind the circumstances and health of their host (or rather, hostesses). Their 'rule' is to expect to be treated as royalty the first day, then as a member of the family, and they should leave after three days at the most (unless invited to stay by invitation).

21

green Islam

'The whole Earth has been created a place of worship, pure and clean.'

(Muslim)

To be 'green' means to care for the environment, the world in which we live, both on the intimate and local level, and in the wider sense of caring for the well-being of the planet. Both aims are specifically a part of Islam, for God required His created humans to be His *khilafah* (pl. of khalifah – ruler on His behalf), in looking after the planet and using it in the best possible way.

'It is He who has made you custodians, inheritors of the Earth.'

(Surah 6:165)

After many centuries of neglect and exploitation by people who simply saw the planet's resources as a free gift to be plundered so that they could get rich quick, it has now become important to be green, and to worry about what has happened. Muslims are required to care for the planet, and not to waste, damage, pollute or destroy it. On the Day of Judgement, they will be asked about their responsibility towards the Earth and its creatures.

Animals

Since Allah loves every creature He has made, the principles of mercy and compassion should be extended to every living creature.

'All creatures are Allah's children, and those dearest to Allah are those who treat His children kindly.'

(Bayhaqi)

It is forbidden for Muslims to be cruel or even inconsiderate to the animals that live and work among them. All domestic animals (whether pets or farm livestock) should be properly fed, housed and looked after.

Beasts of burden should not be made to carry or pull loads too heavy for them, or to labour until they are exhausted, or their flesh has raw patches and sores – a common enough sight in many so-called Islamic societies where Islam is not being carried out.

Hunting

Islam rejects hunting and killing just for sport and amusement; one may take the life of animals only for food or other genuinely useful purpose.

> 'If someone kills (even) a sparrow for sport, the sparrow will cry out on the Day of Judgement: "O Lord! That person killed me for nothing! He did not kill me for any useful purpose!"'
>
> (Nisa'i, Ibn Hibban)

Where animals have a natural hunting instinct (such as hawks or dogs) they cannot be blamed for doing what comes naturally to them – but deliberate cruelty is never encouraged. Animals used for hunting should be well trained, under control, and not clumsy or savage.

If animals are hunted with weapons, they must not be blunt (like clubs for bludgeoning), but efficient and able to pierce the animal (such as spear, sword or bullet) and not such as would club it or throttle it.

Blood sports

Any sport which involves goading one animal to fight another is forbidden in Islam. This includes dog fights, cock fights or bear baiting. All sports involving hunting down and killing animals for fun are also forbidden, such as fox hunting and bullfighting. If a cull or control is necessary, it is not killing for fun and therefore allowed.

The luxury trade

Any destruction of animal life simply to satisfy the vanity of wealthy ladies is abhorrent to Islam. No Muslim could condone the clubbing of baby seals, for example, or hunting beautiful animals simply for their fur, horns or tusks. However, the Prophet ﷺ did not approve of waste, and if an animal died or was killed for food, Muslims were encouraged to use its skin, horns, bones, hair, fur or hide. Animals should never be flayed alive.

Factory farming

Unnatural or cruel methods of farming which deprive livestock of all enjoyment of life are forbidden in Islam, such as keeping them in cramped and dark conditions, force-feeding them unnatural foodstuffs in order to interfere with their natural flavour or fat content, and making them grow unnaturally quickly so that their natural life is unreasonably shortened.

Animal experiments and vivisection

Any experimentation solely for reasons of luxury goods and vanity is forbidden in Islam. Muslims should enquire carefully whether the products they buy have been produced by halal methods – those which do not inflict suffering or cruelty. Any animals used for necessary medical research should be well cared for, and made to suffer as little as possible.

Slaughter

Animal slaughter should always be by the halal method, which Muslims maintain is the kindest possible way. It should be done with a very sharp knife and in an atmosphere that does not cause the animal panic or distress. Animals should not be killed in front of each other.

It is forbidden to deny food or drink or decent living quarters to an animal on the grounds that it is shortly to be killed.

Ownership of land – Mukhabra

Muslims believe that the whole earth, including particular patches of land upon it with boundaries, all belong to God. Only the person who cultivates it has the right to it and its produce. The practice of renting land to others to cultivate against a fixed share in the harvest was known as *mukhabra,* and was forbidden.

All places liberated from the Byzantine and Persian Empires were followed by the liberation of the peasants and serfs. When Persia was liberated feudalism came to an end. Sadly, this ruling of Islam did not survive the rise of the Umayyad Caliphs!

Multinational corporations

The twentieth century was characterized by an unprecedented transfer of power from people and their governments to global institutions and multinational corporations. It is corporate profits that poison our land, air and seas, determine if our rivers are swimmable or choked with toxic by-products and untreated sewage, or if genetically engineered food grown in warehouses will eliminate the small farmer throughout the developing world, just as corporate greed and agribusiness giants have virtually eliminated family farms.

Profit is the primary impetus behind the provisions of GATT (General Agreement on Tariffs and Trade) and the associated World Trade Organization (WTO), which many Musims feel allows massive transnational corporations to dump cheaply produced junk food, junk products and junk culture on any nation in the world, with the right to declare any opposition to that process as an impediment to free trade.

Green individuals

Muslims can follow green principles in all sorts of ways, mainly by being aware of what they are doing and by avoiding waste and pollution. Everyday products should be used and recycled as much as possible, energy use should be cut down, products such as fur or ivory (obtained from the killing of rare or endangered species of animals) should not be traded, nor should products tested on animals captured or bred for this purpose.

Muslims should use biodegradable products as far as possible and prefer unleaded petrol and detergents that do not pollute the water supply.

> 'Whoever plants a tree and diligently looks after it until it matures and bears fruit, Allah will count as charity for him anything for which its fruits are used.'

> (Ahmad)

22
birth

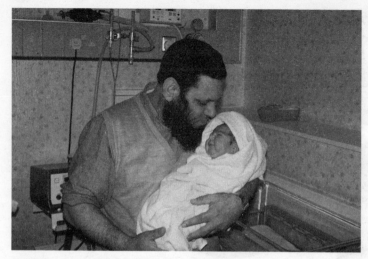

figure 22.1 babies are considered a gift from God

A Muslim welcomes a new baby into the 'family of Islam' or ummah as soon as it is born, by whispering the call to prayer (the adhan) into the baby's right ear, and the command to rise and worship (the iqamah) in its left ear, sometimes using a hollow reed or tube. Thus the word 'God' is the first word the baby hears.

It is sometimes thought to be the case that boys are preferred to girls, but it is a cultural matter, and totally against the spirit of Islam. The Prophet ﷺ loved his four daughters and commended any Muslim men who raised fostered girls.

> 'If anyone has a female child and does not ... slight her, or prefer his male children to her, that will bring him to Paradise. If anyone cares for three daughters, trains them, gets them married, and does good to them, he will go to Paradise.'

> (Abu Dawud)

Tahnik

Tahnik is a little ceremony is the touching of the lips or palate of the baby with honey, sweet juice or pressed dates, accompanied by prayers for the welfare of the child. This symbolizes making the child 'sweet', obedient and kind.

Aqiqah

The *aqiqah* ceremony occurs when the baby is seven days old. Its head is shaved and the equivalent of the weight of the hair in gold or silver is given to the poor and needy. Even if the baby is bald, a donation is still given.

Sacrifice

The sacrifice of an animal is the ancient ritual of thanksgiving. There is a pre-Islamic tradition to share meat in a feast, two animals often offered for a boy and one for a girl. Part of the meat should be distributed among the poor and needy.

Naming

The choice of name is important to a Muslim, and the Prophet ﷺ changed the names of some of his friends when he thought them unmerited, unfortunate, ugly or insulting. Muhammad has now become the most common boy's name in the world, and the second most common is Ali (even before the Christian names Peter and John).

The Prophet's ﷺ actual recommendation was: 'The most pleasing of names to Allah are Abdullah ('servant of Allah') and Abdul-Rahman ('servant of the Merciful One'). If a boy has the name Abdul, this means 'slave of', and should be followed by one of the 99 names of God – for example, Abdul Karim ('slave of the Generous One'), or Abdul-Rahman (see above). Muslim babies are never named 'slave of' any human being, even Muhammad ﷺ. Many Muslim girls take the names of women in the Prophet's ﷺ family, such as Aishah, Fatimah, Khadijah, Ruqaiyyah and Zaynab.

The Prophet ﷺ disapproved of names that suggested in a rather snobbish and conceited manner that the child had certain qualities or attributes (e.g. 'the sweet-tempered one', 'the beautiful one'), when this might not turn out to be the case at all.

Kunya names

When Muslims become parents they rather confusingly sometimes drop their own names and take a *kunya* name; they call themselves 'father of' or 'mother of' the child – for example, a couple named Abdullah and Fatimah, on having a son named Hussain become Abu Hussain and Umm Hussain.

Circumcision

Circumcision, or *khitan*, is the cutting of the foreskin at the end of the penis to enable greater male cleanliness, the practice of all those submitted to Allah, commanded in the revelation to the Prophet Ibrahim ﷺ (Genesis 17.11).

This is usually done at the same time as the aqiqah, if the baby is well. If the child is weak or ill it can be delayed, but should be done as soon as possible. If circumcision is left until the boy is more than ten years old, this is considered shameful, and the parents cruel and neglectful. It is far less traumatic for the child if done while a baby.

In some countries the culture of the land leaves it until the boy is seven to ten years old, and it becomes a serious ordeal for the child, although these days anaesthetics are available. In Turkey, the young boys are dressed up like glittering princes and are circumcised at a public party.

Some non-Muslims have recently campaigned to have the circumcision of boy babies questioned, because it is a form of mutilation and the infant has not been given any choice in the matter. However, Jews and Muslims regard it as one of God's key commands, and maintain that as adults circumcised men will find themselves more able to keep clean, and enjoy more pleasurable sexual intimacy. Some evidence (National Institute for Communicable Diseases, Johannesberg) has suggested it significantly protects men from contracting the HIV virus.

Adult male converts do make the choice themselves whether or not to have this operation. There is no ruling that it is compulsory for them.

Female genital mutilation

Female circumcision (better called female genital mutilation) has nothing to do with Islam but is a barbarous cultural practice that predates Islam. (See page 313).

Bismillah

As soon as a child is able, he or she begins to learn the Qur'an. At the age of four or five a *Bismillah* ceremony sometimes takes place in which a devout senior relative, or perhaps the imam, invites the child to recite surah al-Fatihah and to write the alphabet in Arabic. The successful child feels very happy and proud. After this, the child learns how to perform wudu, and begins to have proper lessons in Islamic studies.

By the age of ten the child should know enough to perform the five daily prayers meaningfully on his or her own, should have started fasting, should be familiar with good Islamic manners and practices, and should have learned to be respectful, modest, clean and aware of haram and halal food.

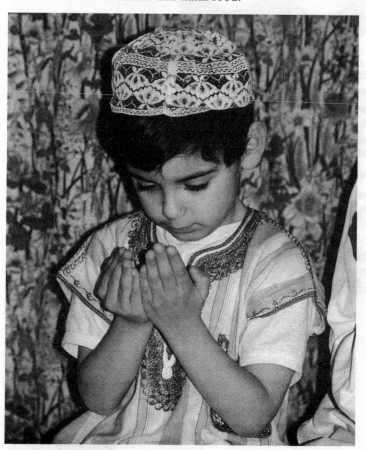

figure 22.2 children study Islam from an early age

23

marriage

In this chapter you will learn about:
- Muslim reasons for marriage
- arranged marriages
- specific Islamic features of marriage
- rules of polygamy.

'And among the signs of Allah is this, that He created for you mates, that you might live in tranquillity with them; and He has put love and mercy between your (hearts). Truly in that are signs (about the nature of Allah) for those who reflect.'

(Surah 30:21)

Marriage is not thought of in Islam as a mystical sacrament 'made in heaven' between two perfectly attuned souls, or as a contract which will only necessarily end at death, but as a social contract which brings rights and obligations to ordinary men and women, and which can only be successful when these are mutually respected and cherished.

It is not Islamic to think of marriages just in terms of a sex life, although this obviously has its important role; Muslims think of wives as potential mothers, and it is in the role of mother that a Muslim woman is most important.

'Do not marry for the sake of physical attraction; the beauty may be the cause of moral decline. Do not marry for the sake of wealth, for this may become the cause of disobedience. Marry rather on the grounds of religious devotion.'

(Tirmidhi)

The importance of family in Islam

Islam teaches that the family is irreplaceable by any other social form or structure. It is the way of life Allah intended for us. Since a good and devout home life is so essential to Islam, making a good marriage is of the utmost importance.

'Whoever has married has completed half of his faith.'

(Bayhaqi)

Muslims believe that the stability of any society or civilization hinges on healthy families. We see all too often the social phenomena of rampant divorce, cyclic family violence, partnership and producing children without marriage, dramatic changes in gender roles, which pose problems for all of us – not just Muslims.

The idea that the pursuit of happiness as a panacea for modern ills, or that unlimited freedom leads to happiness, is one of the mass media's grand illusions. Discontent is fuelled by fairy tales (both Hollywood and Bollywood) of 'love' (what is usually meant is hormonally driven infatuation) that focuses on self-gratification – me first, my rights. The love-struck couple sail through difficulties and 'live happily ever after'; 'Love conquers everything', 'All you need is love.' Some hope! You also need hard work, tolerance and unselfishness.

Freedom based on selfish needs, wishes and desires without mature responsibility is anti-family because it plays down the necessary components of self-discipline, duty and self-denial. Marriage is seen as something easily discarded if a better offer comes along. In Islam, a marriage is a *mithaq* – a firm contract between two consenting adults of sound body and mind, in which everyone is answerable for their own deeds and actions.

It is the mother who sees to the well-being of the family, and generally sets the standard for its morality, politeness, and the children's first learning about Islam. The father is the head of the family, and is responsible for its financial provision, but the mother is the heart of the family.

> 'The best of treasures is a good wife. She is pleasing to her husband's eyes, obedient to his word, and watchful over his possessions in his absence. And the best of you are those who treat your wives best.'
>
> (Abu Dawud, Ibn Majah)

Bringing a new husband or wife into the family is therefore a very serious business and never to be taken lightly. It is intended to be a bonding for life.

Arranged marriages

First marriages are frequently arranged by caring parents of Muslim young people, following the matchmaking traditions of centuries. They seek to find good, compatible partners for their children, since Muslim girls live pretty sheltered lives.

Arranged marriage is not an Islamic requirement, but a cultural practice – of other cultures as well as Muslims. Young Muslims do not usually have the opportunities of Western youngsters to meet and 'fall in love', and in any case, to be under the influence of love is considered to be a state of intoxication that clouds sensible judgement.

In Islam, youngsters have the right to refuse to be married off to proposed mates without giving their consent freely. Some young people trust their parents' judgement so completely, or are so devout they would accept their parents' judgement without quibble. Some see their spouses for the first time at the wedding; but all have the right to say 'yes' or 'no' without pressure, even if the proposed spouse is a relative and harder to reject without embarrassment.

On the other hand, Muslim girls should not arrange marriages for themselves without consulting their fathers or legal guardians, to protect them from rushing into something foolish. If they have no parent or guardian, they are entitled to have access to a protecting adviser (wali), in some places even the ruler of the land (Abu Dawud).

Forced marriages

Islam forbids parents to force their youngsters into marriage with someone they do not like. Aishah recorded that she asked the Prophet ﷺ about the marriages of young girls whose guardians arranged matches for them and whether it was necessary to consult the girl involved, or not. He said: 'Yes, she must be consulted.' (Muslim)

Islam gave women the right to reject spouses they did not want, especially in cases where family money was involved, or where female orphans had guardians who wished to engineer matches to keep wealth within the family. This background no longer applies for the vast majority of Muslim women, and in many cases has never applied.

Any Muslim parents who force or trick their offspring into marriages they do not want are committing haram. Moreover, if either spouse is tricked or forced into marriage, that marriage is actually invalid in Shari'ah law, and may be declared null and void in Western law. In the West, some parents have coerced their offspring into unwanted marriages:

- to bring another relative over to the West
- to get a visa for someone to whom a debt of money or honour is owed
- to keep family money or property in the family.

Previously accepted marriage traditions forbidden by Islam

Several pre-Islamic cultural practices were abusive to women, and therefore forbidden to Muslims:

- Arranging the legally binding future marriage of an unborn daughter to someone's son (obviously without her consent – Abu Dawud 2098).
- *Shighar* – the practice of one man giving his daughter in marriage to another man on the condition that the other gave his daughter to him, without either of them paying the bride-price (Muwatta 28.24, Abu Dawud 843). Shighar might have been convenient for the men concerned, but the brides lost out on their rights.
- *Istibda* – in which a man who failed to make his wife pregnant or who wished his wife to carry a child of a particular noble blood-line could arrange for her to sleep with another man until she did become pregnant. In Islam, married couples should accept Allah's will for them as regards pregnancy, with the proviso that a man could marry a second wife (so long as this did not cause hurt to the first wife).
- It had been considered quite normal for men to adopt or marry orphan girls in order to take over any inheritance they had, and the women involved had little say in the matter. This was now forbidden. (Bukhari 7.2, 71)
- Women were limited to marrying only one husband at a time, as opposed to the pre-Islamic tradition of having up to ten (nomadic) husbands. Men were limited to a maximum of four wives at any one time.

Making use of a wali

Someone needing a spouse is advised to take the assistance of a wali, a supervising guardian. The best superviser is not necessarily one's parent – parents have all sorts of axes to grind. The more unbiased the 'expert' the better. Walis are expected to find out all the necessary details about the proposed spouses, and make recommendations.

The normal procedure is to arrange a few meetings in a chaperoned situation (usually at other people's weddings or family gatherings), where they can meet and observe the prospective partner. If either side rejects the suggested partner, it can be done discreetly, without hurt feelings.

Many Arab and Asian Muslims marry their own relatives, and so their character and background will be well known. These days, Muslims are being alerted to the dangers of first-cousin marriages, especially if this has been the practice for several (or many) generations, as it can increase the chances of inherited defects.

Child marriages

When Muhammad ﷺ reached the age of 52 he married a motherly woman to help raise his daughters, as well as marrying a child, Aishah, who was said to have been only six years old. This action had far-reaching consequences in that it:

- established a precedent and, since his followers are commended for following his example, to this day in rural villages some very young girls find themselves being made to marry men old enough to be their grandfathers
- led to accusations that the Prophet ﷺ was a paedophile
- led to accusations that Muhammad ﷺ could not have been a genuine prophet, for God would not have allowed him to do such a thing.

There is actually controversy over the dates for Aishah's birth, marriage and death. Most Muslims do accept that Aishah was born in the fourth year of the Prophethood, i.e. 614 CE, and that she was therefore engaged to the Prophet ﷺ when she was only six years old. Others have suggested that various dates given in the traditions do not 'add up', and that she could have been born four years before the Prophethood, i.e. 606, in which case she was 13 at her *nikah*, probably the average age for this ceremony in Arabia.

That the Prophet ﷺ had no depraved urge to have sex with a child was proved by the fact that he could have done anything he liked to her, yet there was no physical intimacy between them for several years, and she continued to live in her father's household.

To be married without consummation was not an unusual thing, and to this day it is still accepted that some couples who have been officially married by nikah (even adults) will not consummate their relationship for varying lengths of time, for all sorts of reasons.

In the West today sex is illegal for girls under the age of 16, but this is an arbitrary choice of age,[5] and many girls are sexually active much younger. Muslim culture prefers honourable marriage as soon as pregnancy becomes a possibility to dishonourable sex before marriage with its attendant tragedies and abortions.

Suitable age for marriage

Before the coming of Islam, marriage arrangements could be made from birth (or even from before birth – see page 194), and sexual intimacy was considered acceptable once a girl had become technically capable of childbirth with the onset of menstruation – which could be as early as nine or as late as 18. The usual age for a girl to marry was between 11 and 15.

Islamic feminists point out that there is no Qur'anic text requiring or encouraging men to marry very young girls. If physical intimacy is allowed to take place with the onset of menstruation, it must be primarily dependent upon the Islamic general ruling that no Muslim should ever force any other person to do something that would cause them hurt or abuse, and the specific ruling that men were forbidden to force or co-erce women into unwanted sexual intimacy.

This would in itself rule out young girls being forced to marry any person they did not wish to, let alone much older men. The Prophet's ﷺ marriage to Aishah was in no way forced, but she had seen him every day of her life and loved him dearly, in such circumstances it remains as a sunnah.

The dowry

Islam makes it obligatory for men to pay a dowry (*mahr*) to each of their wives, which remains the property of the wives. If, at a later stage, a wife wishes to divorce a husband who had done nothing wrong and is unwilling to let her go, she could be obliged to return the dowry. If a husband divorced his wife, or

[5]Child marriage was also considered acceptable in the West until very recently. To take two famous examples, Chaucher's 'Wife of Bath' married at 12, and Richard II married Isabel of France when she was seven, a cause for celebration! In 1721 at the age of 11, King Louis XV of France was betrothed to his first cousin, Marie-Anne-Victoire, daughter of Philip V of Spain, the three-year-old Spanish Infanta.

if the wife had normal grounds for divorce against him, she would be able to keep the dowry. Many women, therefore, are glad when a large dowry is negotiated.

The dowry system was not intended as a burden. The sum varies and some women may ask very little or forego it altogether.

> 'And give the women (on marriage) their dower as a free gift; but if they of their own good pleasure remit any part of it to you take it and enjoy it with right good cheer.

> (Surah 4.4)

Others expect a huge sum. Some unfortunate men are obliged to save for years and marry quite late as a result!

A Muslim bride's family should never be asked for money by the husband or his family. This is a Hindu cultural practice, and the very opposite of Islam. The husband has to pay his new wife a negotiated sum which is hers to keep, so that even if she previously owned nothing, she can start her married life with money or property of her own. The only exception should be if the new wife specifically agrees to forgo any settlement.

The wedding

An Islamic wedding or nikah may be a very simple affair, and the bride does not have to dress up or even attend if she does not wish to. If she chooses, she can send two witnesses of her agreement. Normally, the ceremony consists of readings from the Qur'an and the exchange of vows in front of witnesses for both partners. No special religious official is necessary, but often the imam is present.

Many wedding customs, such as the bride's dress, are matters of culture. Many brides these days wear a white wedding dress; Asian brides often wear a beautiful shalwar-qameez outfit (long shirt with baggy trousers beneath) in scarlet, embroidered with gold thread, their hands and feet patterned with henna. This is a cultural practice and nothing to do with Islam.

Muslims living in non-Muslim societies should be aware that to be legal their marriages must also be in accordance with the laws of the land. In the United Kingdom, all marriages have to be registered. A nikah on its own is not a lawful marriage in the UK, and must be registered at the registry office as well. Polygamous marriages are illegal in the West. The marriages of Muslims who married before coming to the West are legal.

figure 23.1 a newly married Muslim couple. The bride is wearing a traditional scarlet dress

Walimah

Islamic marriage is never to be done secretly. If secrecy is attempted, it usually means that some principle of Islam is being broken.

The *walimah* is the wedding party given for friends and family, which makes the marriage public. It usually takes place either at the wedding or within three days of it. In some cultures there is a sumptuous meal, and sometimes families go to enormous expense and invite hundreds of guests. The expense is in part defrayed by the system of the guests giving presents of money, the value of which is carefully recorded; presents of similar value are expected to be given when their relatives get married in turn.

However, it is important to realize that ostentation and expense are directly opposed to the spirit of Islam, and many families struggle to foot the enormous bill quite needlessly. The Prophet's ﷺ arrangements for his own wives and daughters were very simple, involving little expense.

The main reason for the walimah is to make public the fact that the bride and groom are now legally married and entitled to live together. In cultures where the bride is very young, sexual intimacy may be deferred for a considerable time – as for example with the Prophet ﷺ and his young wife Aishah, or with the Virgin Mary (mother of Jesus ﷺ) and her husband Joseph.

Mixed marriages

Muslims may marry any other Muslims, no matter what their race. Muslim boys are also permitted to marry Christian and Jewish girls, but not vice versa. Muslims may only marry Hindus, Buddhists, etc. if the other party agrees to convert to Islam. This might sound harsh for societies used to young people meeting and falling in love at random, but in Islamic societies it would be extremely rare for a Muslim girl to request marriage to a non-Muslim boy.

This is a matter for concern to some Muslim parents who now live in non-Muslim societies, where their teenage daughters attend state schools and mingle freely with boys with whom they might fall in love. This is one main reason why Muslims seek single-sex schools for their children.

Any non-Muslim converting simply to marry a practising Muslim would be accepted, but would probably find it too demanding to live the Islamic way. However, vast numbers have started on the path to Islam through falling in love with Muslims, and have thereby changed their entire lives.

Should husbands be obeyed?

The husband is always the head of the household in an Islamic marriage, but this does not mean that the woman is inferior in any way.

> 'A man is ruler of his family, and he will be questioned on the Day of Judgement about those under his care. A woman is ruler in the house of her husband, and she will be questioned about those under her care.'
>
> (Bukhari)

A woman might be more intelligent, more educated, or more spiritually and morally gifted than her man. It is only to safeguard the smooth running of the home that a Muslim woman accepts a man as her leader. Therefore, a Muslim woman should take great care to marry a man whom she really does respect and who is worthy of her.

Qawwam

> 'Men are the protectors and maintainers (qawwam) of women, (only) because God has given the one more than the other, and because they support them from their means. Therefore righteous women are devoutly obedient, and guard in (the husband's) absence what God would have them guard.'

(Surah 4.34)

The word *qawwam* (guardian) does not imply a domineering boss or master, but rather 'one who stands firm in taking care of the business of others, protecting their interests, and looking after their affairs'. If a man orders his wife to do anything contrary to the will of God, or to condone his doing anything contrary to the will of God – in other words, any nasty, selfish, dishonest or cruel action – then as a Muslim woman she actually has the right and command of Allah to refuse to obey him. Her husband is not her master; a Muslim woman has only one Master, and that is Allah.

Feminist scholars point out that this verse is often translated as 'Men have authority over women because God has given the one more than the other...' They suggest that this is a poor translation, and not an unconditional statement of male authority and superiority over all women for all time, but in reality conveys the notion of responsible providing for women in the context of child-bearing and rearing. It does not necessarily mean that women cannot provide for themselves. Reference can be made to Surah 9.71 which states: '*Believers, male and female, are protectors of one another.*'

Polygamy

In pre-Muslim Arabia polygamy was unrestricted and quite normal for wealthy men. There is even evidence that it was also practised by wealthy women. Islam forbade polygamy for women and limited a man to four wives, but only on certain conditions, namely that:

- the first wife is not to be hurt by it
- later wives must not be a cause of distress to earlier ones
- equal physical intimacy (or loving passion) is not something that is required (or possible), but the giving of equal time is
- all wives must be treated fairly and equally as regards homes, food, clothing, gifts, and so on. Nights have to be spent with each in turn, unless a wife forgoes her turn.

A wife may have it written into her marriage contract that she should be allowed divorce if her husband seeks another wife. Two verses from the Qur'an have led many Muslims to argue that God really intended all marriages to be monogamous:

'Marry such women as may seem good to you, two, three or four. But if you fear that you will not be able to act justly, then marry one woman (only).'

(Surah 4:3)

'You will never be able to deal equitably with your wives, no matter how eager you may be to do so.'

(Surah 4:129)

However, it is a fact of history that the Prophet ﷺ and all his Companions did have more than one wife, and this would not have been possible had they thought it was counter to the will of Allah.

Reasons for polygamy

Polygamy is considered a kindness if a large number of women are left without male protectors and companions, as for example, after a war. Strict monogamy in these circumstances (as after the First World War) would mean that many women would have no chance of marriage at all, and could more easily be tempted into immoral relationships. Many women without menfolk would rather share a husband than face long years of widowhood and loneliness, but it is a very generous, tolerant and understanding already-married woman who would agree to share her husband with another wife.

However, the spirit of Islam is to defend the weak, and not to leave women to fend for themselves if they do not wish to do so. (Of course, if they choose not to marry, that is up to them).

Polygamy is also allowed if a man's wife becomes so physically ill that she is no longer able to look after him or the family, or if she becomes mentally ill. Should a man be expected to live for the rest of his life without any sexual comfort, or should he divorce the unfortunate wife, or marry another?

If a man did fall in love with someone other than his wife, it is considered more honourable to marry the second woman rather than take her as a mistress, and to keep the first wife honourably rather than throw her out. However, although as always one can easily find situations where abuses have taken place, Islamic polygamy should always be with the consent of the wife.

'The rights of a woman are sacred; ensure that women are maintained in the rights assigned to them.'

(From the Prophet's ﷺ Last Sermon)

Muslim men are expected to be able to provide for wives and children at their own expense. A man who takes on several wives with no income or resources should not expect a state system of benefits to finance them, so polygamy is far from the norm, and Muslim men who marry polygamously in the UK and have children on state benefits are committing haram acts and taking advantage of the UK system.

24

divorce

In this chapter you will learn about:
- grounds for divorce
- the 'wife-beating' verse
- different types of divorce
- custody of children.

In Islam, marriages are not regarded as being 'made in heaven' or 'till death do us part'. They are contracts, with conditions. If either side breaks the conditions, divorce is not only allowed, but usually expected. Nevertheless, the Qur'an makes it clear that of all the things God has allowed, divorce (*talaq*) is the most disliked.

> 'Allah has created nothing on the face of the earth more hateful to Him than divorce.'

> (Surah 66.10)

A Muslim has a genuine reason for divorce only if a spouse's behaviour goes against the sunnah of Islam – in other words, if he or she has become cruel, vindictive, abusive, unfaithful, neglectful, selfish, sexually abusive, tyrannical, perverted – and so on.

It is the duty of families and friends to do everything in their power to negotiate and heal the rift that has come between husband and wife. Divorce is considered as a very serious matter as it affects entire families. However, if the marriage contract has been broken and the relationship has failed, Islam does not force people to remain together in misery.

> 'Either keep your wife honestly, or put her away from you with kindness. Do not force a woman to stay with you who wishes to leave. The man who does that only injures himself.'

> (Surah 2:231)

The actual procedure for an uncontested divorce is reasonable, and is less of a strain than the Western legal system.

Muslims living in non-Muslim societies should be aware that to be legal their divorces must also be in accordance with the laws of the land, if their marriages were legally registered. It is very important to keep legal papers safe.

Grounds for divorce

The normal grounds for divorce are usually irretrievable breakdown of marriage, adultery, desertion, cruelty and abuse. Both spouses have grounds for a divorce if one partner deceived the other when they were drawing up their marriage contract or concealed important information concerning the marriage; if the husband is sterile or impotent, if he refuses to maintain her, abuses or ill-treats her; if he becomes insane; if he deserts her or has gone away and not communicated with her for an unreasonable time (usually taken to be four months); or if he has been sent to prison for a very long period.

Khul divorce

If the wife has none of these grounds but still wishes for divorce, or if she presses for divorce whereas the husband does not wish it, it is known as *khul*, or divorce by settlement or negotiation. She may approach an imam to act on her behalf. The husband is entitled to ask for a return of the mahr he had settled on his wife when they married, although she would not be obligated to give it if she no longer had it, or the husband was at fault for the failure of the marriage.

Cultural difficulties

Some societies make it almost impossible for a woman to survive after divorce; others make it very easy for a man to repudiate a wife unjustly. Both of these things are the opposite of Islam. Similarly, it is against the spirit of Islam to condemn a divorced woman to a life of loneliness and unhappiness, either struggling to survive on her own, or to return to her parents' home.

The Prophet's ﷺ sunnah was to choose divorced and widowed women as his wives, and also take their existing children into his household with them. He also approved his Companions who considered the welfare of divorced women, and did their best to see them safely settled in new relationships.

The 'wife-beating' verse

Sometimes Muslim men feel that they have the right to hit or beat their wives because one verse in the Qur'an seems to sanction it. In fact, the only verse in which striking a wife was mentioned was specifically in connection with divorce proceedings in cases of a wife's *nushuz* (refusal to listen to reason).

> 'As to those women on whose part you fear nushuz (disloyalty and ill-conduct), rebuke them, refuse to share their beds, beat (or overcome) them; if they return to obedience, seek not against them means (of annoyance).'

(Surah 4.34)

These are probably the most controversial words in the Qur'an, and a perfect example of how important it is to refer to the sunnah of the Prophet ﷺ to make meanings clear:

- the Prophet ﷺ himself never used this sanction
- he never once struck any woman (or child, or slave or old person)
- he pointed out that a man could hardly hit his wife and then expect her to calmly share his bed later that night
- Aishah reported that 'he never struck anything unless it was in struggling for the sake of Allah' (Ibn Sa'd 1.431–2)
- he regarded those who did so as being far from 'the best' of his followers. In fact, he despised any sort of abuse of those who were weak.

However, if a husband who had not been at fault found that his wife was conducting herself to his shame, then as protector of his household he should not just ignore it, but it was his duty to do something about it. 'Nushuz' (or 'rebellion') meant ill-will, every kind of deliberate bad behaviour of a wife (and vice versa) towards a husband and family (including the children of the family, old people or dependent household staff). With luck, it would be enough for the husband to merely draw attention to it verbally. Communication is everything in a relationship, especially in marriage.

The next verse advised that if the marriage really was breaking up, then the couple should call in the help of two supporters, one for each spouse, who could listen to everything that needed saying and help calm things down. If the couple really wished for peace, God would show a way of reconciliation.

There was never any suggestion that one spouse should ever hit the other out of anger, frustration, irritation, annoyance or disappointment. People would ultimately be held to account for that kind of behaviour on the Day of Judgement even if they got away with it on earth. Furthermore, if a husband bruised his wife he could be sued according to Islamic law.

'A wife has no religious obligation to take a beating. She can ask for and get divorce any time ... If the husband beats a wife without respecting the limits set down by the Qur'an she can take him to court and if ruled in favour has the right to apply the law of retaliation and may have the husband beaten as he beat her.'

(Dr Ahmad Shafaat)

Talaq

Either spouse can declare that they wish for a divorce (talaq). The best way is to divorce with no bitterness or rancour. Either spouse may make the declaration that they no longer wish to remain married, and they then completely abstain from sexual intimacy for three menstrual cycles (*iddah*). If, at any time in those three months, they are reconciled and resume a marital relationship, the divorce is cancelled. However, if, at the end of three months marital relations have not resumed, the divorce is considered valid, and if the couple wish to 'make it up' after that, they would have to be remarried. Muslim men are expected to behave decently during the iddah and do nothing that would prevent the cancellation of the divorce (Surah 2.226–32).

If marital intimacy was resumed, but they then decide to separate a second time, a second divorce declaration has to be made, and they go through another month of separation during which time they could reconcile. If it happens a third time, the divorce becomes irrevocable and if they wish to reconcile yet again after that, the Islamic ruling is that they may not do so until the wife has legally married another man, and been divorced by him. Only then would she be free to remarry the original husband (Surah 2.229–30). Fake marriage arrangements to expedite procedure may happen, but are illegal.

Sometimes men make the three pronouncements of divorce in one sitting, and there is no waiting. There is no provision for this procedure in either Qur'an or sunnah although this abuse has managed to embed itself and is considered valid today in some cultures (notably India/Pakistan). It is an abuse of Islam.

Finally, there is divorce by way of *tafriq* (a judicial divorce) which involves the intervention of the court if the continuation of the marriage would be harmful to the wife's interests or health.

Longer or shorter iddah

If a marriage has not been consummated no iddah or waiting period is necessary; there has been no sexual intimacy, the wife cannot be pregnant, the marriage may simply be dissolved.

If a woman is pregnant, her iddah continues until after the birth of the child, which could be longer or shorter than three months. During this time the wife is entitled to continue living at the house even if she has been divorced, and is also entitled to full maintenance and to receive good treatment. She should not be forced out. After the birth the father has to provide or pay for her food and clothing while she is suckling, for a period of up to two years unless she agrees to make it shorter, or provide the baby a wet-nurse (Surah 2.233; 65.6).

When divorce is forbidden

For the declaration of divorce to be counted as valid, the declarers must be sane, fully conscious and not under pressure from some outside party, or under the influence of alcohol or drugs, or so angry that they did not fully appreciate what they were saying.

Divorce is forbidden when the woman is menstruating, or is postnatal, when perhaps the husband's lack of sexual fulfilment might have made him tense, or led him to a hasty, ill-judged decision.

Also forbidden is *zihar* divorce, a cruel practice that long predated Islam. It involved keeping a wife in a kind of limbo, unable to move away from her husband but being refused a sexual relationship, declaring her to be to him 'like the back of his mother.' (Abu Dawud). This practice was forbidden in Islam (Surah 33.4).

Custody of children

Normally, custody of children is given to the mother, but the responsibility of providing for them remains with the father.

All settlements concerning children should be done amicably and with the best interests of the children at heart. Sometimes, it was even considered best for the child to choose with which parent he or she would live with.

> 'The Prophet ﷺ said to a child: "This is your father and this is your mother, so take whichever of them you wish by the hand." The child took his mother's hand, and she went away with him.'

> (Abu Dawud)

In some circumstances, however, this is not considered wise. Muslim men who have married British women will often seek to keep custody of the children, or may take the children to their mother's household. This is considered better than the very common single parent situation in the United Kingdom, with women sometimes struggling to raise children in poor housing on very meagre finances.

It is very wrong, however, for a Muslim man to cause terrible grief and anxiety to the mother of his children by kidnapping them. All arrangements should be negotiated openly, legally and as amicably as possible and, if possible, both parents should maintain contact with their children. Divorced parents must make sure they love their children more than they hate each other.

25

senior citizens

In this chapter you will learn about:
- the Muslim attitude towards old people
- culture shocks for older Muslims in non-Muslim societies.

'Your Lord orders that you ... be kind to parents. If one or both of them attain old age with you, do not say one word of contempt to them, or repel them, but speak to them in terms of honour ... and say, "My Lord, bestow Your Mercy on them, as they cherished me when I was a child."'

(Surah 17:23–4)

Many old people experience fear, helplessness and loneliness as they grow older and become less capable of caring for themselves. As their friends and companions begin to die, and they become more frail and less able to get about, and their illnesses and wounds hang around longer, it is inevitable for them to turn their thoughts to 'When will it be my turn?' and 'What will become of me?' Loving care of parents is a Muslim's prime duty.

It is particularly frightening for aged Muslims who are obliged to end their days in an environment very different from that of their birth.

So, when does old age begin? It used to be thought that the age of 70 was as much as any person had a 'right' to expect; in some places and times humans were not really likely to live much past the age of 40. But statistics play games, and there have always been those who made it to 90 and over. The Roman Empress Livia died at 93, and some of the Prophet's ﷺ Companions topped 100.

Problems

As people become old, they often become confused, impatient, bad-tempered, or suffer the torment of constant pain that gives them no respite. They may lack energy and become incontinent and increasingly housebound, or even bedridden. Their hearing or sight becomes weaker and more care needs to be taken with their diets so that they do not become malnourished.

They may live alone, and become very depressed, moody and unsociable towards any who try to help them. It is important for them not to be ignored or dismissed as beyond help, but to be checked up on with thorough medical examinations, and be reminded often that Allah is always near to the broken-hearted.

'Do not be like the unbelievers who ... (have) regret and anguish in their hearts. It is Allah who gives life and death. Allah watches over everything you do. If you should die or

be slain whilst in the service of Allah, His forgiveness and mercy will be far better than all the riches you could have saved up.'

(Surah 3.156–7)

The duty to care

Muslim families have a duty to be aware of the problems faced by old people and not to turn their backs on them or regard them as a nuisance. An increase of patience, kindness and real physical help is what is required to cope with these problems.

Muslims do not regard it as kind to relegate the care of their old folk to strangers, unless there is absolutely no alternative. Just as the mother expects to care for and nurse her own child until it reaches independence, so the Muslim 'child' is expected to care for parents who are approaching the end of life and to nurse them safely through into the next life. Since the care of aged parents generally falls to the son rather than the daughter in Asian culture, sons' wives are expected to be very unselfish and loving towards them.

'May his nose be rubbed in dust who found his parents approaching old age and lost his right to enter Paradise because he did not look after them.'

(Tirmidhi)

In fact, the Prophet ﷺ thought care of parents so important that not even personal religious devotion should be used as an excuse for neglecting them.

'A person came seeking permission to participate in jihad, but the Prophet found he had parents living, and sent him away saying: "Go back to your parents and look after them."'

(Muslim – and it is worth noting that these parents were not themselves Muslims at that time)

Old people often feel they are inadequate, a burden on others, and lose their feeling of self-worth and usefulness. Muslims should encourage their elders to continue growing as far as possible through learning, participation in social activities, interacting with a variety of people, finding meaning and fulfilment in helping others. Many senior citizens do all sorts of voluntary work, caring for grandchildren, looking after babies, taking up new hobbies (the internet has been a wonderful new link-up with life for millions). Old people also have the knowledge, the experience, and the time to pass moral and spiritual values to the next generations. The young so often need the counsel, the love and especially the prayers of the elderly – especially those who have spent their lifetimes building up their close relationship with Allah.

Respect

One of the Prophet's ﷺ most famous hadiths concerned the respect a Muslim should show to his or her mother. It was asked:

> 'Who of all people is the most deserving of the best treatment from my hand?' He said: 'Your mother.' The man said again: 'Then, who is next?' He said: 'Again, it is your mother.' He said: 'Then who?' He said: 'Again, it is your mother.' He said: 'Then who?' Thereupon, he said: 'Then it is your father.'
>
> (Muslim)

Muslims feel it is disgraceful to see children ordering their parents about and being rude to them, or treating them as if they were imbeciles. Muslim old folk expect to be treated as wise guides, with a lifetime of experience behind them. No Muslim should ever regard it as being beneath his or her dignity to be kind to old folk. It is considered beneath contempt to hurt or abuse an old person.

> 'He who has no compassion for our little ones, and does not acknowledge the honour due to our elders, is not one of us.'
>
> (Tirmidhi)

Some practical details

Muslims consider it impolite for a young person to call an adult by his or her first name, or to do in front of them anything of which they might disapprove, such as smoking.

Young people should not walk in front of old people, or sit down before they do. They should not interrupt them, or hurry them in their speech, or argue with them – even if they do not agree. They should try to help them before they are asked, and avoid doing anything that irritates them. They should never draw attention to the care and support they are giving them, or point out what they are spending on them, to make them feel a burden, or feel guilty or embarrassed.

Parents are usually much more sensitive to any act of discourtesy towards them from their own children than from any other people. Muslims strive to see to it that their dignity is preserved, and that they should never suffer from hurtful behaviour or speech.

> 'Allah defers the punishment of all your sins until the Day of Judgement except one – disobedience to parents. For that, Allah punishes in this life, before death.'

> (Bayhaqi)

Culture shock for the aged

When living in non-Muslim societies, aged Muslims – particularly those who have migrated to the West – might be terrified of their children abandoning them to non-Muslim care-homes for old people, or to places where they would have great difficulty with language (some old people who have become fluent in English lose it and revert to their original language), lack of halal food, free mixing of the sexes (as in many hospital wards), men and women using the same toilets, women being nursed by men, and so on.

Peer pressure and shame make some aged Muslims highly reluctant to use facilities provided by the State, even when they need to. They expect to be cared for by their families, even though they may barely be able to cope and may be suffering under enormous stress.

Senior Muslims should try to fill their hearts with patience, love and confidence, remembering that no matter how many the sorrows and discomforts of age, if they have done their best to serve Him in this life, in the end Allah will draw out their souls gently and peacefully, and reward them with all the joys of spiritual vigour and youth and beauty beyond our powers to comprehend.

26 death and burial

For a devout Muslim, death should not be something to be feared, although the loss of loved ones obviously makes people sad. Muslims know that the time of their death will not be of their choosing, but when God wishes to call their souls back to Him. Life is God's gift, and the length of one's life is His grant. The true Muslim accepts this as part of the submission to Allah, and greets the possibility of death with the attitude of *'Amr Allah'* – 'At Your Command, O Lord.'

Other people, of course, are very distressed by their sufferings and pray earnestly to have their lives ended, but God knows best and people who are required to live on, despite their hurts and pains, must be patient and try to find the faith to make the best of their circumstances and not concentrate on the worst side of it.

Death is inevitable

It is good for a Muslim to be reminded that no person was more righteous or more loved by Allah than the Prophet ﷺ – and yet there was no miraculous cure for his sickness, and he died, as all humans must die. His friend Umar could not bring himself to accept his death, and Abu Bakr reminded all Muslims of the verse:

> 'Muhammad is but a messenger; there have been prophets before him, and they all died. Will you now turn back?'

(Surah 3:144)

The Prophet ﷺ accepted nursing and medical help, and so other Muslims should not refuse it, or try to rely on prayer and faith alone. Medicine (painkillers, etc.) functions by God's will. A Muslim will always acknowledge that the final outcome is in God's hands. If personal prayers are made for the sick, dying and bereaved, they are never wasted; God always hears us, and something always 'happens', even if it not what the person has prayed for. Euthanasia is forbidden (see page 243).

At the deathbed

Muslims hope to die surrounded by their loved ones, family and friends. However, even if they have to die alone, they should not feel alone, for they know angels will help them.

For those tending the dying, a tactful, respectful and sympathetic atmosphere is recommended as the best way; not becoming so 'holy' that the dying person is irritated, or feels they are being 'hurried' out of this life, and not being so casual that the dying one feels they are not important, or not loved.

If possible, the bed should be turned so that they can be facing Makkah, with the face in the direction of the Ka'bah. Prayers should not be intrusive, but as the dying one finds comfortable. Many relatives will pray using words from Surah Ya-Sin (Surah 36 – 'Surely We will give life to the dead' ...,), though the reciter should pray inaudibly so as not to disturb the dying person. It is always considered the best thing if a believer dies with prayer, or thoughts of Allah.

> 'Whoever's last words are "There is no God but Allah" will enter Paradise.'
>
> (Muslim)

This is not a matter of fanaticism, however, and the dying should not fear that God will be disappointed if these are not their last words; He knows best. What is important is that one dies in the state of belief.

The Prophet's ﷺ sunnah was to settle everything before he died, so that his mind was at rest. Any debts should be paid (or settled by relatives as soon as possible after the death of the loved one), and forgiveness requested for any sins committed against anyone, either sins committed, or sins of omission. Then, the dying one may feel at peace, and may relax and prepare for the next stage of life.

Duties after death

When the loved one has died, the eyes should be gently closed and a prayer said, such as the Prophet's ﷺ own prayer (over his cousin Abu Salamah):

> 'O Allah, forgive Your servant, raise him to high rank among those who are rightly guided; make him as a guardian of his descendants who survive him. Forgive us and him, O Lord of the Universe; make his grave spacious and grant him light in it.'
>
> (Muslim)

Although Muslims believe that the soul departs at the moment of death, and what is left behind is nothing but an empty shell, nevertheless the mortal remains of a Muslim should be treated with dignity and respect, and the last services done to them in a prayerful and loving atmosphere.

The deceased should then be given the final ritual wash as soon as possible. This duty should not be performed by strangers, but by members of the family, preferably male relatives for men, and female relatives for women. A husband is allowed to perform this duty for his wife, and a wife for her husband.

If there is no relative available, the washing is a duty that falls on any member of the community, to see it is done as decently as possible. If males are washing females, or vice versa, their hands should be covered so that they do not touch the naked bodies. If clean water cannot be found (as in some circumstances), sand will suffice. Muslims are not obliged to give the ritual wash to unbelievers, aborted foetuses or dead bodies that have been bomb-blasted. Martyrs are traditionally buried 'with their blood'. In these cases, they are usually shrouded in their clothes. If pilgrims die in ihram, they should be buried as pilgrims, with heads uncovered (for men) and faces unveiled (for women).

For these reasons, Muslims always appreciate hospitals that are aware of their beliefs and customs, and allow the relatives to take their dead away, to do the washing and shrouding, or provide facilities for them to do it themselves in the hospital. If hospital staff wash a body it does not count as wudu.

Shrouding

It is not commendable to use expensive materials, but three white winding sheets for a man, and five for a woman. The shrouding could, however, be two sheets, or even one, provided it covers the whole of the body. A woman's shrouding consists of a cloth to bind her upper legs, waist wrapper to tie it in place, a shift, a head veil (after her hair is plaited, if it is long) and the final winding sheet.

The sheets are spread out, the deceased lifted and laid on top of them and perfumed with incense. Then the edge of the top winding sheet is folded over the deceased's right side, and the other edge over the left side. The second and third sheets are treated in the same way. These are all fastened in place around the deceased and only unfastened when laid in the grave.

The face may be left visible until last farewells have been said.

If no sheet can be found big enough to cover the entire body, then the head should be covered with it, and grass or paper placed over the legs. If the dead are many, two or three may be shrouded together and buried in one grave.

Funeral prayer – Salat ul-Janaza

This is a collective obligation and has to be performed by at least one Muslim. The best person to perform it is whoever the deceased chose personally, providing that person is not immoral or an unbeliever. After that, preference goes to the imam or his deputy, the deceased's father, or grandfather, then son, grandson, or closest male relative. The whole prayer is made standing; there is no prostration as in the normal prayer.

One of the Prophet's ﷺ famous prayers was:

> 'O Allah, forgive him, have mercy on him, give him peace and absolve him. Receive him with honour, and make his grave spacious; wash him with water, snow and hail. Cleanse him from faults as You would cleanse a white garment from impurity. Give him an abode more excellent than his abode was here, with a family better than his family, and a companion better than his companion. Admit him to the garden and protect him from the torment of the grave and the torment of the fire.'

> (Muslim)

The funeral

Cremation is not approved in Islam but not from any fear it would affect the state of the soul. Allah can resurrect as He pleases those destroyed by burning, explosion, being dissolved in acid, or eaten by birds, animals or worms.

People should always stand in respect when a funeral passes whether the deceased is Muslim or not. The Prophet ﷺ recommended that it was more respectful to walk than to ride. (Hiring funeral cars is almost universal in the West. The principle is to be respectful without being ostentatious.) He allowed women to accompany processions, but did not recommend it. The tradition is for processions to move at a brisk pace rather than slowly – to hurry a good person along their road to Paradise, or be rid swiftly of a bad one. Many people may share in carrying the corpse, or may touch it out of respect. Coffins, if they are used, should be simple and not expensive. Muslims prefer bodies to be laid in the earth, rather than in a coffin.

The grave

Graves should also be simple and not ostentatious. Extravagance is distasteful in Islam, and there is no class system for the dead. At the graveside, people should remain standing until the person has been buried (although they may sit to wait if they have arrived before the cortege).

The grave should reach the depth of a man's chest, and preferably have a qiblah niche in it. It is preferable if the cemetery is a Muslim one, or at least a part of it made over to Muslims, so that the graves may be orientated towards Makkah.

A woman's body should be lowered in by men within her family, and all bodies are placed in the grave feet first. The deceased are placed on their right sides, with their faces in the direction of the Ka'bah, and supported so that they do not roll over on to their backs. The fastening of the shroud is undone, and bricks, canes, or leaves set in place so that no earth falls on the body. A little earth is then sprinkled into the grave, saying:

'We created you from it, and return you into it, and from it We will raise you a second time.'

(Surah 20:55)

Then the earth is heaped over, while the people pray. The surface of the grave should be raised a hand's breadth so that it will be recognized as a grave and not trodden on. It is also considered very disrespectful to sit on graves, or lean against them.

The grave may be marked with a headstone, but Muslims should not spend money on tombstones or memorials.

figure 26.1 a simple Muslim headstone

Instead, donations may be given to the poor. Making structures over the grave or plastering them is considered a pre-Islamic practice and is, therefore, disapproved of.

Making graves into shrines

It was, and is, the culture of many places to go to the graves of saintly persons for superstitious motives, to pray to the holy soul to help them or grant them offspring, and so on. This is actually forbidden in Islam. Prayers should be addressed to none but Allah.

Prayers may be said at the graveside for the deceased, but not to them, which is a form of shirk, and the reason for the Wahhabi sect demolishing many much-loved historic graves. Mosques should not be erected over graves.

figure 26.2 praying at the grave of a saint

Grief and bereavement

Death tosses the human being into spiritual turmoil. One of the biggest problems for devout believers is the attitude of so many friends who, because of their sincere faith in the afterlife, simply do not seem to see that people are grieving; or refuse to admit it. They feel that a committed Muslim should accept there is nothing to fear about death, and therefore should be expected to cope wonderfully.

In reality, the mourner may not be coping very well, but because of the attitude of these pious 'comforters', cannot speak up or make it known that help is needed. In fact, religious people who speak like this are quite possibly trying to escape their own emotional involvement, which they find embarrassing or are unable to handle. Everyone feels inadequate, and lacks confidence in what to say for the best to a bereaved person. In fact, a companionable silence is often preferable to false platitudes.

Condolences

Too much mourning implies lack of acceptance of Allah's will or faith in the Life to Come. Muslims are allowed to mourn a husband or wife for four months and ten days. For other deceased, the period is three days and nights. Although one is naturally very sad at a death, the Muslim faith is that people will go to their reward, and the only ones really to be mourned are those who rejected belief in God and lived in such a way that would earn punishment.

Condolences may be offered in any words so long as they lighten the distress, induce patience, and bring solace to the bereaved. Visitors are expected to pay their respects, but it is important that they should not put burdens on the bereaved. Polite visitors bring contributions of refreshments and keep their stays short – unless it is seen that it is helpful to the grieving to plunge into work and conversation.

Qur'an readings

Some Muslims gather for a recitation of the entire Qur'an on behalf of the deceased, either doing it personally or hiring someone on their behalf. This is a tradition, and no sin has been committed if it is not done.

Urs and Rawdahs

The custom of holding *urs* or rawdahs (commemoration services) on the third day, or the fortieth day, or the hundredth day, or the anniversary of someone's death, has no basis in Qur'an or sunnah, but are matters of tradition. They are respectful occasions, but not compulsory.

27

problems for Muslims living in the West

Islam is the fastest-growing religion in the West at the present time, and the number of Muslims in the UK, for example, has now reached around the 2 million mark.

Balancing the converts and number of Muslims born into already Muslim families are the Muslim-born men and women who find the Islamic life too much for them, and in the freedom of Western society, choose to abandon it. It is too early to guess how many of these will come back to their roots in later life.

Schools

Segregated-sex schools

There are lots of issues to do with education. First comes the question of the segregation of the sexes at puberty. Muslims prefer their girls to be taught in an all-female environment, and vice versa, and even when they are sent to single-sex schools, if these are available, there is still the question of the sex of the teacher. Muslims would prefer female teachers for girls, and male teachers for boys. They would also prefer at least some of the teachers on the staff to be Muslim by faith as well.

For these reasons, many Muslims are now attempting to set up their own schools, and encouraging intelligent girls to take up further education so that there will be a good supply of qualified female Muslim teachers.

School dress

Muslims prefer their girls to cover their legs and wear hijab if possible. Some schools do not allow this, but generally the situation has eased in the West, and most schools will now allow Muslim girls to wear trousers as part of their school uniform. Some schools need to grasp that 'Muslim' does not equal 'Asian', and should make the same allowances for Muslim girls of other ethnic backgrounds, including white girls.

Varieties of Islamic clothing have caused confusion; in 2005 the case of Shahina Begum claiming that her faith required her to wear a jilbab drew attention to the fact that female Muslims define Islamic clothing differently. Her case, defended by the Prime Minister's wife, was successful, despite the fact that a jilbab is an outdoor covering garment.

Some countries (notably France) insist upon state schools being secular, and wearing hijab has become an issue. In Turkey hijab was banned from all state-run institutions including schools and universities in 1997, and in 1999 when the MP Merve Kavakci attempted to take her parliamentary oath in a headscarf she was banned and has never been allowed to take her seat. In November 2005 the European Court of Human Rights upheld the hijab ban despite the hopes of Prime Minister Tayyip Erdogan whose party (JDP) had been working to relax the ruling.

Sports

Mixed sports lessons, especially mixed-sex swimming, are not approved of, and Muslim girls are not encouraged to wear revealing swimsuits. For most sports, a track suit is approved, or some modest covering such as a bodysuit with shorts worn over it to 'veil' the private parts. Many swimming baths now make special arrangements for females only, or even Muslim ladies only, and it would be tactful if schools took note of this.

Sex education

Muslims are very wary of their young being taught sexual matters by people whose own morals they are not sure of. It is all too easy these days for teachers to be living together while unmarried, or be homosexual, or to take a lighthearted view of young people enjoying 'relationships', and so forth.

Muslims are also wary of sex education being carried out when pupils are too young or where boys and girls are being taught together. They feel this is something better left to the parents. However, Muslims are not against sex education as such, so long as it is taught in a Muslim moral context.

State school religious education

Since religious education is still compulsory in many schools, this can be another problem area. If the school presents a wholly Christian syllabus, the Muslim child may suffer from the notion that Islam is 'wrong' or that everyone else thinks it is 'wrong', which is depressing. Even where a multi-faith syllabus is taught, there is still the danger of faiths other than Christianity being 'talked down'.

Another problem is that, with the best will in the world, different faiths are sometimes taught by people who know hardly anything about them and, in fact, teach them wrongly. This used to be very common, but with today's highly researched text books the situation is improving. On the good side, Muslims should appreciate that since most state schools do include at least something on the major world faiths, virtually every youngster in the UK will get at least an introduction to Islam.

History syllabus

History lessons generally omit all mention of the Islamic input in world history, and/or depend on books presenting a very biased and colonialist point of view. The peak period of Islamic culture is 'the Dark Ages'.

There is virtually no syllabus coverage of the role of the West in India, Pakistan, Afghanistan, Palestine and Jordan, Iran, Iraq or African countries. If children from diverse backgrounds are to understand each other and feel included, the history syllabus needs to reflect the nature of British society today and validate the historical experiences of minority communities. It is hoped that a new history module might be created to give pupils the choice to study the background of immigrant citizens, and the politics and other causes of their coming to the West.

Special faith schools

Many Muslims now realize that they must establish proper academic Muslim schools in the West, but it is an uphill struggle; there is no tradition of them, and there is active resistance to them from fear they will become breeding grounds for extremism.

The school would be expected to deliver the full State curriculum, plus the Islamic studies, in a calm and devout caring atmosphere. New schools have struggled to produce the required standards of staffing, building or curriculum, and some have languished at the bottom of league tables – but there has been a huge surge of commitment, skills and finances, and now many Islamic schools actually head the league tables.

According to OFSTED there were 118 in January 2005, many with excellent academic success. Notable Islamic schools include Manchester Islamic High School for Girls, the Islamia Girls Secondary School in Brent, London (opened in 1989 and financed by Yusuf Islam, the former pop star Cat Stevens, which topped the exam league in Brent two years running), the Zakaria Girls School, Batley, and many more. The Leicester Islamic Academy achieved a 100 per cent success rate in A* to C passes at GCSE.

So far in the UK, some 33 per cent of Christian, 39 per cent of Jewish but only 0.4 per cent of Muslim children have this choice of schools.

Rather than create special new schools, one idea is to convert existing schools. For example, the non-Muslim Willowbank Primary School in Glasgow, with a 98 per cent Muslim school roll and faced with closure, could be the first flagging primary school to be boosted by a huge influx of Muslim pupils if it becomes Scotland's first state-funded Muslim school.

Madrassah problems

Most mosques try to impart some Islamic knowledge to their young by lessons at the mosque after school or at the weekend. This has potential, but is frequently not really satisfactory. It is acknowledged that some madrassahs bore and stress children without providing any significant degree of knowledge or understanding of the faith.

Non-Muslims do not usually realize that Muslim children are studying at madrassahs, sometimes every night, over and above their normal school studies and homework.

Christmas and Easter

When it comes to celebrating special days, Muslims sometimes feel very awkward because of the emphasis placed on Christmas and Easter. No Muslims would celebrate Easter, for doctrinal reasons. As regards Christmas, although Muslims do accept the virgin birth of Jesus ﷺ, they do not believe that this made him 'Son of God', or that he was 'born to save us from our sins' so Christmas carols and nativity plays are a problem.

Many Muslims would accept the notion of honouring the birth of the Prophet Jesus ﷺ, although others feel it is wrong to celebrate any birthdays, including that of the Prophet Muhammad ﷺ. Others point out that Jesus ﷺ was almost certainly not born on 25 December anyway, but it was a pagan sun festival, and they should not join in (a view shared by Oliver Cromwell). Yet others feel it is harmless and polite to share the celebrations and see nothing wrong in non-doctrinal 'Season's greetings' cards, or giving gifts (even if some families put aside the gifts given to their children until Eid days).

Time off for Friday prayers and Muslim Feast Days

Many Muslim males would like to attend the compulsory Friday prayers at the mosque, but are not able to leave school or their workplace. Some employers are more sympathetic than others about the hour or so an employee would be missing from work depending on travelling time. The actual gathering is usually about 30 minutes. At school, it is sometimes possible for Muslim youngsters to gather together to pray, but there are not always facilities for this, or for the washing that comes before prayer.

Many Muslims have to do their best to enjoy their Feast Days without being excused from work or school.

Music

Some Muslims believe that all music is disapproved of or even forbidden in Islam, and some ban all instruments except drums, but will accept songs (*nashid*) for the unaccompanied voice. Yet there is no ban mentioned in the Qur'an and it therefore falls into the category of that left to the conscience of the individual. Indeed, the Qur'an tells of Allah bestowing the gift of song upon the Prophet-king Dawud (David) ﷺ, and the mountains echoing him and the birds praising God along with him (Surah 28.79, 34.10).

Islam has a long tradition of music and song used as a medium to express joy in the faith. There is no 'typical' Muslim music, for there are different styles from Africa, Uzbekistan, Bosnia, Turkey, Spain and India. Certain types of music are certainly disapproved of as they lead towards the haram:

- pop music with sexual lyrics or sexually provocative rhythms
- nationalistic and jingoistic music ('God save the Queen' is acceptable, 'Rule Britannia' is not)
- music which is intended to stir up tolerance for haram substances or behaviour.

Medical treatment

Muslims prefer women to be treated by women, and men by men, and this is not always possible in hospital/medical situations. However, it is usually possible to choose one's general practitioner (GP). Hospitals are not always very sympathetic to mass visiting from large families and there is sometimes a language problem, with very frightened patients unable to understand what is going on, although nowadays people can usually be found who can speak the Asian language of most local Muslims.

When a Muslim dies in hospital, the family is grateful for sympathetic authorities that allow relatives to take the dead away quickly for washing and burial.

Dogs

Muslims do not dislike dogs, but if their saliva touches clothing, it is considered unclean for prayer, and the Muslim would have to go home and change.

Sniffer dogs are increasingly used to find hidden drugs and explosives. Planes going to the Middle East often use sniffer dogs. This annoys many Muslims who like their aircraft to be ritually clean so that they can pray in them when it comes to the appropriate times.

Racism, Islamophobia and intolerance

Sadly, this can always be found in any country. Muslims have to be tolerant themselves, and understand that if some individuals make life unpleasant for them, there are countless others who are ashamed of the racism and intolerance these ignorant people show. In his lifetime the Prophet ﷺ was vilified, insulted and abused countless times, yet did not retaliate against personal insults, and prevented followers who sought recriminations. His generous and forgiving attitude converted many of his enemies.

Distortion of the image of Islam by the media

Since the end of the Cold War and the collapse of Communism, many Muslims feel they are now being demonized as the world's major enemy of peace and stability and that many equate Islam with terrorism. Muslims are naturally distressed that the nature of Islam as a religion of reason, tolerance and justice does not reach people as it should.

Lazy, unexamined assumptions are made about Islam – 'they' threaten 'our' freedom', 'they' want to destroy 'our' values. Who are 'they'? The 2005 UK suicide bombers enjoyed British freedoms and way of life as much as anyone else. Is propaganda constantly peddled because it allows politicians and commentators to focus on 'Muslim beliefs' as the cause of violence rather than the real circumstances and injustices that lie behind it? Incorrect statements about Islam convince the Muslim world that the West is an implacable enemy.

Muslim fears and conspiracy theories

Many feel there is a deliberate conspiracy against Islam, and suggest that distortions of its image by the media may well stem from the fact that Islam has to be presented as an evil leading to oppression and violence in order to mobilize public opinion against it.

The distortion of the image of Islam and Muslims takes a variety of forms. Occasionally, it genuinely results from reporters' ignorance of Islam. Very often, however, it does seem to represent a deliberate effort by certain news agencies and reporters who use their free speech to discredit Islam and defame Muslims. They:

- deliberately distort Islamic world views and practices with half-truths and downright lies
- associate the views and practices of fanatical groups and individuals with Islam itself
- give out subtle messages and tactics by the use of such phrases as 'Muslim bomb' or 'Islamic terrorism', whereas violence by Christian individuals and groups is virtually never referred to as 'Christian terrorism' or a 'Christian army'
- ignore the huge contribution of Muslims to Western society and simply present Islam as a source of threat and menace
- justify imposition on, and aggression against, Muslims
- give media accounts that refer to Muslims as 'believers in Allah' as if they are referring to some false god and not simply the Arabic word for God.

Shooting oneself in the foot

Western media have a long tradition of seeking out sensation, corruption, hypocrisy, evil and catastrophe as the content of the news. Muslim fanatics seem quite unconcerned that their activities, statements and even clothing only serve to make all Muslims look irrational, hateful, oppressive, abusive and downright odd.

The vast majority of criticisms of Islam made in the media are not actually criticisms of Islam at all, but of that weird type of Islam promoted by these sectarian and bigoted people. It is the responsibility of the Muslim community itself to present Islam accurately, so that the small minority of those who seem to enjoy embarassing all other Muslims with their narrowness of vision may be seen in perspective.

Westerners, who are on the whole tolerant, sometimes feel irritated that Muslims seem to make a big fuss over unimportant matters, such as newspaper cartoons and disrespectful adverts, instead of important issues like world poverty and human rights.

28

the Shari'ah

In this chapter you will
learn about:
- the Muslim 'way' – Shari'ah
- right and wrong
- working out Shari'ah
- schools of thought.

Din and Shari'ah

The din (pronounced 'deen') is whole faith and dedication of one's life to Islam. The Shari'ah is Islamic law, the detailed code of conduct or the canons comprising ways and modes of worship, standards of morals and life, laws that allow and prescribe and that judge between right and wrong.

The five categories of Shari'ah

The Shari'ah does not limit behaviour to just two categories – right and wrong – but five:

1 Fard or *wajib* – things which are compulsory and must be done, such as keeping the five pillars.
2 *Mandub* or *mustahab* – actions which are recommended but not compulsory, such as making extra voluntary prayers.
3 *Mubah* – actions which have to be decided by conscience because there is no clear guidance.
4 *Makruh* – actions which are not actually forbidden, but are disliked or disapproved of, such as divorce.
5 Haram – things which are forbidden and should never be done, such as committing adultery or eating pork.

Anything which Allah made compulsory or forbidden is clearly and specifically stated in the Qur'an, and there is no ambiguity. Whatever is not actually forbidden is permitted, under the guidance of Islamic principles and conscience. Most problems pertaining to modern life fall in the mubah section.

Fiqh

The technique for working out Shari'ah law is called *fiqh* from the word for 'intelligence' or 'knowledge'. Fiqh is detailed law derived from the Qur'an and hadith, covering the myriad of problems that arise in normal everyday life.

Ijtihad, qiyas and ijma

How can a law laid down 14 centuries ago in the Middle East meet all the complex demands and pressures of modern technological civilization? How can anyone know whether it is right or wrong to watch TV, play pop music, use birth control, etc?

Ijtihad means working out Muslim principles, individuals using reason and judgement to decide on the course of action most in keeping with the spirit of Qur'an and sunnah. *Qiyas* means analogical reasoning, using past analogies with their decisions as precedents in each new situation. Decisions made in this manner are called ijma, or consensus. In making decisions, account must always be taken of the opinions of respected people present and past; previous decisions and the reasons for them; the general sense of justice; concern for the public good; and a most practical consideration that is sometimes overlooked by ambitious leaders and politicians – the acceptance of the masses.

However, consensus does not mean the opinion of the masses, or even the majority or collective opinion of learned Muslim scholars – the *ulema*. Even if hundreds of scholars passed a law unanimously, if it contradicted the principles of Qur'an and sunnah, it would be anti-Shari'ah and rejected by Muslims. The principles behind Shari'ah deter any pressure groups – even highly religious ones – from imposing burdens and duties on people which go beyond the spirit of Islam, and become tyrannical.

Ijma are not regarded as totally binding like a Qur'anic command, since they are based on human opinions. The only ijma accepted as binding are those ancient ones made by the first Caliphs, who had been the Prophet's ﷺ closest Companions.

Closing the doors of ijtihad

After the death of the Prophet ﷺ, any qualified legal scholars could study a question, apply independent reasoning (*ijtihad*), and issue a nonbinding *fatwa*. In the eleventh century, however, when the legal judgments of the *ulema* were crystallized into schools of Islamic jurisprudence, progress stopped. Independent interpretation was effectively banned. With the 'doors of ijtihad closed', the traditionalists imposed their own conservative positions on mainstream Islamic jurisprudence, which remained largely frozen for almost a millennium.

The spirit rather than the letter – Istihan

Modernist Islamic scholars place their emphasis on the concept of *istihan*. This means that justice can only prevail when legal scholars are able to take a broad approach to the law by keeping its 'spirit', rather than sticking to its letter, so that it does not become burdensome or seem outrageous. Justice must be seen to be just, the law should not 'be an ass'. This is the concept of istihsan, the practice of using legal reasoning to interpret the law based on the Qur'an and hadith literature in different ways, in the light of the general principle of serving the public good (*maslahah*).

Muslims who insist on strict adherence to the 'letter' of the law as opposed to the spirit certainly desire to maintain its purity, but risk the danger of the Shari'ah seeming archaic and inadequate for dealing with developing issues (see Chapter 33).

Madhhabs

Following the death of the Prophet ﷺ hundreds of scholars (including female ones) had followers or 'schools'. By the third century after the life of the Prophet ﷺ four major schools (known as *madhhabs*) had emerged in Sunni Islam, and still remain – the **Hanifi, Maliki, Hanbali** and **Shafi'i**, named after the most eminent jurists of that early period. Their students attended particular colleges, received training in a particular methodology of juristic inquiry, and developed a specialized technical language. The main Shi'ite schools of thought are the **Ja'fari** and the **Zaydi**. Two other schools were significant – the **Ibadi** and **Thahiri**. Thus, on each point of law, there can be at least ten different opinions (*ikhtilaf*) and considerable debate.

Sunni and Shi'ite Muslims differ in their beliefs of who is permitted to interpret Shari'ah law. The Shi'ites believe that living religious scholars, known as *mujtahids*, have an equal right to interpret Divine Law as those scholars of the past. They also believe that there was a time when the spiritual leadership of the world depended on the descendants of the Prophet's ﷺ daughter Fatimah, and these imams had the right to exercise ijtihad freely. Esteemed religious scholars earned the title *ayatollah* or 'sign of God', and the most famous modern one was undoubtedly Ayatollah Khomeini of Iran, who led the people's revolt against the Shah of Iran.

What are fatwas?

A fatwa is a legal opinion or verdict, which is issued by a qualified jurist, theologian or legal pragmatist. The word has become notorious in Western media when taken to mean a death-threat, but it is really a clarification whenever new and unprecedented cases arise – cases for which there is no clear directive either in Qur'an or sunnah. A fatwa is not required when Islam's position is already clear and unequivocal. The word comes from *fata* or 'young boy' and is used in Arabic as a metaphor for anything young, new, unfamiliar and unprecedented.

Tasawwuf

Whereas fiqh deals with the apparent and observable conduct of Muslims, or the actual fulfilling of duties, *tasawwuf* is concerned with the spirit behind them. For example, the performing of correct ablution, facing Makkah, the times the prayers are said and the number of rakahs performed are all matters of fiqh; whereas the intention, concentration, devotion, purification of soul, and effect of prayers on our morals and

figure 28.1 Tasawwuf is concerned with the intention and spirit behind our prayers

manners are matters of tasawwuf. Fiqh governs the carrying out of commands of the minutest detail; tasawwuf is the measure of the spirit of obedience and sincerity.

It has been said that a worshipper devoid of spirit, although correct in procedure, is like a handsome man lacking in character; and a worshipper full of spirit but defective in performance is like a noble man deformed in appearance.

29

the sanctity of life

In this chapter you will learn about:
- the Muslim attitude towards human life
- contraception, abortion and infanticide
- suicide and euthanasia.

To Muslims, human life is sacred.

> *'Whoever saves a life ... it shall be as if he had saved the life of all humanity, and whoever takes a life, it shall be as if he had taken the life of all humanity.'*

(Surah 5.32)

Muslims believe that no human has an automatic right to life – it is God's gift. If God wills otherwise, that person will cease to be, or will not be granted life in the first place.

The time span

> *'Allah decrees the time span for all things. It is He Who causes both laughter and grief; it is He Who causes people to die and to be born; it is He Who causes male and female; it is He Who will recreate us anew.'*

(Surah 53:42–7)

The human body is part of the world of matter, but the individual soul is God's 'loan' to that body, for so long as He wishes; it is in a sense a visitor, a guest. Moreover, God knows the exact length of the individual's lifetime, even before his or her conception.

Just as the decision to grant life is God's prerogative, so is the time span for that life, and the ending of the soul's occupation of the body. Muslims believe it is gross presumption for any human to try to interfere with that decision, no matter how well meaning, or even to try to find out when it will be. That is not a matter granted to human knowledge.

Muslims should be grateful to Allah for their life, whatever the circumstances in which they are born, or whatever hardships they may have to face. But they should never forget it is God's gift, and it is a Muslim's duty to live every day so that they are ready to hand their life back with easy conscience, should God demand it.

It is when facing death that a believer has a great advantage over a non-believer, for the peace of mind and hope that it brings. The choice of whether or not to believe in life after death is one of the freedoms granted to humans during their earthly life; that freedom no longer exists after the moment of death, because they are confronted with the new situation, whatever it is, and must cope with it as best they can. All humans must die, and it is pointless and futile to resent the inevitable end of the human body.

'When your time expires, you will not be able to delay the reckoning for a single hour, just as you cannot bring it forward by a single hour.'

(Surah 16:61)

Muslims believe it is a foolish gamble to assume that there is no afterlife and that all God's messengers who have taught of the life to come have been misled.

'Do you think that We shall not reassemble your bones? Yes, surely, yes – We are able to restore you even to your individual fingerprints.'

(Surah 75:3–4)

Many people desperately try to prevent their deaths and pray for Allah to grant them some miracle that will keep them alive, but Nature runs its course and miracles are not granted. On the other hand, many people long to die because they are so unhappy or in such pain, but Allah requires them to go on living. It is, however, important to realize that there is a difference between dying (over which you have no control) and killing yourself (which is an act of your own free will).

Contraception

Islam permits birth control, so long as both mother and father have consented to it, and provided the method is one which prevents a woman conceiving in the first place and not one that aborts a conceived child. Thus, a condom or a conception-preventing pill would be acceptable, but the coil or morning after pill would not. In all cases, Muslims believe that Allah's will would override whatever the parents did if He desired a particular child to be born.

Abortion

'Do not slay your children because of poverty – We will provide for you and for them.'

(Surah 6:151)

Muslims do not allow abortion of an unwanted foetus, except in the case where a mother's life would be put at risk, in which case the actual life of the mother takes precedence over the potential life of the unborn child. There are two schools of thought regarding terminating pregnancy in its early stages.

Some believe the soul enters the foetus after 40 days (six weeks), and others that the soul does not enter the foetus until it 'quickens' at around the sixteenth week, and therefore if an abortion was absolutely necessary, it could be performed before that time.

Others maintain that no one really knows what the soul or spirit is, and when the Prophet ﷺ was asked to define it he was instructed by Allah to say that knowledge of it belonged to God alone. Therefore the foetus represents a potential life from the moment of conception, and should be protected and given all the rights of human life.

Some women argue that it is a woman's right to decide what she does with her own body, ignoring the rights of her unborn child's body and the fact that she may suffer an enormous burden of guilt later. The Qur'an reminds these mothers that on Judgement Day these infants will require to know why they were killed.

> '*When the souls are sorted out, when the female infant buried alive is asked for what crime she was killed . . . when the World on High is unveiled . . . then shall each soul know what it has sent ahead.*'

> (Surah 81:7–9, 11, 14)

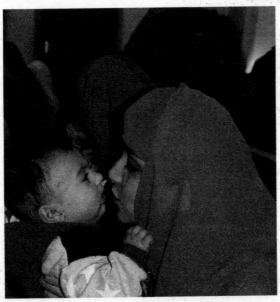

figure 29.1 Islam teaches that all human beings are loved by God

Infanticide

The usual practice of birth control among the Arabs before the time of the Prophet ﷺ was to let the woman give birth then leave the babies exposed to die naturally, or from wild beasts, or to bury newborn infants (generally girls) face down in the sand before they drew breath. These practices were totally forbidden in the Qur'an.

Femicide

Today, modern technology such as ultra-sound scanning has made it possible to determine the sex of a baby long before birth, and this has led in many countries to the aborting of females. This is the case in cultures where the cost of raising daughters is high, either due to the need to accumulate a large dowry which is paid to the husband upon marriage (as in India), or where males are more valued than females. In the long term, it will create a serious imbalance of the sexes. The practice is forbidden in Islam.

(For honour killing please refer to page 311.)

Suicide

To kill yourself is just as forbidden as to kill any other person unlawfully. People who commit suicide are presumably very depressed and beset by problems that seem to have no answer. But to kill oneself is no escape whatsoever, for the torments suffered in increased awareness after death are much greater than those endured while still living – for now they realize who really loved them, and experience the hurt of those left behind, while being able to do nothing to alleviate their awful pain for the rest of their lives.

> 'He who kills himself with sword, or poison, or throws himself off a mountain will be tormented on the Day of Resurrection with that very thing.'

> (Muslim)

Life may be full of hardships, sufferings and loneliness, but Muslims are taught to accept these as part of their test, and to face them with patience and humility, and not lose faith.

> 'None of you should wish for death for any calamity that befalls you, but should say: "O Allah! Cause me to live so

long as my life is better for me, and cause me to die when death is better for me."'

(Abu Dawud)

Deliberate and calculated suicide is considered a total lack of faith in God and a terrible sin. It is a rare occurrence in Islam, for Muslims should not even consider it. Even 'honourable' suicide, done out of shame for crimes committed, is not acceptable. It would be better for the 'sinner' to live on, accept responsibility, and put right the wrongs committed. To commit suicide to escape punishment would be futile, and would merely postpone it to God's justice in the Life to Come.

Of course, nearly all people who commit suicide do not do it of their own free will but as the result of mental illness, or when the balance of their mind is disturbed. It is important to realize that such people are in a different category, and are not counted as responsible for their actions, and are always forgiven by God, in His compassion.

(For 'suicide bombers' please refer to page 301.)

Euthanasia

Sometimes a person's life seems such a burden or so painful that well-meaning people consider it would be better to end it. Just as one would not stand by and see an animal suffering, but would put it out of its misery, so they consider euthanasia (a 'good death') for humans, to end their sufferings. Euthanasia is usually thought of as being 'put to sleep' painlessly, perhaps by drug overdose.

Many hospital cases are considered hopeless, and doctors may decide that to keep on trying more and more drastic measures to keep the patient alive is pointless, and will only prolong their suffering. In these cases, the notice 'NTBR' ('Not to be resuscitated') appears on their medical sheet, the doctors taking the point of view that it is better to let nature take its course, and that they 'should not strive officiously to keep alive' when to continue fighting for that life only causes increased distress.

Some people consider that putting a gentle end to human life should be considered when an infant is born severely disabled or mentally ill, when the prospective lifetime in front of it would be grim. It seems kinder to the child and to the family that loves it.

Some consider it would be kinder to put an end to old people when they become 'vegetables', or to anyone who has been in a coma for a long period, rather than keep them alive indefinitely, and create a lack of hospital beds for 'ordinary' patients.

These dilemmas are faced every day by doctors called upon to 'play God'. All these things are forbidden in Islam. They are highly emotive issues, and it is one thing to discuss such things, and quite another to be requested to end a loved one's life.

Muslims reject euthanasia, because the reason for the disability or suffering will be known to God, and 'mercy killing' frequently does not allow the dying individual any choice in the matter. Muslims find the thought that anyone should be put to death out of social convenience appalling. Our tests may indeed seem unfair to us when we do not know the reasons, but Allah knows, and He is never unfair.

The Muslim attitude is to bear personal tragedies with love and fortitude, and to make life as comfortable as possible for the suffering person. The Prophet ﷺ taught that any suffering of a person in this life would remove penalties in the life to come, and therefore did serve a purpose, and was part of Allah's plan.

Capital punishment

The death sentence does still exist as a possible punishment on the statute books of Islamic law in many countries.

> 'Do not take life, except for just cause.'

> (Surah 17.33)

In Islam there are three crimes which are considered 'just cause' for meriting the death penalty in law – murder, sexual intercourse performed in public and apostasy, when accompanied by treason or murder (see pages 256–9).

30

justice, crime and punishment

In this chapter you will learn about:

- the principles of Islamic justice
- the importance of judges
- the nass principles
- the spirit rather than the letter of the law
- categories of crime and punishment.

'O believers, be staunch in justice, witnesses for God, even though it be against yourselves, your parents or your kindred, whether the case be of a rich person or a poor person – for God is nearer to both (than you are); so do not follow passion, lest you lapse (from truth), and if you lapse or fall away, then lo! God is ever informed of what you do.'

(Surah 4:135)

In Islam, all people are equal before the law. No citizen should be beneath the protection of the law, no matter how humble. Every citizen should have equal rights, including the right of defence if accused of something. No citizen should ever be above the law, no matter how powerful, rich or influential. If any person can buy his or her way out of a rightly deserved punishment, then that society is corrupt and should be challenged.

Is Islamic law barbaric?

Many non-Muslims feel that Islamic justice is cruel and barbaric, requiring numerous executions, floggings, and mutilations. Such things grab the headlines and horrify a public that has grown accustomed to a society in which criminals can be treated very leniently, and drunkenness and adultery are rife.

Two comments have to be made. First, many things regarded as 'Islamic' are not in the least Islamic, but are the actions and culture of rulers and governments that may well govern Muslim people, but who flout the laws of Islam and may actively go against them. Islamic law is also sometimes abused or misinterpreted by people with a variety of motives (including a tyrannical zeal for an extremist form of Islam which is not sunnah).

Second, in any society in which Islam was truly being practised, there would be no drunkenness with its associated catalogue of crimes; no drug addiction or theft; no adultery or sexual freedom with its accompanying distress and consequences; no battering of children or old people; no cheating or swindling.

Islamic motives

Muslim justice is the powerful desire to see peace, right and order prevail, by removing the failing, weakness or enmity that lies behind the wrong. If someone has been wronged, Muslims are expected to do everything possible to put things right. Muslims can never think it acceptable to turn a blind eye to injustice, or let it go unchallenged. That is seen as weakness, and counter to the will of God. Allah is always merciful, and He understands human weakness. He will indeed forgive any person who is sorry; but if they have wronged another person, then the other person's demands for justice also have to be fulfilled. If the unjust 'get away with it', then the victims are assured that Allah will give them recompense after death.

Muslims who have been wronged are requested to be merciful if they are able:

> *'The entitlement for an injury is an equal injury back; but if a person forgives instead and is reconciled, that will earn reward from Allah.'*

(Surah 42:40)

The importance of Islamic judges

When Islam governs justice, the judge should be above corruption and bribery, and should not fear the power of his prisoner. He should be highly skilled and competent enough to interpret Islamic law correctly. A good judge would rather set a criminal free than wrongly risk punishing an innocent person and should always delay a trial while angry, hungry, restless, or absorbed in some other matter.

The rights of the accused

Islamic justice should not be administered blindly, but be tempered with mercy, following all the principles of fairness without favour or fear (Surah 4.135 and 5.8).

- No person should be arrested, convicted and punished all on the same day.
- A defendant should not be denied legal representation.
- Accused people should not be treated as criminals before they have been proved guilty (Surah 24.15 and 39.7).
- No one should ever be imprisoned unless they have been properly convicted of a crime by an unbiased court[6].

[6]Muslims feel very justified in objecting to such practices wherever they find them, including under various authoritarian Muslim regimes, and the USA holding people without lawyers etc. at Guantanamo Bay.

- No one should be threatened, punished or imprisoned because of the fault of others, or in order to intimidate others.
- The defendant should have the right of appeal (Surah 24.24, 82.11).
- Shari'ah law should always be carried out publicly, not for the sake of brutality or to please a bloodthirsty audience, but because it is vital that justice is seen to be done, and that the bounds are not exceeded. Muslims cannot approve of trials and punishments being carried out in secret, with the possibility of inhumane treatment and torture.

Always not guilty

The Prophet ﷺ ruled that certain categories of people were never legally responsible, and these conditions gave ample scope for defence lawyers. These people include:

- those not conscious of what they had done
- those whose balance of their mind was disturbed
- those who had not yet reached puberty.

Two categories of crimes

In Islam each Muslim is answerable not just to a human judge but to God. Thus the Shari'ah classifies crime into two distinct categories:

- crimes against Allah and
- crimes against individuals.

Muslims are granted the right of privacy within their own homes (Surah 24.27). Any behaviour committed by consenting adults in private which falls short of the moral code laid down by Allah, is a matter left between those individuals and Allah. Private sinning most certainly indicates lack of belief in the real existence of God, and that the sinner cares little or nothing for the consequences to face in the Life to Come – but spying and searching out people's faults, or sending round vigilantes or 'religious enforcers' to intrude on any person's privacy, or administer punishments on the spot, is against the spirit of Islam.

Private behaviour and bad habits are matters which could alter at any time. Judgement is left open in the hope that the wrongdoer might come to taqwa, and genuinely repent, in which case Allah would always forgive – until that person's last breath.

It is a very different matter if the person breaks laws in public, or if the private sinful behaviour involves abusing or harming or causing offence to any other individual, who most certainly has the right of complaint and of being protected and given justice.

Three categories of punishment

For those convicted of an offence after a court hearing, their punishment falls into one of three possible categories – *jinayah* (retaliation or compensation), *ta'zir* (a discretionary penalty) or *hadd* (specific penalty).

Jinayah

Jinayah penalties cover homicide and bodily harm, which are punishable either by:

- *qisas* – exact retaliation based on the principle of 'an eye for an eye'
- *diyah* – payment of blood-money or compensation to the victim or his/her surviving kin.

Ta'zir

Ta'zir (corrective) penalties are normally the least serious and can be applied under three circumstances:

- where the revelation does not provide a specific hadd or qisas penalty
- when the proof is based on a strong assumption of guilt but is not enough to impose specific penalties, or
- where those are barred by doubt.

Penalties can include fines, imprisonment, community service, tagging, probation, etc.

Hadd

The hadd (pl. *hudud*) are specific laws of extreme 'limits', penalties laid down in the Qur'an for specific crimes, whose purpose is general deterrance or prevention. The penalties for some crimes can be very severe – the amputation of the hand of a thief (followed by amputation of other limbs if thieving continued), a flogging for illicit sexual intimacy, and the death penalty for murder, apostasy where it involved treason or warfare, and publicly witnessed adultery (see next chapter).

When human justice fails

Every Muslim believes that human judgements can so easily be wrong, or influenced by bias or ignorance of the circumstances, but Allah sees and hears everything. No person can ultimately escape the true judgement on their life. The Prophet ﷺ knew the frailty of human judgement and warned his followers that if anyone knowingly allowed judgement to be given against someone they had accused wrongly, they would pay for it before the justice of Allah:

> 'When you bring your case to me, some of you may be more eloquent in expressing their side than others. I will judge based upon what I hear, and if I happen to give someone something belonging to his fellow citizen, he should not take it, for I would be giving him a piece of the fire!'

> (Bukhari, Malik, Ahmad)

On that day, no one will be able to make excuses for another – we will all stand alone, as individuals, with the true record of our lives.

31

the Hudud – Limit Laws

In this chapter you will learn about the hadd penalties for:
- drinking alcohol
- theft
- kidnapping, armed robbery and terrorism
- public indecency
- false accusation
- apostasy.

The hadd penalties

The hadd (pl. hudud) penalties cover six specific matters:

- *sukr* (consumption of alcohol)
- *sariqah* (larceny or theft, or taking by stealth)
- *hirabah* (taking with force, kidnapping, armed robbery, terrorism, waging war against the state)
- zinah (adultery and fornication)
- *qadhf* (slander, false accusation)
- *riddah* (apostasy).

(Sukr and sariqah are usually treated as lesser ta'zir crimes because no clear specific penalty for them was given in the Qur'an. Rape has been included under zinah in some cultures (notably Pakistan), but is more properly included under hirabah).

There are two main interpretations of hadd penalties:

- that they are the automatic penalties laid down by Allah for specific crimes
- that they are not intended as the automatic penalties but are the extreme limit of the punishment a judge could ordain, the severest penalty the law is entitled to inflict.

Far from the extremes of hadd being harshly pursued, the Prophet ﷺ taught mercy if it was possible, an attitude he would never have taken if the hadd penalties were to be automatically applied:

> 'Avert the infliction of the hadd penalties on Muslims as much as you can, and if there is any way out, let the person go – for it is better for a ruler to make a mistake in forgiving, than to make a mistake in punishing.'

> (Tirmidhi)

Allah had told him:

> *'My mercy prevails over my wrath.'*

> (Hadith Qudsi)

In fact, it was expected of the hadd verses that the warnings should be sufficient, and the punishments should be unnecessary in a truly Muslim society, since Muslims would find it beneath them to steal or commit adultery or murder. The biggest deterrent for a Muslim is not the fear of savage punishment, but the knowledge that Allah can see everything you do, and it would be recorded against you for the Day of Judgement.

Flogging for drunkenness

Shari'ah law can order a flogging for drunkenness. This seems particularly harsh to societies in the West that have grown accustomed to most adults (and many children) consuming alcohol, and nobody facing corporal punishment in our legal system.

The Prophet ﷺ did not seek out or spy on people who consumed alcohol in private, but was prepared to give the penalties for public drunkenness or any behaviour that offended, hurt and abused or disrupted the rights of others, caused by alcohol.

The effects of alcohol on society are very well known, as are the associated criminal activities; everything from drunken driving to public disorder and causing public nuisance, from wife-beating to burning the house down accidentally, to lessened responsibility with its attendant ill-mannered and loutish conduct.

Muslims generally find the behaviour of drunks highly distasteful. The sight of young Westerners (including scantily clad girls) vomiting or lying down in the street after a Saturday night binge, or the behaviour of tourists at so many Muslim coasts, does nothing to improve the stereotype image of Westerners in Muslim eyes.

Cutting off the hand for theft

Cutting off the hand is the hadd punishment for theft, a deterrent intended to give deliberately callous thieves just punishment for the hurt they have caused, as well as warning the community there is a thief in their midst. A second big deterrent is the shame that knowledge of your theft would bring not only on you but your entire family (or whole village, if you lived in a small community). A thief might expect very rough justice in many places. However, the Middle East is not full of one-handed people.

If a thief is taken before a merciful Shari'ah judge, the amputation of the hand is not meted out casually or automatically, but follows certain rules. There have to be witnesses. The cause should be examined, and if it could be proved that the reason the person stole was in some way the inadequacy of the state or local ruler or community (say, for example, that someone stole food for their family because they could not find work to pay for it), then the thief should not be held at fault, and the thief's hand could be 'cut off' from stealing by work being provided.

If there was no excuse and no remorse, and it was simply a case of someone being addicted to picking up other people's property with no qualms or conscience, then a Shari'ah judge could indeed order amputation, and if the thief persisted, continue on to other limbs. (Even Jesus ﷺ said: 'If your hand causes you to sin, cut it off. It is better for you to enter life maimed than with two hands to go to Hell.' (Mark 9:43).

The Prophet ﷺ commented that he would carry out this punishment himself against any deliberate thief, no matter how highly placed and influential, even if it was his own beloved daughter Fatimah (Muslim 1688).

Many modern scholars suggest the cutting of the *yad* (meaning hand or power) could also be interpreted as cutting off the thief's power to steal by his removal from society (i.e. imprisonment), or by creating a society in which theft is unnecessary.

Hirabah

The classical jurists considered many different crimes to be hirabah or terrorism. Many included armed robbery, assassination, arson and murder by poisoning as crimes of terror and argued that such crimes should be punished vigorously regardless of the motivations of the criminal. No matter what the desired goals or ideological justifications of a *muharib*, (one who commits hirabah, or fights society), the terrorizing of the defenseless was recognized as a huge moral wrong and an offence against society and God (see terrorism page 302).

Kidnap

Kidnapping, enslavement by force, hijacking and unlawful hostage holding are all forms of hirabah, and if carried out in order to damage one's state, are acts of treason and could carry the death penalty. The appalling events of 2005 in which several innocent people were taken by force, and some put to death (including the terrible beheading of Kenneth Bigley and others) cannot be justified in Islam. Kidnappers who murder face a death sentence where this penalty is still in force – whether in the USA or Saudi Arabia.

Rape

The crime of rape (*zinah bi'l jabr*) is enforced sex; this could be either rape of a female, or male anal rape. It includes sex without the consent of the victim, or with consent when that was obtained by putting the victim in fear of death or hurt, or by deception if the woman believed she was validly married to the man.

A man whose depraved sexual urges led him to commit rape, whether of girl, boy, woman, wife or another man, is certainly guilty of lust and zinah, but this is hardly the case for the victim of the rape. On the contrary, victims would have suffered appalling fear, probable actual bodily harm, traumatization that could last a lifetime, and in some societies social consequences that could stigmatize or shame them.

It is now generally recognized that rape is a form of hirabah, does not require the testimony of four witnesses, and could include capital punishment as a penalty. The rapist looks for victims who cannot defend themselves.

Alternatively, the crime could be categorized as *jirah* (wounding or bodily harm), which might even be applied to domestic abuse and marital rape, and could result in damages or financial compensation for the wounded woman.

Murder

Murder is actually not a hadd crime, but to this day, Islam accepts the justice of taking a life for a life for the crime of murder, although individuals are not allowed to take the law into their own hands. The execution of a murderer should only take place after a proper legal trial, which fully examines the provocation, state of the murderer's mind, and so forth.

> '*Do not take life, except for just cause. If anyone is wrongfully killed, We have granted the right of retribution to his heir, but let him not carry his vengeance too far in killing the culprit through taking the law in his own hands, as he is supported by the law.*'

(Surah 17:33)

'The law of equality is allowed for you in cases of murder.'

(Surah 2:178)

In any case of doubt (*shubhah*), the sentence of hadd was barred and commuted to that of a ta'zir crime.

The right to overrule the judge

Even if the death penalty is granted, Islam differs from Western law in that the judge's sentence is not the final word. Allah granted the heirs of the murdered person the right to overrule the highest judge in the land by forgiving any murderer sentenced to death, or to accept money compensation (diyah) instead. If they could find it in their hearts to forgive, that was the best way.

Thus murder, grievous bodily harm and damage to property were permitted to be avenged legally by personal retaliation, but if the aggrieved party relinquished this, revenge was transformed into an act of merit for the merciful person.

Zinah

Zinah is any sexual intercourse outside marriage, whether before or after marriage. It is fornication when neither party to the illicit sexual liaison is married (i.e. premarital or post-divorce), and adultery when the persons are married. The penalty laid down for zinah in Surah 24.2–3 is flogging, and the refusal of permission for Muslims to marry any person found guilty of acting lewdly:

> *'The woman and the man guilty of zinah, flog each of them with a hundred stripes: let not compassion move you in their case in a matter prescribed by Allah if ye believe in Allah and the Last Day: and let a party of the believers witness their punishment. Let no man guilty of zinah marry any but a woman similarly guilty, or an unbeliever, nor let any but such a man or an unbeliever marry such a woman: to the believers such a thing is forbidden.'*

(Surah 24.2–3)

Adultery was considered an appalling dishonour towards a devout innocent partner, although it seems to have occurred often enough and was apparently treated lightly by many until the revelation of Islam. Divorce was the norm once a marriage had failed, and partners who gave in to sexual liaisons or temptations willingly were despised.

It is interesting that for this crime alone nearly insurmountable restrictions were placed on the giving of evidence. A person could not be found guilty of zinah without four eye witnesses to the actual sexual penetration. The witnesses had to be adult, sane and of upright character, not children or people whose right-mindedness could be questioned, or people of dubious morality and, if their evidence was obtained by violating a defendant's privacy, it was inadmissible.

These are obviously very difficult requirements to fulfil, since such acts are virtually always performed in secret and privacy. With such restrictions, the aim in general must have been to encourage good morals but to limit conviction to cases where the two parties committed the act in public, in the nude – thereby making it an issue of public indecency.

No other law had this stringent requirement. There were no cases in the Prophet's ﷺ entire lifetime based on the evidence of witnesses as laid down in the Qur'an.

The death penalty for adultery

The death penalty was commonly given for adultery in pre-Islamic times, and since it is known that the Prophet ﷺ was involved in several cases, there is to this day debate over whether or not there was ever a 'verse of *rajm*' or stoning in the Qur'an. There was such a verse in the Jewish Torah (Deuteronomy 22.22–27), but there is most certainly no such verse in the Qur'an as it existed by the end of the Prophet's ﷺ lifetime. Therefore, if it ever did exist it must have been abrogated; it was impossible to 'forget' a verse, since so many people knew the entire Qur'an by heart. Any law contrary to a clear Qur'an law should be rejected outright by all Muslims.

In two cases Jewish rabbis brought the Prophet ﷺ test cases, and he condemned them by their own law. In the famous case of Ma'idh b. Malik, this man insisted on admitting his guilt and being punished – to have a 'clean record' when he faced the Life to Come. However, when his stoning commenced he changed his mind and tried to escape, but the people carried out the sentence anyway. The Prophet's ﷺ significant comment when told was that he wished they had let him go, for he would certainly have repented and been forgiven by Allah (Abu Dawud).

The Prophet's ﷺ sunnah was that he was never eager to sentence anyone to death, and the reluctance must surely indicate that he regarded this punishment as the extreme limit of punishment for adultery.

False accusation or slander – qadhf

No Muslim should ever cast doubt upon the character of a woman except by formal charges with very specific, secure evidence. Whoever falsely accused a chaste person of zinah was to be punished. If direct proof that a woman had disrupted public decency did not materialize, then those who charged her were liable to physical punishment for slander, they would no longer be eligible as witnesses for anything in the future, and the public in general were obliged to assume the woman's innocence (Surah 24.16–17). Even if the charge happened to be true, any single witness not accompanied by another three would be liable to punishment.

> '*And those who launch a charge against chaste women and produce not four witnesses (to support their allegation) flog them with eighty stripes: and reject their evidence ever after: for such people are wicked transgressors.*'

> (Surah 24.4)

The Prophet ﷺ knew from personal experience the trauma of having a beloved wife accused of adultery, and the seed of suspicion planted in his own mind. His wife Aishah was accused of adultery simply because she had been left alone in the desert and had accepted a lift home from a young man she had known from childhood. Allah gave him this personal revelation as a specific result of this case.

Li'an – divorce after swearing an oath

If there were no witnesses but an accusing spouse had caught his partner in the act of adultery, the procedure was that the accuser would be allowed to swear four times that the adultery really had been committed, and then the accused would have to swear four times that lies were being told against them. The fifth oath would bring the curse of God upon whoever was not speaking the truth. The divorce would then take place – and the punishment for adultery would be avoided in this world and left over to the next (Surah 24.6–9).

Apostasy

Apostasy (*ridda* or *irtidad* – literally 'turning back') does not mean insulting God or the Prophet 🕌. It is the sin of deciding to give up Islam, or belief in Allah, after having previously been a genuinely believing Muslim. If a person's faith in Allah was not really genuine to start with, then they count as hypocrites, and if such leave Islam they are not apostates. Apostasy is not a matter that applies to non-believers at all.

It only applies when a person has been a believing and practising member of a Muslim community, and then chooses of his or her own free will to give up that belief, a serious matter for the neighbouring believers to cope with. Needless to say, if a person did not speak or act in any way that hurt others and, finding life in Muslim society too difficult for them, chose to move away, it is obvious that any penalty for that is a matter between that person and God in the Hereafter. No death penalty for apostasy was given in the Qur'an. The very notion runs contrary to the clear Qur'anic order: '*Let there be no compulsion in religion.*' (Surah 2.256)

Apostasy was mentioned in no less than 13 verses of the Qur'an. Surah 3.86–91 is possibly the most definitive of these passages:

> '*How shall Allah guide those who reject faith after they accepted it and bore witness that the Apostle was true and that clear signs had come unto them? Allah is not the Guide of unjust people. The reward of such people is that the curse of Allah, the angels and all humanity is upon them. They shall remain under it for ever; neither will their punishment be lightened nor will they be given respite. But for those who repent after this and mend their ways, then truly Allah is indeed Forgiving, Merciful.*'

These verses were all revealed while the Prophet 🕌 was ruler of Madinah, and was clearly in the position of being able to carry out any punishment Allah had laid down, but not once was any legal punishment specified. The verses all speak of punishment as God wills, in the Life to Come, and until they passed away they were given every chance to repent and be forgiven.

The Prophet 🕌 only ever sentenced an apostate to death if the crimes of treason or murder had been committed.

Blasphemy

As regards the wish of some pious persons that the death penalty should be imposed for leaving the faith, or vilifying Allah, or speaking abusively about Allah or his Messenger ﷺ, this is not laid down in the Qur'an. The attitude of the Prophet ﷺ himself, when so frequently abused or hurt or jeered at, was to stand firm and accept the unpleasantness with patience, hating the evil, but never hating the people who had been overtaken by evil, for if God willed they would see the noble qualities and behaviour of the Muslims, become ashamed of their former ways, turn to God in repentance, and be forgiven and welcomed into the ummah or community of believers.

Muslim countries that have made blasphemy a punishable offence (e.g. Iran and Pakistan), have presumably done so by interpreting the Qur'an's clear denunciation of *fitnah*, anything that causes dissension or civil strife.

Salman Rushdie/cartoons of the Prophet ﷺ

Salman Rushdie's book, *The Satanic Verses*, was regarded as obscene, a terrible slur upon the Prophet ﷺ and his wives, and resurrected an old unproved theological tradition about the possibility that Satan could dupe him into including verses in the Qur'an which were not genuine, which would have undermined the veracity of the entire Qur'an. Since Rushdie claimed to be a Muslim, his abuse did amount to apostasy.

Cartoons of the Prophet ﷺ published in a Danish newspaper in 2005 caused a tremendous outcry. One cartoon showed the Prophet ﷺ wearing a bomb for a turban, and another showed him standing on a cloud refusing entry to martyred *mujahideen* because they had run out of virgins. The cartoons caused enormous dismay and protests around the Muslim world because it is forbidden in Islam to depict God, angels or messengers of God, so such cartoons were regarded as blasphemous. It was a scurrilous association of the Prophet ﷺ with terrorism and it reinforced Islamophobia in that it poked fun at Muslim beliefs, without awareness that there is nothing in the Qur'an about the supply of virgins in Paradise as rewards for dead soldiers.

Both publications provoked the expected passionate results. However, freedom of speech is also cherished by Muslims, who defend it in principle while vociferously objecting to its abuse.

Most non-Muslims had no idea what all the fuss was about, and Muslim speakers were quick to condemn their own 'fundamentalists', pointing out that far more damage was done to Islam by the media coverage of the irate protesters, some of whom caused damage and made death threats, than by the insults to God or the Prophet ﷺ.

32

Sufism

In this chapter you will learn about:
- the meaning of Sufism
- the aims and goals of Sufism
- details of some leading Sufis
- the criticisms of Sufism.

Sufism, or Tasawwuf, is Islamic mysticism. As a movement, it developed as a reaction against dry Islamic legalism, but it has always played a fundamental part in the religious experience of those Muslims (like the Prophet ﷺ himself) who devoted themselves to a lifetime of prayer and closeness to God. Although many non-Sufi Muslims are suspicious of it, it cannot be separated from Islam, for it is basically the 'awakening of the heart' by means of submission.

Some Muslims regard it as the most important aspect of Islam, whereas those who distrust the emotional and intuitive side of religious experience (with its obvious scope for abuse and ego-tripping) relegate it virtually to the sidelines. It depends on what type of person the Muslim is. Sufism has been called the heart or spirit of Islam by those who grasp its value; but it is regarded with suspicion by Muslims who base their faith on obedience to the correct ritual performance of Islam, and who fear *bida* (innovation).

The name 'sufi' may come from the Arabic *suf* meaning 'wool', in which case it refers to their simple garments of undyed wool. The basic wool robe was worn as a sign of ascetic living, of giving up the luxuries of life – food, dress and shelter – and accepting simplicity and poverty.

Another possible origin of the word is from the Greek *sophos* which means 'wisdom'. Others think it comes from the root *safa* which means 'purity', or from the verb *safwe* to mean 'those who are chosen'.

Aims and goals

Sufis have many aims. Basically, they are:

- to abandon the desire for worldly wealth and luxury
- to search for an inner, spiritual life
- to 'purify the heart' and achieve 'union with God'
- to overcome the appetites and desires of the human body with its concern for self.

Ali said:

'Ascetism is not that you should not own anything, but that nothing should own you.'

figure 32.1 a Naqshbandi Sufi at Peckham Mosque, London

Conflict with rulers

Sufism encourages renewal and revival in the hopes of restoring the pure and original message of the Prophet ﷺ, placing leadership in the hands of those who are closest to emulating his way of life. The ruler should be the most qualified person in spiritual terms, the most evolved in consciousness, pious, humble and accessible to the people – not someone who lives in arrogance, contempt and luxury. This, obviously, is a great threat to the decadent and extravagant lifestyle of many so-called 'Muslim' rulers.

Conflict with the orthodox schools

During the ninth and tenth centuries when jurists began teaching Shari'ah in a more formal and standardized manner, the Sufis saw their role as keeping the spirit and full meaning of Islam alive rather than adhering to the formal and ritualistic aspect of the 'State' religion which was ominously taking shape.

Some Sufis, however, adopted so outspoken and ecstatic a lifestyle that they attracted a notoriety which really set them apart from orthodox Islam. Their claims that their souls had merged with God had overtones of shirk; furthermore, music, chanting, dancing or recitation of poetry were increasingly used in order to induce transcendental experiences, and these were not practices encouraged by orthodox Islam.

Female Sufis

Although the most famous, Rabi'a al-Adawiyya (b. 95/714 or 99/717–8, d. 185/801) was not the first, but a culminating representative of female Sufism. She was not a highly strung and emotional recluse, but a rational, disciplined teacher who demonstrated her mastery of important mystical states, such as truthfulness (*sidq*), self-criticism (*muhasaba*), spiritual intoxication (sukr), love for God (*mahabba*) and gnosis (*ma-rifa*).

Rabi'a has often been called the founder of Sufi love-mysticism, but this was actually not a particularly important aspect of her teaching. She had a reputation as a specialist in jurisprudence. Her pupil, Maryam of Basra, was noted for her lectures on love, going into ecstasies on hearing someone speak of love, and finally dying in a swoon during a discourse on love.

By the beginning of the tenth century, Sufi women could be found throughout the Muslim world from Egypt to Khurasan, but most had become disciples of Sufi men as opposed to having women teachers. Sufi women mixed freely with men, travelled long distances in order to study, and occupied positions of authority and respect. But they no longer seemed to have been spiritual masters themselves.

Some accepted the 'spiritual marriage', also part of Christian practice, in which a couple lived together but the sexual relationship was set aside. It was also permitted for unrelated men and women to live together as 'brother and sister' in a spiritual union, caring for each other with no sexual intimacy. The woman was usually expected to act as the servant of Allah by serving and attending to her male companion. Rabi'a bint Isma'il had this relationship with her husband Ahmad b. Abi al-Hawari. She encouraged him to take other wives if he needed sexual satisfaction. In the view of some, this made such a woman superior to her husband, who still had the need for sex.

Male Sufis

Muhyiddin Ibn al-Arabi (560/1165–638/1240)

Ibn Arabi was born in Andalus in 560/1165 and brought up in Cordoba, Seville and Granada. He travelled east, settled in Cairo in 596/1201, and moved to Makkah two years later. He also visited Baghdad, Jerusalem, and Damascus, where he died and was buried in 638/1240.

He was the most speculative of Islamic thinkers. His key theory was the pantheistic 'unity of all existence', (*wahdat al-wujud*), and his key emphasis was on love rather than justice.

- God is One, Absolute, the Source of all being, whose existence is Being.
- The world is created so far as it exists in space-time, and eternal in that it is in the knowledge of God.
- Man never becomes God, nor God man, but it is possible through knowledge to achieve spiritual unity with God.
- Every prophet is *a* word of God and Muhammad ﷺ is *the* word of God, the focal point of all other prophets.
- The purpose of creation is *al-insan al-kamil* (the perfect man), who is also the microcosm reflecting the glory of God the Macrocosm.

- In so far as the previous prophets were reflections of the perfect man, they were the *awliya* (sing. *waliy* or friend) of God. This quality was higher than prophecy.
- Ibn Arabi thought himself the *khatim* (seal of last) of the friends of God, as Muhammad ﷺ had been the khatim of the prophets.

Abu Hamid al-Ghazzali, 1058 –1111 CE

Sometimes called the Thomas Aquinas of Islam, his outstanding contribution was to present Sufism in terms an orthodox scholar could accept. He claimed for himself the right to make fresh interpretations of the Qur'an and Islamic law instead of following traditional interpretations (*taqlid*).

He reaffirmed the view that tasawwuf was both knowledge and action, and rebuked those who sought fast-track methods of reaching the mysical experience. He disapproved of any claim that a Muslim was not obliged to observe all the rituals and other laws of Shari'ah. Ghazzali would never accept Sufism except on the conditions that it kept within the bounds of Islamic law and traditional belief, and thus secured its accepted place within Islam.

Jalal ud-Din Rumi (the Mevlana of Qonya)

The thirteenth century is usually regarded as the golden age of Sufism, and its chief exponent was Jalal ud-Din Rumi of Qonya (1207–73) who founded the order of whirling dervishes. These sought ecstasy through gyration accompanied by music that was intended to represent the order of the heavenly spheres.

Acceptance of God's will, whatever it might be, was the highest form of sacrifice of self, the highest proof of love. The Mevlana taught that one should not ask for personal requests in prayer, but should strive to be content. This was pure Islam, pure submission. Love was what mattered, not knowledge, or greatness or striving. To achieve love meant understanding unity, God's light shining into all the dark places of the earth and making them one.

Some of the Mevlana's famous sayings

'God speaks to everyone . . . He speaks to the ears of the heart, but it is not every heart which hears Him. His voice is louder than the thunder, and His light is clearer than the sun, if only one could see and hear. In order to do that, one must remove this solid wall, this barrier – the Self.'

'There are many roads to the Ka'bah . . . but lovers know that the true Holy Mosque is Union with God.'

'The sun lights up a thousand courtyards. Take away the walls, and you will see that it is all the same light.'

'You belong to the world of dimension, but you come from the world of non-dimension. Close the first shop and open the second.'

(Rumi)

Tariqahs

The Sufi science of self is called a *tariqah* ('way' or 'path'). All Sufis claim a chain or linkage or revelation (called the *silsilah*) which goes back to the Companions and to the Prophet ﷺ himself. There were two kinds of membership: the initiates (or inner circle) and the associates (who attended occasionally). Any initiate on a particular path was known as a *murid*, a disciple who owes absolute allegiance to his or her particular *shaykh*. This close relationship with the shaykh is a vital part of Sufism, and a dying shaykh usually elects his successor (if a suitable person is available), to whom obedience and loyalty is transferred.

Zawiyahs

Zawiyahs (or *Khaneqahs*) are places of spiritual learning and concentration where Sufis meditate and remember God, and train their disciples. They are also known as *tekkes* in Turkey, and *ribats* in North Africa. They are centres of missionary work, and frequently the shaykhs associated with the particular tariqah are buried there. To this day, they are visited by thousands of pilgrims. Examples are the famous shrines of Abdul Qadir Gilani in Baghdad; Muinuddin Chishti in Ajmeer, India; Shah Halal in Sylhet, Bangladesh; Jalaluddin Rumi in Qonya, Turkey; and Shams-i-Tabriz in Multan, Pakistan.

Sufi Orders in the West

The two main Orders of Sufis practising in the West today are the Naqshbandis and the Murabitun. The Naqshbandis are Sunni, and follow the Turkish Shaykh Nazim, the fortieth shaykh in line from Abu Bakr. Their UK headquarters is at Peckham Mosque, South London. The Murabitun follow the Scottish Shaykh Abd-al Qadir. Their headquarters is in Norfolk. Both tariqahs have followers all over the country. There are also many immigrant Muslims now who belong to all the Orders of their countries of origin.

Music in Sufism

Music plays a great part in many Sufi movements, and is particularly emphasized in the Chishti path to spiritual attainment. Music is *Ghiza-i-ruh*, the food of the soul. *Qawwali* are special songs sung at their contemplative musical assemblies.

The qawwalis sing distinctly, so that every word is clear to the hearers, and the music may not hide the poetry. The *tabla* (drum) players emphasize the accents and keep the rhythm even, so that the being of the Sufi joins with the rhythm and harmony of the music. The condition of the Sufi becomes different – emotion has full play, and there is a feeling of joy that cannot be put into words, language being inadequate to express it. This state is termed *Hal* or *Wajad*, the sacred ecstasy, and is regarded with respect by all present in the assembly.

Sometimes, if deeply touched, feeling finds vent in tears, or even motion or dance, which Sufis call *Raqs*.

Semi-Sufis

Some 50 per cent of the Pakistani population follow the Barelvi school founded by Ahmad Raza Khan (1856–1921) of Bareilly. It was founded to defend the existing beliefs of Muslims of South Asia that were deeply influenced by Sufism and incorporated many unorthodox beliefs against the reformation movements influenced by the Hanbali school that emphasized Shari'ah and Qur'an. The critics of Barelvism accuse them of practising many non-Muslim innovations (*bid'at*) and therefore deviating from the true path.

The Barelvis believe the Prophet ﷺ was not just a human being made from *bashar* (flesh and blood) but was also *nur* (light) at the same time (as was the angel Jibril), infallible, free from all imperfections and sinless (as are all prophets), and is still present with us. He also has the ability to be *hazir* (present) – to go physically and spiritually anywhere in the created universes that he pleases, whenever he pleases, and to be in more than one place at the same time.

Barelvis believe in intercession between humans and Divine Grace. This consists of the intervention of an ascending, linked and unbroken chain of holy personages (*pirs*), reaching ultimately to the Prophet ﷺ, who intercede on their behalf with Allah.

Criticisms of Sufism and its practices

Orthodox Muslims are often suspicious, critical, and even highly antagonistic of Sufism, for a mix of these reasons:

- **Tawhid challenged** – by the Sufi desire to 'become one with God'.
- **Erotic and distasteful language** – physical terms such as embracing, hugging and talking to God, or erotic language is distasteful to most Muslims.
- **Khamr** – some Sufis used alcohol or drugs to induce mystic states.
- **Music and dance** – many Muslims insist these are forbidden.
- **Fana** – replacing belief that life in this world is God's arena for human spiritual development with the notion that it is not important, just a brief journey to the beyond.
- **Unity threatened** – the unity of the ummah is threatened, as Sufis withdraw into sects in which they are tempted to think themselves better Muslims than others.
- *Kashf* – rational scientific knowledge is abandoned in favour of mystical experiences, and critical analysis ignored for the authoritarian pronouncements of a shaykh – which would inevitably be limited by the knowledge, experience, and talents of the shaykh, and could even be the ravings of an unsound mind.
- *Ta'ah* – the unwise, even dangerous, total obedience to a shaykh.

- *Karamat* – teaching that miracles are possible in the state of union or communion with God, and are indeed favours granted by God to the most pious.
- **Ologies** – mathematics becoming mixed up with numerology, astronomy with astrology, chemistry with alchemy, etc.
- **Magic** – teaching that *dhikr* or repeated prayers are 'shortcuts' to results; encouraging people to hope for manipulation of supernatural forces, thus opening the door to gullibility, magic, talismanship and charlatanism.
- *Ta'abbud* – deliberately giving up the fulfilment of normal obligations, for the sake of ritualistic worship such as chanting of phrases, and lengthy contemplation.
- *Tawakkul* – trust in Allah degenerating into trust that God will make your desired things happen; replacing the study of God's inexorable laws with superstition.
- **Pantheistic metaphysics** – that all created things from the level of inanimate objects to the highest of conscious beings were all part of 'the one'.
- **Teaching that all religious paths are of equal value** – all inspired by the same divine source.
- **Egotism** – seeking to be saved oneself rather than caring for others.
- **Tomb-shrines** – praying at the tombs of 'saints' for miraculous intervention in healing, pregnancy, or worldly success.
- **Urs festivals** – the anniversary of the death of a *shaykh* becoming the occasion for great gatherings of people and major festivals.
- **Charlatans** – at worst, Sufism offers an opportunity for pretenders of spiritual excellence to take full advantage of the gullibilities of eager but unwary disciples.

The important role of Sufism

Many people consider that Sufism saves Islam from being over-influenced by 'legalism'. True Sufis, with their humility, sincerity and devotion, character and conduct, fight to keep the love of God and the Prophet ﷺ alive.

However, Sufis have frequently been misunderstood and persecuted. For these reasons, they have sometimes gone 'underground' in order to safeguard and continue their teaching discreetly, either through fear of tyrannical rulers, or of the power-mongering religious scholars who felt challenged and undermined by the popularity of the Sufis.

They were and are the champions against materialism, and still play an important part wherever rule-keeping, rather than movement of the spirit, threatens to take over the ummah. Their influence within Muslim nations remains enormous, and it is rare to find a Sunni Muslim ruler who is not affiliated to one or other of the Orders.

33

Islamic reform – Fundamentalism, Salafism and Neo-Sufism

In this chapter you will learn about:
- Islamic reform
- Fundamentalism
- Wahhabism
- secularism and Modernism
- Salafism
- Islamic Revivalism
- Neo-Sufism.

The basic aim of Islamic reform has nothing to do with politics; it is the recognition that Islam means little if it is not taken seriously, both in matters of belief and personal practice. It is the powerful urge for personal spirituality, grounding believers in the reality of Allah's presence, compassion and intimacy with us as individuals, so that laziness, selfishness, ignorance and hypocrisy no longer have room in the Muslim heart, which becomes full of fervour and desire to serve God in every aspect of life.

Muslims are urged to acknowledge that the problems of their world stem from secular influences, laxity in personal religious practice, and ignorance which can both lead to blind obedience (taqlid) to preachers and speakers who could be wrong, and following practices thought to be Islamic which are not, and could even bring about the opposite of Islamic principles. The path to peace and justice lies in a reform to touch the hearts of Muslims as individuals, a personal revitalization by returning to the fundamentals, the original simple message and practise of the faith.

Fundamentalism

The first principle of a fundamentalist is to believe that the vast mass of material accumulated over centuries of Islamic jurisprudence is more of a burden to the pious believer than a help. There is too much, it is too complicated, and only other scholars can really grasp it all.

The second principle is that, in any case, any scholar – no matter how well educated – is only a human being with human limitations, and their conclusions are only as good as their particular skills and brain-power. There are madhhab-revering Muslims who think something is not permissible because Imam Malik, for example, forbade it – yet however great, learned or important a scholar he was, he was human and not infallible. To a fundamentalist, any rulings based on any individual's intellectual capacity, logic and reasoning, are unsafe. Muslims should rely solely on the actual sacred words of the Qur'an and the sunnah of the Prophet ﷺ and nothing else. They contain all the religious and spiritual guidance necessary for salvation.

This, of course, means rejecting not only the entire history of Islamic scholarship but also everything seen as innovation (bida), including Sufi teaching and practice.

The opponents of fundamentalism are therefore going to be:

- those who value the work of traditional scholars and support their madhhabs
- Sufis and those who enjoy esoteric mysticism, devotional practices and Sufi literature
- Muslims who are not saints and cannot manage all the ritual requirements
- Intellectuals and liberal modernists who wish to keep abreast of the modern world by 'opening the doors of ijtihad' and using reason and logic to interpret Shari'ah by looking to the spirit and principles of Islam rather than the letter of the law
- those who wish to embrace and utilize the modern sciences.

In the West, the word fundamentalism is also used of those who assert their views through politics, violence or militancy, even though most fundamentalists are non-violent, and some are entirely apolitical. For example, the Tablighi Jama'at is a missionary-like organization whose aim is only to increase the personal piety of Muslims.

The link-up comes because Fundamentalist Muslims (as all devout Muslims) regard defending their faith to the point of offering their own lives as the highest sacrifice of devotion, and the extreme fringe might be prepared to sacrifice others if it was felt that God, Islam or the Prophet ﷺ were being attacked or abused.

Islamic Fundamentalism should perhaps rather be called Islamic Conservatism, part of the spectrum of modern movements in Islam of which Fundamentalism and Liberalism define the two poles.

Ibn Taymiyyah (1263–1328)

Ibn Taymiyyah, generally credited with being the founder of fundamentalism, was also a major leader in the revivalist campaign to open the doors of ijtihad. A leading Hanbali scholar, his erudition soon went beyond its confines, leading him to conclude that blind adherence (taqlid) to any one madhhab was too limiting. But he distrusted human intellect ('aql) as a reliable means of attaining religious truth, and rejected the arguments and ideas of both philosophers and Sufis.

Wahhabism

Four centuries later **Muhammad ibn Abdu'l-Wahhab** (1703–92), an intensely pious puritan, founded a movement to rid Islam of all the corruptions he believed had crept into the religion. He also believed it was vital to return to the fundamentals, and his attitude towards the whole vast edifice of scholastic material was to dismiss it. He took a very narrow view, exhibiting extreme hostility towards intellectualism, Shi'ism, any other sectarian group, with especial antagonism towards Sufism.

The wording of the Divine law was universal and timeless, so any attempt to 'dilute' it by limiting pronouncements to their historical background or context were rejected, and scholars seeking new interpretations were regarded as arrogant self-idolaters. Humanistic fields of knowledge were branded 'the sciences of the devil.' Religion was used to oppress women and minorities and tolerance became an unpopular word.

The ruling house of Saud has been bound to Wahhabism since Abdu'l Wahhab signed a pact with Muhammad ibn Saud in 1744. Wahhabi rebellions of the nineteenth and twentieth centuries were very bloody because they indiscriminately slaughtered and terrorized Muslims and non-Muslims alike. To its adherents, Wahhabism is not a school of thought within Islam but *is* Islam, and therefore even the term Wahhabism is considered derogatory. In their literature, Wahhabi clerics have consistently described themselves as *Salafis* (traditionalists).

The rise of political Islam

One impetus for reform began with Napoleon's invasion of Egypt in 1798.[7] The Muslim rulers of the Ottoman Empire acknowledged that the West's power was based upon its superior technology and weapons, and wished to acquire these things for themselves. Students were sent to Europe to study languages, science, and politics; European experts were drafted in; printing presses were introduced to make technical information more accessible. European legal codes became the basis for reforms, and Islamic law was restricted to personal status or family law (such things as marriage, divorce and inheritance). The state (or a small political elite) increasingly asserted its right to regulate and administer religious matters,

---

[7]Napoleon was highly sympathetic towards Islam, and actually took the name Ali.

creating ministries of religious affairs and endowments to control organizations and institutions that had previously been outside their authority, including Sufi orders, mosques, Shari'ah courts, and religious schools.

Muslim societies both felt and were marginalized by the imposition of Western value systems, way of life and methods of government. Imperialism and colonialism were not received as blessings by the conquered. It was noted that oppressive feudal and colonial rule caused moral degradation, political instability, economic exploitation and spiritual bankruptcy –the last seen as the root cause of destroying the moral fibre of society.

Secularism

Secularism means different things to different people. The Western concept is 'this-worldly', largely due to the fact that their secular states were formed after the revolt against exploitation by the religious hierarchy of Roman Catholicism during the Reformation. In fact, secularism develops in two ways – either towards disbelief in anything beyond this world and hostility towards all religion (as in Communism), or a separation of state and religion, or at least non-interference by the state in the religious life of different communities or of their priestly class in politics and state affairs. In other words, tolerance of religion so long as it does not interfere in politics. In many Western secular states there is respect and recognition of religious pluralism, and today's aim is for equal rights of protection and respect for people of all faiths.

Democracy

A diversity of voices within the Islamic world began to debate issues of democracy, or political participation of the people:

- **Secularists,** who might be extremely religious, argued for the separation of religion and state.
- **Rejectionists** (both moderate and militant Muslims) rejected democracy, feeling it was not in keeping with Islam.
- **Extremists** condemned any form of democracy as haram, forbidden, an idolatrous threat to God's rule (divine sovereignty). Their political activity was increasingly intended to topple kings and governments in order to impose a pure authoritarian Islamic rule according to their interpretation of Islam.

Modernism

The main principle of Islamic Modernism is to acknowledge that today's issues require a multi-disciplinary approach with expertise in all areas of science, politics, economics and international affairs, to show how Islam is perfectly in keeping with the sciences and should be making use of science in order to bring progress. Modernists emphasize Muslim pride, unity, solidarity, freedom of thought and the quest for truth through multiple sources – rationalism, human experience, critical thinking and so on, in order to re-interpret and re-apply the principles and ideals of Islam to the modern situation. Directly opposed to Wahhabism, they argue that re-interpretation and reform are not blasphemy but a vital necessity. Most also wish to pursue an anti-colonialist agenda, the ultimate goal of which is national independence.

They also assert the right of well-informed Muslims who are not trained *ulema* to interpret Islam. An intellectual lay-person might be more saintly and have better skills than a mediocre *mullah*.

Salafism

The founders of Salafism were fundamentalists in that they agreed that Muslims should always return to the Qur'an and the sunnah of the Prophet ﷺ and his Companions (the *salafiyyah* or *as-salaf as-salih,* the pious forefathers) and also rejected being slavishly bound to the interpretations of earlier Muslim generations or madhhabs. They differed from Wahhabis in that they regretted the loss of Islam's spirit of science and inquiry that was so spectacularly demonstrated by such giants as Ibn Sina, Ibn Rushd, al-Farabi, al-Biruni, al-Haytham, etc. A desire for all forms of knowledge needed to be revived if Muslims were to revitalize and have a niche in world history once more.

Salafism is not necessarily anti-Western. In fact, its founders strove to project contemporary institutions such as democracy, constitutions or socialism into the foundational texts, and to justify the modern nation-state within Islam. Many of the pioneers lived at the end of the nineteenth century, at the end of the imperialist era, when the Ottoman Khalifate was the 'sick man' of Europe, and all kinds of nationalist, modernist and secularist movements were springing up.

Salafi pioneers

In Egypt a number of reformers appeared, some concerned more with law, others economics, and yet others the challenges posed by Western civilization. These included **Jamal al-Din al-Afghani** (1838–97) who had observed British imperialism in India, noted how Muslims were systematically discriminated against, joined the resistance movement against the British in Afghanistan, then went to Cairo where he became the great champion of Pan-Islamism, the movement it was hoped would unite the Islamic world politically as well as in faith. If Afghans could defeat the forces of Britain, what an impact the unity of all Muslims under a charismatic ruler could have. His call for Muslim solidarity influenced Egypt's nationalist movement, Turkey's *Tanzimat* reforms, as well as Iran's constitutional and Islamic revolutions.

One of his influential students was the Egyptian religious scholar **Muhammad Abduh** (1849–1905), often called the founder of Islamic Modernism, who became the rector of the Cairo al-Azhar University, and argued that the social aspects of Islamic law could be reformed in such areas as marriage, divorce, and inheritance (for example, he argued that the Qur'an supported monogamy, not polygamy, and supported education for women).

Another leading voice was the radical Syrian **Muhammad Rashid Rida** (1865–1935), who held a position closer to that of Abdu'l-Wahhab and stood for the strict application of the Shari'ah. He called for the unity of Islamic nations and the revival of true Islamic Caliphate (which had been abolished by Mustafa Kemal Ataturk in Turkey in 1924). He was one of the most influential Muslims scholars through his books and many articles in the Egyptian journal *al-Manar* (the Lighthouse) which he founded in 1898 and published throughout his life.

Islamic Revivalism

For many Muslims, Islamic Revival simply means becoming a more religiously observant Muslim. Most Muslims oppose Islam's manipulation for violent or revolutionary ends, but the political and economic climate in so many Muslim countries fuels Islamist movements to go beyond reverence and promote political strategies. For them, Islamic Revival is about creating a more just, moral, Islam-based society/world, and Islamism represents a last-ditch effort to better their situation after decades of living in impoverished states that have already experimented with socialism, Arab nationalism, military dictatorships and monarchies, and observed little discernible improvement.

Hassan Al-Banna (1906–49) and the Ikhwan al-Muslimun

Al-Banna's message was also that Egypt had lost its soul and become secular, politically sub-servient and economically dependent on the West because it had strayed from the path laid down by God. His campaign was therefore to bring the Muslim masses back to their personal relationship with and awareness of the Almighty. In 1928 he founded the Ikhwan (or Muslim Brotherhood), to promote personal piety and encourage practical kindness and charity. It became the largest and most influential Sunni Revivalist organization in the twentieth century, and also the first overtly political movement to oppose secular and Western ideas in the Middle East.

Radical tendencies soon asserted themselves; a 'secret apparatus' (al-jihaz al-sirri) engineered a series of assassinations of enemies of the Brotherhood. The Egyptian government, concerned with its increasing popularity and fearing it was plotting a coup, outlawed the Ikhwan, impounded its assets, and sent scores of its members to jail. In response the Egyptian Prime Minister was assassinated, which in turn prompted the murder of al-Banna, presumably by a government agent, in February 1949, when he was only 43 and at the height of his career.

Since then, the Brotherhood has remained a significant force in the politics of several Arab countries, either directly or through the movements it inspired. It is at present the major opposition party in Egypt.

Neo-Sufism

Neo-Sufism also arose in the eighteenth century, an alternative response to modernism and secularism, neo-puritan Islamism, the corrupt authoritarian Sufism of colonial times, and partly in response to colonialism itself. For example, anti-French resistance in Algeria was spearheaded by the brilliant Sufi shaykh **Amir Abdu'l Kader**.

In India, faced with sectarian conflict, low moral tone, and poor understanding of the Qur'an, it was feared that political collapse would be accompanied by religious disintegration. That this did not happen, but rather an era of religious regeneration commenced, was due largely to the activities of **Shah Wali Ullah** (1707–62), who campaigned to bring Muslim society back to the concepts of basic social justice, translated the Qur'an into the language of the people so that those without Arabic could understand it, and after studying the writings of each school of thought worked out a system upon which all but extremists could agree.

In the nineteenth century Islamic assertion took several different forms ranging from the **Mahdi movement** of the Sudan and the **Sanusiyyah** in North Africa which both fought wars against European colonizers, to educational movements such as that of Aligarh in India founded by **Sir Syed Ahmad Shah**.

34

the rise of
militant Islam

In this chapter you will
learn about:
- the rise of Islamic militancy
- Maududi and Qutb
- Khomeini
- anti-Americanism.

Wahhabism and Saudi Arabia

Wahhabi ideology was resuscitated in the early twentieth century under the leadership of **Abdu'l-Aziz ibn Saud**, the founder of the modern state of Saudi Arabia. With the discovery of oil beneath the sands, and the mining skills of Americans soon present to exploit it, the House of Saud was soon to gain enormous wealth and power, and the Wahhabi clerics got the state backing that would enable them to promote their ideology across the globe.

The Saudi wealth has been used to make enormous contributions to the spread of Islam and Muslim space in the West, but at the same time hardline Wahhabism has horrified Muslims the world over – not least by presiding over the systematic destruction of the Muslim heritage in and around Makkah in the fear that places of historic interest and religious landmarks could give rise to idolatry or polytheism. Cynics note that following the destruction come commercial developers to fill the voids with lucrative high-rises.

The rise of militant Islam

Given the existence of undemocratic and corrupt regimes all over the Muslim world, it is not surprising that for much of the twentieth century the dominant form of political dissent in these countries has been revolutionary Marxism. (The end of the Soviet Union and the Cold War has largely discredited leftist ideologies and strengthened Islamic parties.)

The huge problem confronting militant Muslims is their feeling that the governments of Islamic countries may be all made up of Muslims and Muslim leaders, but they are seen (rightly or wrongly) as corrupt, and therefore not proper Muslims. Politicized reformist Muslims are therefore feared by their own governments, and often face what is virtually or actually a police state – one that undermines, prohibits or cancels any kind of attempt to build an Islamic political party or movement.

Political Muslims are not only feared but also used by the governments they oppose, for their own ends. For example, in republics of the former Soviet Union, such as Tajikistan, Kyrgyzstan and Uzbekistan, anti-fundamentalism is used to justify horrendous human rights abuses. Any person who is even moderately religious is labelled a fundamentalist and imprisoned, or at least abused, and it has been very difficult for Muslim political parties to have any political effect.

Abu'l Ala Maududi (1903–79)

Maududi is regarded by many as the major influence for militant Islam. He was not a traditional jurist but a self-taught pious man. He concluded that one reason for the decline of Muslim power in 'British' India was the long-established practice of interfaith mixing which had watered down Islamic thought. The solution was to purge Islam of all alien elements, and sever all social and political ties with Hindus. He and others founded the Jama'at-e Islami Party in Lahore in 1941.

Apart from pious personal practice, Maududi also saw Islam as a revolutionary force. A nascent Islamic *jama'at* (society, group) could begin and grow from a period of weakness to gather strength before waging jihad, just as Muhammad's ﷺ jama'at was weak and persecuted in Makkah and gathered strength in Madinah before returning triumphantly to Makkah. The revolutionary jama'at would be a vanguard, remaining outside the government until the ultimate goal of the jama'at was realized – the establishment of an Islamic State, a 'theo-democracy'. His ideal Islamic state would have a president, an elected *shura* council (consisting of Muslims elected only by other Muslims), an independent judiciary and a cabinet. *Dhimmis* (non-Muslims living under Muslim protection) would only have the right to vote in lower level elections.

At first Maududi strongly opposed the idea of creating Pakistan as a separate Muslim country, but after the Partition in 1947, he migrated there and relentlessly criticized any secular policies. He was an intensely controversial figure, and counter-criticism came not only from secularists but also from many of the *ulema*. He also found himself persecuted and imprisoned for his political beliefs.

In 1953, his pamphlet criticizing the Qadiyani[8] sect resulted in widespread rioting and violence, and a military court sentenced him to death for sedition, although he was eventually pardoned.

[8]The Qadiyanis are a subsect of the Ahmadiyyah Movement founded by Mirza Ghulum Ahmad (1839–1908) who, in 1891, declared himself the promised Messiah (masih) of Islam, and claimed descent from Jesus ﷺ (who had not died at his crucifixion but survived, travelled to India, produced offspring, and was buried in Srinagar). Although Ahmadis regard themselves as Muslims and observe Islamic practices, most Muslims in Pakistan deny this. There is now an Ahmadiyya presence in 166 countries, but in Pakistan they have been made subject to discriminatory laws and an atmosphere of intolerance and violence, much of which is instigated by organized religious extremists.

Maududi's influence gave rise to the two most important mujahideen factions in the Afghan civil war, that of Ahmad Shah Masud (who leavened his Salafism with traditionalism), and Gulbuddin Hikmatyar.

Sayyid Qutb (1906–66)

In Egypt, Sayyid Qutb was a prominent Revivalist whose thought was deeply influenced by Maududi's revolutionary radicalism. In 1948, the year of the creation of the state of Israel, Qutb (a brilliant writer and employee in the Egyptian Ministry of Education), was sent to the US to study American educational institutions. There, he was deeply offended by the racism he observed (and experienced first-hand) and noted with disgust how their youth flirted, dressed and danced even at church gatherings, and how Americans seemed blind to thousands of Palestinians being made permanent refugees, and the Muslim death-toll. Were Arab lives worth less than European Jews? His experiences partly formed the impetus for his rejection of Western values and increasing radicalization. On his return to Egypt he resigned from the civil service, joined the Ikhwan, and became perhaps their most persuasive publicist.

An attempt on Nasser's life in 1954 led to large numbers of the Muslim Brothers being rounded up and Qutb experienced arrest, torture and conviction of anti-government conspiracy. In 1964, having suffered ten years of incarceration, he published his best known work, *Milestones*, (or *Signposts*) that inspired some of the most extreme expressions of Islamic Revivalism, such as Islamic Jihad and Takfir wa'l Hijrah.

One of his central concepts was to apply the term *jahiliyyah* (originally humanity's state of ignorance before the revelation of Islam) to modern-day Muslim societies which had turned away from Islamic values under the influence of European imperialism. Qutb also urged the creation of a 'vanguard' (*tali' ah*) of believers who would lead the way in the war on jahiliyyah, a clear call for Islamic militancy.

His natural conclusion that his torturers were subhuman infidels turned to extremism, and the infidels stretched to include the entire state that had ordered this brutality, plus even those Muslim civilians who passively lent their support to Nasser's regime. Thus his justification of the killing of 'infidels' so long as it was done in the name of Islam now included practically everyone. All non-Islamic states were illegitimate. He was never released, and was eventually executed by Nasser in 1966.

Qutb's thought played a key role in the emergence of the Awakening Movement (*sahwa*), a blend of Qutbist ideas and radical Wahhabi thinking, which grew out of the work of exiled Muslim Brothers from Egypt and elsewhere beginning in the 1960s and which achieved prominence in Saudi Arabia in the 1980s.

Qutb has been interpreted, particularly in Western media, as the intellectual precursor to various Islamic militant movements from the 1980s to the present day, including the notorious international organization, al-Qaeda.[9]

Ayatollah Khomeini (1900–89)

In Iran, Ruhollah Khomeini was a leading and distinguished cleric, a famous ascetic and teacher. Before his exile, seeing the religious establishment losing ground in the face of Modernist secular challenges and corruption, Khomeini took refuge in mysticism, especially in the notion of the 'Perfect Man' who would be able to guide society from corruption to a life of absolute perfection.

By the early 1960s, Khomeini was resisting the modernizing reforms proposed by the Shah's 'White Revolution', using the term 'westoxification' (*gharbzadigi* – from the Arabic root *ghraba*) to describe what he considered the poisonous influences of Western culture. He was arrested by SAVAK (the Shah's secret police) and later sent into exile, ending up in Paris, where he pursued his mission by utilizing 'modern' means, churning out tapes and cassettes which were eagerly snapped up and disseminated by his loyal supporters. Two weeks after the Shah left Iran in 1979, dying of cancer, Khomeini was recalled, and returned to construct his revolutionary 'reign of virtue' according to his principle of the *velayet e-faqih* ('vice regency of the theologian').

[9]Qutb's brother Muhammad moved to Saudi Arabia where he came a professor of Islamic Studies. One of his students was Ayman Zawahiri, who later became the mentor of Usama bin Laden.

Khomeini was the first revolutionary Muslim cleric to actually create an Islamic government, welcomed with joy by his devotees, but criticized as based solely on his own personal conception of what such a government should entail by his detractors. His revolution inspired both Sunni and Shi'ite Revivalist movements around the world, including Hizbullah in Lebanon.[10]

Anti-Americanism

Before 1967, Islamic militancy had been a relatively small movement. However, Israel's swift success over Egypt, Jordan and Syria in the Six Day War spelled the end of Arab Nationalism as an effective political movement, while their conquest of Jerusalem transformed Israeli-Palestinian strife from a regional conflict into one that affected all Muslims. Other crises throughout the Muslim world – the upheaval in Malaysia in 1969, Pakistan's invasion of Bangladesh in 1971, the revolution in Iran and the Lebanese civil war all fuelled the belief that the West had failed Muslim societies not only as an ally but as a viable model of development.

Extremism also found an origin in wars that the United States decided to support. Radical Islam was not a force in Lebanon before the Israeli invasion of 1982; Hamas owes its emergence and influence to the fact that the Palestinian territories are still occupied in defiance of UN rulings.

Muslims feel that the corrective to militant Islamism is to properly integrate mainstream Islamists into the political process of their respective countries. They cannot be ignored because they present some of the most powerful voices in the political life of their countries. Radicalism would be defused if the US shifted its focus from trying to crush Islamic movements militarily to pursing policies that made their development redundant.

[10]By the end of the twentieth century, with much of Iran's youthful population too young to remember Khomeini and impatient with the theocratic rule of the mullahs, the mood has changed. One Baghdadi who described the 2004 American invasion of Iraq as a 'liberation' was Khomeini's own grandson, Sayyid Hussein Khomeini, who said that people in the region welcomed freedom wherever it came from, even a country which his grandfather had dubbed 'the Great Satan'.

Recent surveys show that over 80 per cent of Muslims would like to have democracy – except for those radical Islamists who reject any form of governance in favour of the Caliphate.

People vote with their feet. Many Muslims have moved to the USA and Western Europe, either as refugees or in search of betterment and freedom, but not everyone is confident about the USA's goal of democratization and 'freedom' for their homelands. Smart tyrants have generally tended to be allies of the USA if they wished to remain in power. Only when Muslims are empowered to choose their own leadership and policies freely, and are able to reject USA-supported choices of leaders can the blight of violence begin to wind down.

The real test will be when democratically-elected Islamist parties are genuinely able to come to power through the ballot box – as happened with Hamas in Palestine in January 2006. For democracy brings not only power but also accountability. Movements which previously had the luxury of criticizing from the sidelines will have to deliver the goods.

35

Modernism and moderate Islam

Why Salafism is rejected by many Muslims

Salafism undoubtedly stems from noble and pious origins, but in their efforts to defend their 'purist' system of beliefs from the onslaught of Westernization and Modernism, an unfortunate side-effect has been to produce unsmiling zealots whose arrogance and hatred for those they should be missionizing is all too clear in their faces, with a fantasy-like level of confidence and a supremacist attitude. Salafism seems to appeal to a certain type, often impervious to self-criticism, and displaying a self-righteous arrogance towards the West, non-believers in general, Muslims of different sects and women.

By emphasizing the presumed Golden Age in Islam, Salafis ignore the actual recorded history in the hadiths and tend to idealize the time of the Prophet ﷺ and the characters of his Companions beyond reality. Nobody may risk criticism of any of the Companions, for they were the 'best of people'.[11]

Untutored scholarship has resulted in today's plethora of pseudo-scholars and uninformed preachers who effectively undermine any notions of qualified juristic authority in Islam. It becomes open for all to think themselves justified to speak on behalf of the Divine Will, even those who have only been Muslims for five minutes, yet are suddenly more righteous than everyone else, and feel perfectly competent to instruct others.

Liberalism

Liberalist and Modernist scholars point out that in circumstances where the Shari'ah has been limited to strict Fundamentalist interpretations, or where training schools are limited only to the resources approved by particular sects, the knowledge base of how the Shari'ah has been/is interpreted by other schools of thought is greatly narrowed, and might even be in danger of being lost. They maintain that Fundamentalism itself constitutes a sort of bida, since its very limiting form of Islam never existed in the past.

---

[11]A speaker can be heckled, for example, for suggesting that the Prophet ﷺ was a human being with human frailties or limitations, or that the behaviour of certain Companions was not perfect, that they had weaknesses, ignorance, made mistakes, etc.

This situation is rendered even more grave if classical texts are altered and 'censored' of 'un-Islamic' aspects, with the trainees dependent on those resources perhaps being quite unaware that they have been altered. It is certainly one good reason to cling to the practice of placing the Arabic text of the Qur'an alongside any translations, and to urge as many Muslims as possible who have a talent for languages to learn Arabic for themselves. Failing that, it is good practice to compare more than one translation.

The way forward – Istihsan

Modernists insist that Muslims must look not just at the text, but at the context of the text, and to re-apply sacred texts to the realities and challenges of the times in which we live. What are the broader principles and values underlying the language of the Qur'an on specific issues, or the decisions and actions taken by the Prophet ﷺ? How would these be understood in a contemporary setting? Key priorities of modernist ijtihad are justice and equity (istihsan) and the general welfare or public interest.

There is a critical distinction between Shari'ah, the divinely mandated laws and principles that are universal and timeless, and fiqh, the human interpretations and applications that develop in response to specific historical and social contexts. Often the phrase 'Islamic law' blurs this distinction, thereby sacralizing the corpus of the fiqh and the *fuqaha* (legal scholars) themselves.

So, some verses were specific to the Prophet's ﷺ time (e.g. the curse addressed to Abu Lahab, rules given specifically to the Prophet's ﷺ wives), and others were eternal in purpose. Should we make Abu Lahab timeless, or make it clearer that other verses are historically specific? If a verse was directed at the wives of the Prophet ﷺ, was it compulsory for all Muslim women everywhere, or just those addressed?

Moreover, while Muhammad ﷺ was the last human nabi (prophet), we are still being taught by history and science. Muhammad ﷺ talked about our moon and sun as if they were the only moon and sun. Today we know Allah created billions of galaxies. And if we need to reinterpret the Qur'anic verses on sun and moon in the light of our new understanding of astronomy and the cosmos, why can we not reinterpret Islamic verses about ancient punishments (hudud)? The expansion of human knowledge is not just about stars, but also about human beings and their behaviour, psychology and genetics.

Some thoughts on modernizing Islamic criminal law

We now know far more about the causes of crime, the limits of culpability and guilt. We know that poverty, bad parenting, a sense of injustice, racial discrimintion, chemical imbalance in the human body, a bad neighbourhood and bad social environment can all be contributing factors that turn a human being toward crime. Fourteen centuries ago there were no police, prisons, forensic science or knowledge about DNA. Since then, God has taught us more about crime, its causes, the methods of its investigation, the limits of guilt and the much wider range of possible punishments and deterrents.

Islam and freedom of thought

Ironically, the great hindrances blocking renewal and creativity in Islamic thinking today are still the absence of intellectual, political and social freedom in most Islamic societies, except in the West, and the conservative religious establishment's firm grip on the training of religious leaders, and on religious discourse, doctrine and practice.

Muslim Reformers, seen by their followers as saints, are naturally often perceived as a threat by conservative leaders, religious institutions and even the devout students in these institutions. Muslim Modernists can find themselves silenced or removed from their teaching positions, with their livelihoods and even lives threatened, forced into exile, caught between authoritarian regimes that are prepared to imprison and religious extremists prepared to kill. A huge gulf is opening up between the adherents of the two types of Islam.

Who or what is a moderate Muslim?

In today's climate, the definition of a moderate Muslim depends very much on who you ask and what their agenda is, their politics or religious positions. 'Moderate' is a relative term, understood differently by different people. It might include:

- any Muslim who believes in democracy, tolerance, a non-violent approach to politics and equitable treatment of women
- those who accept that the Qur'an and hadiths were written for a time and place very different from today and are therefore open to re-interpretation
- those who reject the idea that any one group or individual has a monopoly on defining Islam, and who respect the right of individuals to disagree, or to worship Allah the way they choose, or even not to worship and not to believe
- those willing to co-exist peacefully with peoples of other faiths, to seek dialogue with them, and emphasize the common ground and not the differences
- those who would be prepared to separate politics and religion
- those who would try to bring people into Islam by logic and love, example and discussion, rather than by threats, coercion or force of arms
- those who would condemn suicide bombings and terrorist operations, and abhor 'preachers of hate', even though they still might not condemn all occasions of political violence against authorities who occupy Muslim lands by force.

In internal debates, a more extreme Muslim might use the term 'moderate Muslim' pejoratively (and unjustly) to indicate one who is more secular and less Islamic than the norm, which varies across communities. People who are moderate solely on the basis of their politics could be understood as opportunists and self-serving.

In the USA

In the USA the litmus test for being a moderate Muslim is tied to foreign policy issues, and how critical the Muslim is of American policy, interests and preferences within the world order, who accepts that Islam has no role in politics, and avoids any confrontation – even political – with Israel. Some Muslims seen as moderate by the Muslim world are called radical by the Bush administration. Leading modern moderates such as Yusuf Qaradawi, Tariq Ramadan and Yusuf Islam, for example, were all treated with suspicion in 2005.

36

Khilafah and the Islamic State

In this chapter you will learn about:
- unity and division
- the Islamic State
- the meaning of khilafah
- jihadist sects.

Unity and division

Islam shuld be one ummah but, unfortunately, it is all too obvious that the family of Islam suffers from splits, rivalries, jealousies and nationalism. Far too many issues divide the Muslims of different countries and cultures, which is not the fault of Islam itself, and certainly not the aim or desire of the Prophet ﷺ. While the Prophet ﷺ was alive he regretted the divisive instinct that spoiled the peace of his own community of believers.

> 'Believers are one single brotherhood (ummah), so make peace and reconciliation between two contenders, and revere Allah, that you may receive mercy.'
>
> (Surah 49:10)

The Prophet ﷺ commented: 'The devil is a wolf to humanity, catching the one which is solitary, the one who strays from the flock, and the one which wanders off. So avoid the branching paths, and keep to the general community!' (Ahmad)

The Prophet ﷺ hated sectarianism and exclusivism; he disapproved of extremists pushing themselves forward and causing fitnah (discord) including rivalry and hurt feelings and enmity. However, although many Muslims do fall far short of the ideal, nevertheless the ideal of the ummah is there to be aimed at.

An Islamic State and its relationship to Shari'ah

A united ummah would in essence be an Islamic State (dawlah islamiyah), a united people, or territory, where governance was under a Caliph and according to the principles of the Shari'ah. In practice, since this does not yet exist, there are several attitudes towards existing states and whether or not they are Islamic enough for Muslims to accept them. Some argue that a true Islamic State can only be one in which the Shari'ah is formally implemented. Others might argue that in some such states the Shari'ah has become cruel and misinterpreted, and in opposition to the true spirit of Islam. Some Muslims might find a state acceptable if none of its laws was contrary to the basic tenets of Islam. Yet others might accept a State in which Islamic law is *one* of the available sources of law.

Difficulties with non-Muslim law

Under non-Muslim governments devout Muslims inevitably face a conflict of loyalties in that secular law systems frequently negate the standards by which they are required to live. Adultery, prostitution, pornography, homosexuality, gambling, interest on loans and consuming liquor cannot be made legal in Islam.

What is Khilafah?

Khilafah is the concept of all Muslims being united under the rule of one elected Muslim man of superb character, the khalifah (Caliph), who would be totally committed to bringing about the will of God on earth as it is in Heaven. He would be appointed by Muslims through an electoral process known as *bay'ah* (mandate), a pledge on the Book of Allah and sunnah of His Prophet ﷺ. Many would prefer this leader to be a descendent of the Prophet ﷺ, of whom a large number exist to this day.[12]

What would be his aims?

He would seek to establish unity among all the Muslims on earth in a community which would be regarded as the 'best community' (Surah 3:110). This Islamic State would consist of all those submitted to Allah – it could exist along the lines of united geographical states (like the United States of America or the old Union of Soviet Socialist Republics), or as pan-Islam, a rule of all Muslims wherever they happen to live. The Caliph's rule on behalf of Allah would be dedicated to the common good of all humanity, and would transcend race, language, colour, and geography.

He would do this by demolishing the rules of *kufr* (unbelief) and transforming the land to *Dar-al-Islam* (land of Islam), and carrying the message of Islam to the world, unfinished business until Muslims govern the whole earth.

No forced conversions

Some groups urging for khilafah also support jihad. However, spreading the will of God on earth does not imply forcing

---

[12]They include, incidentally, our Queen and her offspring.

people to believe what they patently do not believe. This is the very opposite of God's will; Allah ordered no compulsion in matters of faith, and pointed out that had He willed everyone on earth to be Muslims, He would not have created them as individuals (see Surah 10.99–100 and Surah 18.29).

Is Khilafah feasible?

Considering the present state of the world, most Muslims regard khilafah as a concept that belongs in the realm of ideals rather than reality. They feel it is more sensible to acknowledge the status quo and get on with following the compulsory aspects of Islam, living good Muslim lives, with or without a khalifah, since the concept is not universally accepted by scholars as a necessary part of Islam. It is not one of the 'five pillars', was not always successful, even in the earliest days, and its absence does not make Islam impossible.

Jihadists

Others feel the move to establish khilafah should be the prime aim of all Muslims. These Muslims often become sectarians, with a reputation for aggression, a desire for jihad, and – being prepared to lay down their lives for what they see as the service of Allah – the glory of martyrdom. They inevitably cause distress and embarrassment in their communities (which reaction they ignore since they despise those outside their groups as not proper Muslims), and their aggressive activities are frequently picked up by the media. Moderates feel angry and frustrated, object to the fitnah (discord) they cause, and consider the whole of Islam to be tarnished by these antagonistic brethren who think they are the only Muslims doing their duty and serving Allah properly.

For moderate Muslims ijtihad and istihsan are the preferred methods of choice for sociopolitical change and military jihad the last option. For militant Muslims, military jihad is the first option and ijtihad is not an option at all.

Moderate Muslims are dismissed by them as being 'asleep', lazy, and unwilling to make the required sacrifices for Allah. Their opinions are dismissed as corrupt, debased, lax, irrelevant, inadequate, or just plain wrong.

In Islam the sure sign of a bigot is *takfir* – the accusing of all those who do not agree with their interpretation (even people known to be devout believers and practising Muslims) of being *kuffar* (non-believers), the attitude that Islam has not been properly understood by anyone since the Prophet Mohammed ﷺ and the early Muslims – except themselves.

The quiet majority of Muslims is shocked by their ill-mannered tactics and intolerance, and the most charitable view is that 'they will grow out of it' when their texts wrested out of context are studied more carefully. However, this is seen by the jihadis as patronizing, and simply irritates them all the more until there is a risk they might become dangerous politically, or even willing to undertake terrorist activity.

Hizb ut-Tahrir and the Muhajirun

Hizb ut-Tahrir, and its offshoot the Muhajirun, are modern examples of Islamic sectarian groups of vociferous zealots, who insist that working to re-establish the Islamic way of life depends on promoting khilafah, since in their view Islam is incomplete without it and therefore is not really Islam. They point out a hadith of the Prophet ﷺ that khilafah would cease (which it did, in Turkey in 1924), but would eventually return. They share the zeal of those of other faiths who are obsessed with the end of the world. The Muhajirun sect was officially disbanded in 2004.

Al-Ghurabaa (the Strangers) and al-Firqatun-Najiyah (the Saved Sect)

These are new extreme groups, widely believed to be the reformed Muhajirun. *Ghurabaa* is a derivative of *gharaba*, meaning to go away, depart, absent or withdraw from, leave. The singular, *ghareeb*, means strange, foreign, alien. The reason for the name is two hadiths:

> 'Truly, Islam began as something strange, and it will return as something strange the way it began. So give glad tidings to the strangers.'

> ' Paradise is for *al-Ghurabaa* (the strangers).'

The concept is that the existing ummah of Islam has failed or become inadequate in one way or another, and the members of this sect have been selected to live a specially purified life – the true Islam (a similar concept to Pharisaism at the time of Jesus, and the Old Testament notion of a 'Righteous Remnant').

The Saved Sect, which theatrically stormed a Muslim general election event in April 2005, takes as its founding hadith:

> 'If the people of Isra'il were fragmented into 72 sects my ummah will be fragmented into 73 sects. All of them will be in Hell Fire except one. They (the Companions) said: "Allah's Messenger, which is that?" Whereupon he said: "It is one to which I and my Companions belong."'
>
> (Tirmidhi, Abu Dawud)

Members of al-*Ghurabaa* take this to mean themselves, the select few who truly follow Islam, whereas the mainstream of Islam naturally considers it means the mainstream! The sectarians pervertedly take pride in the fact that people will condemn them, speak ill of them and slander them, none of which will be able to hinder them from their path, nor shake their determination to be a 'small group of pious people in a large group of evil people. Those who disobey them outnumber those who obey them.' (Ahmad)

37

terrorism in the name of Islam

In this chapter you will learn about:
- the extremist threat
- suicide bombers
- causes of terrorism
- hopes for peace.

The extremist threat

One hallmark of extreme puritan movements was and is to divide the world into mutually exclusive categories – the forces of good and the forces of evil, the world of belief (*dar al-Islam*) and that of unbelief (*dar al-harb*) which is fair game for conquest. Those who are not with them, whether Muslim or non-Muslim, are the enemy; they are to be fought and destroyed in a war with no limits.

The role of Islam in the political sphere

Since the 9/11 attacks on the USA there has been debate about the different interpretations of Islam, its impact on Muslim politics, and the relationship between Islam and the West, a debate that gained renewed vigour after the London attacks on 7 and 21 July, 2005. Many insecure governments have used the threat of global terrorism as an excuse or green light for increasing their authoritarian rule, as the politically angry radical Muslims exacerbate the already rampant anti-Americanism in the Muslim world and encourage terrorist responses to real and perceived injustices.

Suicide bombers

To detest oppression, injustice and suffering is an Islamic obligation, and no amount of legislation will prevent Muslims from doing so. When people try to resist State injustice verbally those states invariably attempt to outlaw such dissent, to prevent exposure of the nature of their oppression. Hence bans on 'incitement to hatred', political groups, inviting people to speak about oppression, leaflets, etc. Even watching videos exposing the sufferings of Muslims is suspect.

However, the appalling acts of suicide bombers horrify and shame Muslims. Killing and maiming the innocent is terrorism, and such twisted hatred and bitterness have nothing whatsoever to do with Islam, God, or the message or example of the Prophet ﷺ. Terrorism can only succeed politically by losing morally, since suicide bombers assume that their enemies care about the innocent lives they rip apart.

When Muslims choose to kill themselves for political reasons, they may be hoping to make a statement – even though they must know suicide is totally forbidden in Islam. When they kill innocent bystanders along with themselves it is nothing less than murder.

These bombers may perhaps have been duped into thinking of themselves as martyrs for Allah, or for their cause, but a martyr is someone who has been put to death by an oppressor because of their faith. Suicide bombers not only commit murder and will have to face the consequences in the Life to Come, but have also caused fitnah (dissent and damage) and committed a physical attack upon Islam itself by the damage they have done to its image.

The Prophet ﷺ made his message crystal clear:

'That person who defects from obedience and separates from the main body of the Muslims, ... if he dies in that state ... he will die the death of one belonging to the days of jahiliyyah (i.e. would not die as a Muslim). One who fights under the banner of a people who are blind (i.e. do not know whether their cause is just or otherwise), ... if he is killed (in this fight), he dies as one belonging to the days of jahiliyyah. Whoever attacks my ummah, killing the righteous along with the wicked, sparing not (even) those staunch in faith ... he has nothing to do with me and I have nothing to do with him.'

(Muslim)

It is perhaps worth noting that the New York World Trade Centre destroyed by the terrorists used to host a Friday prayer that drew some 1,500 Muslims.

al-bara'a (self-exoneration)

There is no power of excommunication in Islam so terrorists cannot be formally banned from the community – but the community can distance itself from them by the Islamic principle of *al-bara'a* (self-exoneration). This means that Muslims must not just remain quiet, but must publicly dissociate themselves from terrorist acts.

The real causes of terrorism

The real fuel for terrorism is not radical preaching, but simply flows from the reality of what is going on in the Muslim world – the occupation of Palestine, subjugation of Kashmir, installation of puppet regimes throughout the Muslim world and so on, which all cause anger. If the Muslim ummah feels marginalized and persecuted, hate-filled preachers are not needed to tell them this – they may just watch the news on their TVs.

Usama bin Laden and al-Qaeda appeal to grievances that exist among many mainstream Arabs and Muslims, from foreign policy issues to domestic complaints against repressive and corrupt governments and failed economies. They twist Islamic values about good governance, social justice and the requirement to defend Islam when under siege, to legitimize their use of violence, warfare and terrorism.

Military, political and social causes of terrorism

There is no way that terrorism, the hadd crime of hirabah, can be justified in Islam, but it is easy to understand the numerous root causes of terrorism. These include:

- The feeling of being pushed around – the traumatic experience of non-Muslim colonialism invading Muslim religious and cultural space, which explains why terrorists often attack seemingly innocuous targets such as banks (*riba*), cinemas and hotels (sexual licence, etc.).
- Frustration and fury – despotic and often corrupt governments clamping a tight lid down on dissent and freedom of expression.
- Outrage for a righteous cause – the establishment of the state of Israel, and expulsion of the Palestinians.
- No level playing field – the fact that favoured governments can assassinate, impose collective punishments, flout numerous UN resolutions and develop nuclear power with impunity.
- Evidence twisted, lies told, abuse – the eventual discovery that there were no weapons of mass destruction in Iraq. Abu Ghrayb, Guantanamo, crude photographs of abused prisoners.
- Possible cover-up for real motives – the 'war on terror' really being a pretext for Western control of oil and world economics.
- The feeling that Americans and Europeans value their lives more than those of Muslims. The deaths of tens of thousands of innocent Muslims in Afghanistan and Iraq were not even counted, the Western media infuriating the Muslim media by the incredible tactlessness of reporting casualties in single figures when graphic digital evidence of Muslim loss and humiliation was available to anyone with a computer.

- The belief that a tacit conspiracy exists between the West, its agencies and its multinational corporations on the one hand, and local business and military cliques in the Third World on the other, to assume complete control of certain countries and 'develop' them on a joint venture basis. It is human rights violations that make these countries attractive to business.
- The bigotry of sectarian groups who wish to wage jihad on all with whom they disagree.
- The callous use of malleable individuals by criminals with no religious interest at all.

Hypocrisy

The West claims to uphold values of freedom, justice, rule of law, democratic and representative government (all actually Muslim values) but apparently cannot see that various governments they support – which are themselves supposed to uphold these principles – brazenly undermine them in a whole range of countries and instances.

Rather than strengthen democracies, US leaders have actually overthrown numerous democratically elected governments and crushed many populist-nationalist movements fighting against intolerable regimes.

Algeria is a case in point. When Algeria voted for Islamic parties in free democratic elections, the military intervened, rescinded the election result, and the upholders of democracy and freedom endorsed the military's action – with the consequence that violence ensued, a bloody civil war began, and large numbers of radicalized Algerians fled to the West as refugees and asylum seekers.

Children learn from their parents the grief and anguish of year upon year of unrequited injustices inflicted on vulnerable people in Muslim lands.

Undermining human rights

The commitment to human rights is seen as being selectively undermined. The UK Anti-Terror laws proposed after the 7 July bombings has mobilized those defending civil liberty as well as workers in race relations.

The normal presumption in the UK has always been that a person was innocent until proved guilty, and trial at civilian courts had to show evidence of guilt to satisfy a judge and jury. Since 9/11 many Muslims have been locked away without charges being presented or a date for their trial. Scores are incarcerated not knowing what evidence is against them, or whether they face extradition or an open-ended term in prison on the basis of secret 'evidence' which even their legal representatives cannot challenge.

No interviews take place upon arrest, so technically there has been no arrest – since an arrest under Criminal Legislation would provide a person with rights.

Hopes for peace

It is seriously hoped that the Muslim outcry against terrorism will make fundamentalist and jihadi groups discard the notion that anyone who is not a Muslim is an 'infidel', reject the attitude that since the goal of converting humanity to Islam is a noble one, any means to do so are justified, but accept diversity and that they must compete in the 'global market-place' of faiths through normal channels rather than attack others.

The Saudi reform effort

In its own efforts to promote the path of *wasatiyya* (the 'middle path') the Saudi regime is attempting to fight tafkir (accusing other Muslims of apostasy) by re-education of extremists. Two large-scale projects are under way – a counselling program for outreach to Saudi security prisoners, and the Sakinah Campaign, an independent initiative for online dialogue with Islamists. Some 40 ulema (religious teachers) and propagators of Islam with internet skills enter extremist websites and forums, and converse with the participants in order to bring them to renounce their extremist ideas.

Some practical thoughts

Is it time to abandon wearing the sort of Muslim 'uniform' that is unwittingly used as 'advertising space' for extremists (as the Union Jack became advertising for the BNP)? Should men give up the type of beards and long shirts and baggy ankle length trousers, (the *khaksari* (down-to-earth) style first popularized by Maududi)? Muslims who wear such clothes in the belief it shows their piety are, in most cases, unwittingly giving succour to a brand of Islamist extremism.

Should Muslim women reconsider their motivation for wearing face-covering veils? These do not suggest modesty to Westerners but are seen as threatening – covered faces usually suggest terrorists (e.g. IRA), bandits, people out to attack, rob or rape you – who have obvious reasons for hiding their faces. You cannot be greeted with a smile, easily understand what a veiled person is saying to you, or sometimes even know whether the veil conceals a woman or a man.

Muslim leaders have the task of convincing terrorists that even though they may feel their cause is just, and the lack of other viable alternatives makes descending to these levels of immorality permissible – it is not. The challenge is to advocate a 'higher morality.' Secondly, they must address the political situations in which Muslims find themselves, including the arrogance of powerful figures in major governments, and thus remove the fuel that fires the so-called 'preachers of hate,' who are considered responsible for manipulating impressionable and vulnerable Muslim youth.

Muslims should perhaps make common cause with other individuals and groups who seek a just and peaceful world, unite with non-Muslims, organizations like the Stop the War Coalition, Trades Unions, political parties, etc. As regards interfaith forums, they should practise what the Prophet ﷺ ordered, and 'come to what is common' between them.

38

Islamic feminism

In this chapter you will
learn about:

- problems to be addressed
- pioneers and reforms
- female imams.

Muslim women worldwide are now seizing opportunities to look deep into the spirit of the Qur'an and find there the gender justice they believe was the original intent of the revelation. By gaining knowledge they are also gaining in influence and authority. Hundreds of women's groups have sprung up all over the world.

It requires courage and conviction for religious leaders to question and possibly oppose entrenched positions and suggest they are based on wrong conclusions. But for those who care that the spirit of Islam should be honoured in practice, this is necessary and worth any risks in order for women to achieve liberation through Islam as originally intended.

The following is a list of major problem areas that need to be addressed:

- Marriage and divorce laws that reinforce the image of the rights of the husband superseding those of the wife, and prevent women from getting fair treatment.
- Violence against women in the home, community, and as a consequence of warfare, which is claimed by some to be allowed by Islam – when it is not.
- Abuse of practices that affect women negatively, like polygamy and temporary marriage, when applied out of context and without abiding by Islamic restrictions.
- Failure to promote proper education and health provision for females; tolerance of femicide, child marriage, female genital mutilation, slave and child labour.
- Excluding women from religious activities such as attendance in the mosque, or serving on mosque committees.
- Failure to promote the importance of a woman's contribution to society beyond child-bearing, and a lack of awareness of the importance of men giving a good example within the family, sharing household responsiblities and child-rearing.
- Failure to enable women to take advantage of rights of property ownership, dowries and inheritance as outlined by Islam.
- Subjecting women to harassment, intimidation or discrimination, especially as regards rights to have friends, leave the house, go to work, mix in society, and not be obliged to wear certain forms of clothing.

'And thus does their Lord answer their prayer: I shall not lose sight of the work of any of you, be it man or woman: You are members, one of another.'

(Surah 3:195)

Women as leaders

A disputed hadith reported that when the Prophet ﷺ was informed the Persians had crowned a woman as their ruler, he said: 'A people with a female ruler will never be successful.' (Bukhari) Many traditional Muslim societies have been unwilling to allow women to rule for this reason, and some have even forbidden them from working in the government, despite the verses in the Qur'an about Queen Bilkis of Sheba (Saba'), who was interviewed by the Prophet Sulayman ﷺ and not asked to relinquish her rule.

Islamic feminists argue that women may be heads of state, judges, and so on. Many of the women who have broken the glass ceiling and made it to the rank of female president or prime minister have been Muslim women. Of the world's female prime ministers, we have seen Benazir Bhutto in Pakistan (the first woman prime minister of a Muslim country), Khaleda Zia in Bangladesh, and Tansu Ciller in Turkey. Megawati Sukarnoputri is the female head of Indonesia, which has the largest Muslim population in the world. Iran has had a female vice-president and there are seats reserved for women in the parliaments of Pakistan, Iraq, UAE and others.

Women judges

Islam has a tradition going back to Caliph Umar of women serving as judges and magistrates, even if it has been neglected in many Muslim places. Iraq's first female judge, Zakia Hakki, was appointed in 1959 (she is currently a prominent member of parliament). In the longest-standing Islamist state, Iran, women legislators are included in the Majlis. In Morocco, 20 per cent of all judges are women, more than in the US.

Keeping women on the bench elsewhere is not always trouble-free. In 2003, the US authorities appointed Nidal Nasser Hussein as the first female judge in the Shi'ite city of Najaf, a decision met with widespread outrage and several senior conservative clerics issuing fatwas. She has yet to take her seat on the bench.

The right to vote

Until recently most Muslim nations did not have democracy. Many mainstream Muslims now believe it to be an evolution of the Islamic concept of shura (consultation), and most Muslim nations today allow their female citizens to have some level of voting and control over their local government with a few exceptions, namely Kuwait, Saudi Arabia and Lebanon (which requires proof of education for women to vote). In 2005 Kuwait passed a ruling that will allow women to vote in 2007.

Feminist pioneers and successful reforms

Among the pioneers of Islamic feminism are the Moroccan writer Fatema Mernissi and the Pakistani scholar Riffat Hassan, although neither is entirely comfortable with the label, disliking the Western cultural baggage it brings. These scholars simply see themselves as Muslims pursuing rights for women within an Islamic discourse.

A London group, Women Living Under Muslim Law, was founded in 1984 to oppose the harsh interpretation of Shari'ah emerging in Algeria. One case cited was the incarceration of three Algerian feminists jailed without trial and kept incommunicado for seven months for discussing laws unfavourable to women.

A joint effort by Muslim and Coptic women has helped end the practice of 'honour killing' in Upper Eqypt. Rana Hussaini, a Jordanian women's activist, heads a task force seeking to reform laws governing these crimes in Jordan. With the coming of Islam, killing women suspected of sexual indiscretion was totally forbidden and the so-called 'honour-killings' that have taken place in various societies have nothing to do with Islam, and are in fact murder of an unconvicted female by a father or brother or uncle.

Organizations such as Mara al Jadida in Egypt are fighting domestic violence, while women-run orphanages and adoption agencies in Morocco, Tunisia and Egypt deal with abandoned children. Other groups, such as Parsa Kabul, an NGO (i.e. non-governmental organization) based in Kabul with an office in the US, are quietly sending aid to the isolated women of Afghanistan.

In Indonesia Fatayat, the women's wing of Nahdlatul Ulama now trains its members in Islamic jurisprudence so that they can hold their own in religious debates. Musdah Mulia, the chief researcher at Indonesia's Ministry of Religious Affairs, called in

2004 for important changes to Shari'ah in areas such as marriage, polygamy, and the wearing of the hijab, with meticulous references to Islamic jurisprudence. The Indonesian Society for Pesantren (religious schools) and Community Development also uses fiqh to encourage Indonesian women's reproductive health and family planning.

The African Charter on the Rights and Welfare of the Child specifically gives girls the right to be protected from early marriage, on the grounds that being forced into such marriages not only robs them of their childhood and any chance of an education, but risks exposing them to exploitation and violence.

In rural Iran such child marriages were not only sanctioned by tradition, but in the aftermath of the 1979 revolution, Iran's new government quickly suspended the country's progressive family law, disallowed female judges, and strongly enforced the wearing of the hijab. Within a few months, the marriage age of girls was lowered to nine and boys to 14, polygamy was permitted, unilateral divorce allowed for men but not women, and fathers were given sole custody of children in the case of divorce. Now, however, the law requires court approval for the marriage of any girl under 13 or boy under 15. One female reformist, Fatemah Khatami, said that the new law was particularly due to the efforts of women law-makers who sought to increase legal protections for girls and women.

Indian/Pakistani Muslims have perhaps been the most resistant to any reinterpretation of Muslim law to suit modern times. The Sarda Bill against child marriage was supported by both Allama Iqbal and Muhammad Ali Jinnah as early as the 1920s, but the ulema opposed it. However, the 1961 Muslim Family Law Ordinance in Lahore banned child marriage and set a minimum age for the marriage of boys at 18 years and girls at 14.

Morocco recently raised the marriage age from 15 to 18, abolished polygamy, equalized the right to divorce, and gave women the right to retain custody of their children. The conservatives opposed this, but Morocco's modernizing king, Muhammad VI (a direct descendent of the Prophet ﷺ), backed the reformers and defended the changes with copious references to the Qur'an.

Women in Egypt recently celebrated the passage by the People's Assembly of *khula*, or consensual divorce. Women are now free to ask for and get a divorce if they are willing to return their dowries; the law was justified on religious grounds. The khula right was clearly stated in the Islamic Shari'ah all along, but it had to be pointed out.

Female genital mutilation

Muslim scholars have long emphasized that there is no Islamic basis for this very harmful practice, which causes many deaths among young girls each year.

According to UNICEF (the United Nation's Children's Fund) more than 130 million women around the world have undergone the procedure. Female circumcision is practiced in 28 African countries (notably Somalia, Ethiopia, the Sudan and Egypt) although it is now illegal, but the procedure is also increasingly found in Europe, Australia, Canada and the USA, primarily among immigrants from these countries. So far, according to Amnesty International, only 14 of the overall 53 African countries have adopted laws banning the practice.

In 2005 a conference organized by the Organization of Islamic Conference (OIC) and the Islamic Educational, Scientific and Cultural Organization (ISESCO) called upon all Muslim states to 'take the necessary measures to eliminate all forms of discrimination against girls and all harmful traditional or customary practices, such as child marriage and female genital mutilation.'

Female imams

All the functions of an imam, such as religious education, and spiritual and social counselling, have always been open to Muslim women, but they are not allowed to lead men in prayers. Three of the four Sunni schools, as well as many Shia, agree that a woman may lead a female-only congregation, although the Maliki school does not allow even this.

Those who support the move for female imams cite the precedent of the Prophet's ﷺ Companion Umm Waraqah. 'The Prophet ﷺ used to visit her in her own home; he appointed a mu'adhin for her, and ordered her to lead the members of her household (in *Salah*)' (Abu Dawud). Since Umm Waraqah's household included men, this can be used to support the claim that women can lead men in prayer; the word translated as 'house' (*dar*) might even be taken to refer to her whole area (else, they reason, why appoint a mu'adhin?) However, most scholars regard this as an invalid deduction, or that this privilege was given only to Umm Waraqah and was not applicable to others.

In the Hanbali madhhab, women are not allowed to lead the five salat, but may lead the optional tarawih prayers in Ramadan if there is no man knowledgeable in the Qur'an present, they are senior women not young, they are well-versed in the Qur'an, and they stand behind the men, in the women's rows, rather than in front.

Female imams of female-only congregations

Several hadiths report that the Prophet's ﷺ wives Aishah and Umm Salamah led congregations of women. The female imam stands in the middle of the front row of the congregation, instead of alone in front of it.

The Hui people of China have a tradition of mosques solely for women, and women have been trained as imams in order to serve them. In recent years, efforts have been made to establish similar mosques in India and Iran.

In practice, everywhere that women are obliged to pray in separate rooms from the men has virtually created separate mosques for them. The barrier or wall counts as a sutrah, often making it impossible for the women to see the imam or follow him, and virtually relegates them to a separate prayer-congregation, which should, perhaps, have its own leader.

In early 2005, Amina Wadud (professor of Islamic Studies at Virginia Commonwealth University, USA) led a congregation in Friday prayer in New York, sponsored by the Muslim Women's Freedom Tour. Muslim Jurists in America responded by issuing a fatwa reiterating the traditional view that women may not lead the Friday prayer nor deliver the sermon, and that the prayers of whoever takes part in such a travesty are null and void. Supporters of the event insisted that, to the contrary, it was a long overdue change; Khaled Abou el-Fadl (professor of Islamic Studies at University of California) said that, 'What the fundamentalists are worried about is that there's going to be a ripple effect not just in the US but all over the Muslim world. The women who are learned and frustrated that they cannot be the imam are going to see that someone got the guts to break ranks and do it.'

39

Islam in the twenty-first century

In this chapter you will
learn about:
- Islam and the West
- Islamic awareness
- projections for the future.

Islam and the West

There is immense spiritual and intellectual ferment taking place among the world's Muslims today. Ordinary people now have unprecedented access to sources of information and knowledge about their faith and, with mass education and mass communication, the days have gone when governments and religious authorities can control what their people know, and what they think. Even when there are state-appointed religious authorities – as in Oman, Saudi Arabia, Iran, and Egypt – with the discussions in newspapers, on the internet, on cassettes and CDs, and on television there is no longer any guarantee that their word will be heeded, or even that they themselves will follow the lead of the regime.

Islam is now the fastest growing religion in the West, and the second largest faith-group in Europe, the USA and Australia. Some 400 million Muslims have relocated during the twentieth century, and USA Muslims will soon constitute the world's most educated, influential and wealthy Muslim population. It is no longer 'Islam versus the West'.

Islam is growing very fast through conversions – not through the off-putting activities of over-zealous Islamic missionaries, but through reading and personal study, observing the polite, decent and hospitable way of life of ordinary Muslim people. Some have become fascinated with Islam through what they have observed while on holidays abroad. Others have appreciated the spiritual richness of Sufism, or the dedication of shopkeepers to follow a discipline of purity, prayer and fasting, and submitting all the minutiaea of their lives to Islamic practice. Some have come to admire the faith through the character of those who have suffered appalling disaster, whether in warfare or through natural catastrophe such as the 2004 tsunami. As often before in Muslim history, soldiers sent to fight and aid workers going to help the stricken in Muslim lands have been converted by those with whom they came in contact. No jihad is necessary.

In the UK, there are Muslims in the House of Lords and the Commons, which institutions are becoming increasingly knowledgeable in the modern interpretations of the Shari'ah.

Radical Muslims will hopefully come to realize they are not the 'only true Muslims', and let other exemplars of Islam carry on making quiet progress with their service to Allah. Hopefully, it will soon not matter if Muslims are vilified by the media etc., for ordinary people will be able to see and judge for themselves the standards of decent Muslim life.

Leaders needed

Leaders (Islamic as well as politicians in general) can only expect moral status if they provide genuine moral leadership, show self-restraint in the face of provocation and resist the temptation of following the easy, if counterproductive route of venting their anger on their oppressors. Muslims should strive to give the moral example that insists that one wrong does not justify another.

Reticence to push oneself in front of one's peers may have previously prevented mainstream and moderate Muslims from standing up and speaking out on behalf of the concerns of the Muslim community – but the need is now acknowledged and being rapidly addressed.

Islamic awareness

Islamic awareness events try to put across to the general public what it is Muslims would like any educated citizen to be aware of as regards Islam. These points include:

- Allah is not a different God from Jehovah or 'Our Father, Who art in Heaven', but there is only One Supreme God, no matter what people call Him or what they believe about Him. Allah means 'the Almighty'.
- The word 'Muslim' means a person who is submitted to God.
- Muslims are not 'against' Jews or Christians who are all peoples of the Book (*Ahl al-Kitab*) with revelations from the same Divine Source, but they are 'against' shirk and Zionism.
- 'Muslim' does not mean Arab or Pakistani (or brown-skinned or bearded). Certainly the Prophet ﷺ was an Arab, but there are now believers in every country in the world – from Eskimo to Aborigine. There is no 'chosen race' – all races are God's creations and are loved by Him. Many brown-skinned people are Hindu, Buddhist, Sikh, Christian, etc., or of no faith at all. Muslims are every shade from white to jet-black, and millions do not have beards.
- Muslims are not all the same – just as Christianity has its Roman Catholics with incense, statues and priests wearing

lace, the Salvation Army with uniforms and brass band; the Quakers with silent meditation, and so on, so Islam has its Sunnis, Shi'ites, Isma'ilis, Salafis, Sufis, Jamaatis, Deobandis, Barelvis, Hizbullahis, Hizb ut-Tahriris, Naqshbandis, and so on.

- Muslim character types are representative of all human types. They are not usually like the media stereotypes, and they do not all think, eat or dress in the same way.
- Muslim women do not all define hijab in the same way – some choose the complete privacy of seclusion, some cover their faces and even their eyes, others simply wear the modest dress of their own societies.
- Muslims are not just 'backward Third World' people – there are millions of highly educated Muslims. Many Muslims in the UK, for example, are physicians, dentists, lawyers, microbiologists, computer technologists, etc.
- Muslims include in their number just as many saintly and noble people as other faiths. They also include just as many weak, corrupt and lax people, arrogant, bumptious, bigoted people and ignorant, self-opinionated idiots.
- Muslims and Islam often get the blame for notorious practices that are actually the opposite of Islam, but culturally accepted in some societies that have accepted Islam.
- Muslims cannot force anyone to come to Islam – this is not only forbidden to them, but it is in any case impossible to force anyone's heart and mind.
- Islam is a very high vocation and calling – you cannot force people (even Muslims) to pray five times per day, fast the month of Ramadan (sometimes in appalling circumstances) to become modest, or to feel distaste for irresponsible sexuality, etc.

Which way will it go?

The battle for Muslim hearts and minds continues. Should Muslims concentrate on their personal faith and lives and disentangle them from politics, or should campaigns for world-wide justice, unity of Muslims under one leadership, and the spread of Islam throughout the non-Muslim world continue to be passionate ambitions?

Will Sunni and Shi'ite Muslims be able to come together and find common ground that will be of benefit to both sides? Will Wahhabis be able to mellow towards Sufism, and Salafis towards liberalism and tolerance?

Will extremism eventually be perceived as being so radical that it will have little impact on Islam – like the Christian rejection of the Reverend Jim Jones' suicide cult, or the Branch Davidians at Waco?

The path of enlightened moderation

'Truly, Allah does not change the condition of a people until they change what is in themselves.'

(Surah 13.11)

The Organization of the Islamic Conference (OIC) summit of December 2005 published the following targets:

- to prepare a strategy and plan to enable the Islamic ummah to meet the challenges of the twenty-first century
- to promote enlightened moderation, and re-educate militant Islamists
- to condemn terrorism in all its forms and manifestations, reject any justification for it, and declare solidarity with member states that have been victimized by it
- to renew emphasis on conflict resolution, inter-faith dialogue, human rights and good governance
- to combat Islamophobia and media misrepresentation, and consider the possibility of developing a media channel that can rebut misinformation
- to use funds from oil-rich countries to optimize economic resources, which when pooled together could make a massive difference to development, and free Islamic economics from the West – with the possibility of a common Muslim currency and a common economic approach, with the rich assisting and improving the status of the poor
- to experiment with document-free travel across Muslim borders
- to create a knowledge fund to support and improve the quality of education, especially in underdeveloped parts of the world, and to both create new and upgrade existing Institutions of Excellence for research and development, and support and encourage Muslim experts in non-Muslim universities.

A few modern ventures

In 2004 the International Prize for the Promotion of Dialogue between Islamic and Western Civilizations, endowed by the Sultan of Brunei, was presented to the Prince of Wales for his work on behalf of Islam. The Oxford Centre for Islamic Studies (thanks to the persistent efforts of Prince Turki al-Faisal and colleagues), will soon be relocated from its existing premises to a purpose-built college with its own mosque, lecture theatres, exhibition gallery and library.

Kuwait is to establish the first Islamic Economy University in the world, to cope with the growing demand for specialists and experts in Islamic economy as well as the increasing number of Islamic investment companies and banks.

Prince Walid ibn Talal, has donated 20 million dollars each to the USA's Harvard and Georgetown Universities, to fund courses dedicated to Islam and pay for new researchers on the subject. He is also donating 15 million dollars to establish the first centres for reciprocal American Studies in Beirut and Cairo.

Islam in the twenty-first century

Will the faith of Muslims in al-Ghayb (the Unseen) – the existence of God, angels and a Life to Come – be defeated by the onslaught of secularism, science and materialism? Will Islam be engulfed in a process of assimilation? Will it be forcibly ejected from the West, or could it become the dominant religion of the next century? Allah knows best.

Atheism and materialism have had a long run, but people have not rejected the spiritual, as expected, but are thirsting for truth, reality, hope, compassion, charity and excellence. Muslims naturally hope they will discover and come to love and accept the universal religion of submission to the One Almighty God. To be Muslim is to believe in God, and dedicate one's life in submission to the will of God.

It may even be that in this century people who all worship the same One True God by many different names and practices will come to realize that, as Mevlana Rumi said, 'we see the sunlight shining into many different courtyards. If we take away the walls, we will see it is all the same light.'

glossary

adhan call to prayer
akhirah life after death
amal action
ansars the Helpers of Madinah
aqiqah cutting the hair of new babies
ashurah 10th Muharram (death of Hussain)
asr the mid-afternoon prayer
ayah Qur'an verse
ayatollah leading shi'ite imam
burqa fully covering garment
chador covering sheet
du'a personal prayer
eid al-adha feast of sacrifice
eid ul-fitr feast to end Ramadan
fajr the pre-sunrise prayer
fard obligatory
fiqh study of Islamic law
ghayb the unseen universe
ghusl complete bath
hadith sayings of the Prophet ﷺ
hafiz (pl. **huffaz**) knows the Qur'an by heart
hajj pilgrimage
halal permitted
haram forbidden
hijab the veil
hujr al-aswad the black stone
ibadah worship
ihram pilgrim garments
ihsan realization
ijma consensus of legal opinion
ijtihad working out Islamic principles

imam leader of congregation
iman faith
iqamah second call to prayer
isha the night prayer
jahannam hell
jama'ah congregation
jamrah pillar representing devil
jannam heaven, Paradise
jihad striving or struggle to do God's will
jinn lesser spirit beings
Ka'bah Makkah cube-shaped shrine
Khalifah (Caliph) successor
khamr intoxicant
khitan circumcision
khutbah sermon
kiswah the black cloth over the Ka'bah
kunya parent's name taken from child
laylat ul-bara'at Night of Blessing (full moon before Ramadan)
laylat ul-isra wal miraj Night of Prophet's ﷺ ascent to heaven
laylat ul-Qadr the Night of Power (descent of the Qur'an)
madhhab school of Islamic law
madrassah mosque school
maghrib the nightfall prayer
masjid mosque
mihrab niche showing direction of Makkah
minaret tower for call to prayer
minbar pulpit for sermon
mu'adhin (muezzin) person who calls to prayer
mubah action left to conscience
muhajirun the Emigrants from Makkah, those who 'emigrate' to God
mujtahid religious scholar
mutah temporary marriage
nafs soul
niyyah intention
polygamy multiple marriage
purdah seclusion of women
qadr predestination
qisas 'eye for eye' revenge
Qur'an Holy Book
rakah unit of prayer movements
Ramadan fasting month
rawdah gathering to commemorate the dead
riba interest on loaned money, extortion

risalah prophecy
salah ritual prayer
salat ul-janaza funeral prayer
sawm fasting
shahadah statement of belief, bearing witness
Shari'ah the Way of Islam
Shi'ite sectarian party of Ali
shirk the division of the unity of God
subhah prayer beads
Sufi religious mystic
suhur dawn meal before fasting
sujud prostration in prayer
sunnah the Prophet's ﷺ example
Sunni mainstream Muslim
surah Qur'an chapter
taharah purity
talaq divorce
tajwid art of correct pronunciation
tarawih Ramadan prayers
tariqah Sufi 'way' or 'order'
tasawwuf spiritual insight in Islam
tasbih prayer beads
taqwa God-consciousness
tawhid the One-ness of God
tayammum 'dry' ritual wash
tilawah reading with intent
ulema religious teachers (sing-alim)
ummah the 'family' of Islam
umrah pilgrimage not at Hajj time
walimah wedding party
wudu (wuzu) ritual wash
wuquf the 'stand' at Arafat
zakah religious tax
zawiyah Sufi training centre
zinah adultery, illicit sexual intimacy
zuhr the mid-day prayer

Recommended reading

Atlas of the Islamic World – Frances Robinson, Oxford, 1996

Hadith Literature, its origin, development and special features – Muhammad Zubayr Siddiqui, Islamic Texts Society, 1993

In The Shade of the Tree: A Photographic Odyssey Through the Muslim World – Peter Sanders, Starlatch Press, 2005

Islam between East and West – Aliya Izetbegovic, American Trust Publications, 1984

Islam, its meaning and message – Khurshid Ahmad (ed.), Islamic Foundation, 1976

Islam, the Way of Submission – Solomon Nigosian, Crucible, 1987

Islamic Awakening between Rejection and Extremism – Yusuf al-Qaradawi, International Institute of Islamic Thought, 1991

Morals and Manners in Islam – Marwan Ibrahim al-Kaysi, Islamic Foundation, 1986

Muhammad – Martin Lings, Islamic Texts Society, 1983

No God But God: The Origins, Evolution and Future of Islam – Reza Aslan, Random House, New York, 2005

Only Half of Me: Being a Muslim in Britain – Rageh Omaar, Viking, 2006

Purification of the Heart: Signs, Symptoms and Cures of the Spiritual Diseases of the Heart – Hamza Yusuf, Starlatch Press, USA, 2004

Tell me about Hajj – Saniyasnain Khan, Goodword Books, 2000

The Elements of Islam – Shaykh Fadhlalla Haeri, Elements, 1993

The Elements of Sufism – Shaykh Fadhlalla Haeri, Elements, 1990

The Lawful and the Prohibited in Islam – Yusuf al-Qaradawi, Shorouk International, 1985

The Muslim Woman's Handbook – Huda Khattab, Ta-Ha, 1993

The Oxford History of Islam – John Esposito, Oxford, 1999

The State We Are In: Identity, Terror and the Law of Jihad – Hamza Yusuf Hanson, et al, Amal Press, 2006

Thinking about God – Ruqaiyyah Waris Maqsood, American Trust Publications, 1994

Western Muslims and the Future of Islam – Tariq Ramadan, Oxford University Press Inc, USA, 2005

What Every Christian Should Know About Islam – Ruqaiyyah Waris Maqsood, Islamic Foundation, 2000

What is Islam? – C. Horrie, Star, 1990

Women and Gender in Islam – Leila Ahmed, Yale University, 1992

Websites

There are many excellent sites, but I would caution students not to accept the information on all sites blindly, particularly if they have an arrogant, strident or unpleasant tone or stray from plain facts and concentrate on controversial opinion or on an overtly political agenda. I would also urge new Muslims to avoid email forums or chat rooms about Islam. There are some nasty people lurking there – self-styled pseudo-scholars preaching hellfire, doling out personal abuse and decrying sincere Muslims as non-believers.

www.islamonline.net
www.eastlondonmosque.co.uk
www.islamic-foundation.org.uk
www.ummahnews.com
www.ummah.com
www.muslimteachers.net
www.muslimnews.co.uk
www.mwlusa.org (i.e. Muslim Women's League)
www.maryam's.com (Islamic feminism)
www.themodernreligion.com/index2.html
www.mchc.org.uk
www.muslimnews.co.uk
www.muslimhands.org
www.islamfortoday.com
www.beliefnet.com
www.cair-net.org
www.theamericanmuslim.org
www.renaissance.com.pk
www.salaam.co.uk
www.therevival.co.uk
www.soundvision.com
www.sufism.org
www.isna.net/horizons
www.islamcity.com/Hajj
www.islamic-relief.com
www.islamic-world.net
www.iflibrary.org.uk (Islamic Foundation Library)
www.islamcan.com
www.islamiCity.com
www.islamic-awareness.org
goasia.about.com/b/a/2006_01_07.htm–pix of hajj
Sr. Ruqaiyyah's website – www.members.aol.com/Ruqaiyyah